In Search of Soul

In Search of Soul

Hip-Hop, Literature, and Religion

Alejandro Nava

UNIVERSITY OF CALIFORNIA PRESS

University of California Press, one of the most distinguished university presses in the United States, enriches
lives around the world by advancing scholarship in the
humanities, social sciences, and natural sciences. Its
activities are supported by the UC Press Foundation and
by philanthropic contributions from individuals and
institutions. For more information, visit www.ucpress.edu

University of California Press
Oakland, California

Library of Congress Cataloging-in-Publication Data
Names: Nava, Alejandro (Author on hip hop), author.
Title: In search of soul : hip-hop, literature, and religion /
    Alejandro Nava.
Description: Oakland, California : University of
    California Press, [2017] | Includes bibliographical
    references and index.
Identifiers: LCCN 2017007876 (print) | LCCN 2017010142
    (ebook) | ISBN 9780520293533 (cloth : alk. paper) |
    ISBN 9780520293540 (pbk.) | ISBN 9780520966758
    (ebook)
Subjects: LCSH: Soul—Christianity. | Soul—Judaism. |
    Hip-hop—Religious aspects—Christianity. | Soul in
    literature. | Music—20th century—Philosophy and
    aesthetics. | Music—21st century—Philosophy and
    aesthetics.
Classification: LCC BT741.3 .N38 2017 (print) |
    LCC BT741.3 (ebook) | DDC 233/.5—dc23
LC record available at https://lccn.loc.gov/2017007876

Manufactured in the United States of America

26   25   24   23   22   21   20   19   18   17

10   9   8   7   6   5   4   3   2   1

La sombra de mi alma
huye por un ocaso de alfabetos,
niebla de libros y palabras.

—Federico García Lorca

Contents

Acknowledgments

I've been teaching courses on religion and hip-hop for many years now, so I want to begin by acknowledging my students at the University of Arizona. The conversations in the classroom—touching on issues of culture, music, religion, and literature—have added richness and depth to the themes and concerns of this book. When I first proposed a course on hip-hop more than ten years ago, it took some convincing that the subject had merit and intellectual weight. Things are different now; there are hundreds of courses on hip-hop throughout the country, and the University of Arizona has even developed a minor in hip-hop studies. I've been both surprised and delighted to witness this turn of events.

Of course I'm deeply grateful to the first readers of my book, especially Adam Bradley and Ilan Stavans. Adam Bradley read a very early draft of this book and showed tremendous patience, insight, and wisdom in his evaluation. He offered invaluable advice and direction. I'm grateful for his enthusiasm for this project. Ilan Stavans, too, provided me with tremendous support and encouragement. Although he is a busy scholar and public intellectual, he still found time to read my manuscript, and I'm very thankful that he did. And for many years now, Richard Rodriguez has challenged me to think and write outside the box of academic norms, to be more daring and creative in my scholarship. Although part of me will always remain tethered to academic fields of study, I take his counsel seriously and strive to loosen the restraints—sometimes as tight as a straitjacket—that prevent many scholars from stretching and extending our minds.

At the University of California Press, I want to thank Eric Schmidt for reaching out to me and choosing to publish my manuscript. At every stage of the journey, from proposal to review process, he was quick, courteous, and professional in his responses and provided me with many critical and supportive suggestions. My copyeditor, Sharon Langworthy, was fantastic and very helpful in correcting many of my worst tendencies in writing.

In the theological circles that I run in, I want to thank Roberto Goizueta, Tim Matovina, Daniel Groody, Benjamin Valentin, Carmen Nanko-Fernández, Gustavo Gutiérrez, and David Tracy. For years I've cherished the scholarship of each name above, but I've probably learned as much from their depth of character and devotion to the poor. I wrote my dissertation—and first book—on the thought of Gustavo Gutiérrez, and I can honestly say that his voice continues to ring and boom in my ears. Even when unacknowledged in this study, his influence on my theological vision has been profound. At the University of Chicago, I had numerous teachers who stirred my curiosity and sense of wonder, but David Tracy certainly stands out as an exceptional presence in the life of my mind and spirit. I have been blessed to count him as a teacher and as a friend, and I value his brilliance, learning, and generosity. Other teachers at the University of Chicago included Anne Carr, Bernard McGinn, Adela Collins, John Collins, Friedrich Katz, Homi Bhabha, and Jean-Luc Marion—all have been bright lights in my education. For the purposes of this study, I also received helpful advice from the current dean of the University of Chicago, Richard Rosengarten. Thank you, Rick, for your suggestions on the matter of "soul."

Finally, I want to thank my immediate and extended families for their unwavering love and support. My adopted family and their children—Rukia, Abdi, Abdullahi, Isha, Madina, Wiliye, Amina, Zeinab, Fatima, Yaya, Nasteha, Noorto, Husein, and Halima—have been a true gift and blessing in my life. I cherish the time we spend together and consider each of you my blood and kin. Of course, my mother and father gave me parts of their soul in raising me and my siblings; I'm grateful for their unconditional love. For their strong presence in my life and their inestimable support and encouragement, I thank my brother, Andy, the former b-boy and current physician (of Royal Rockers fame); my sister, Melinda; my sister-in-law, Bettina; my nephews, Zeta, Bianca, and Paloma; my uncle Carlos and aunt Bertha; and my cousin, Robert

Robinson. Numerous friends and relatives also have played key roles in my writing and life: Rick and the Duran family, Miguel Ferguson, Jim and Mimi Dew, Annie Reay, Elise Hansen, Brooke Sabia, Isabel Shelton, Bridget Longoria, Thomas Witherell, Carlos Nava, Eric Arvayo, and Mark and Sara Ryan. I'm very fortunate to have so many wonderful family members and friends who constantly enrich and nourish my soul.

Abbreviations

The following abbreviations are used in parentheses in text to refer to works by these authors in chapters 4 and 5.

FEDERICO GARCÍA LORCA

CP: *Collected Poems,* ed. Christopher Maurer (New York: Farrar, Straus, and Giroux, 2002).

DS: *Deep Song and Other Verse,* ed. and trans. Christopher Maurer (New York: New Directions, 1975).

G: Ian Gibson, *Federico García Lorca: A Life* (New York: Pantheon Books, 1989).

IL: *Impressions and Landscapes,* ed. and trans. Lawrence Klibbe (Lanham, MD: University Press of America, 1987).

SL: *Selected Letters* (New York: New Directions, 1983).

SV: *Selected Verse,* ed. Christopher Maurer (New York: Farrar, Straus, and Giroux, 1995).

RALPH ELLISON

CE: *The Collected Essays of Ralph Ellison,* ed. John Callahan (New York: Modern Library, 1995).

GTT: *Going to the Territory* (New York: Vintage Books, 1986).

IM: *Invisible Man* (New York: Vintage Books, 1995).

JT: *Juneteenth,* ed. John Callahan (New York: Vintage Books, 1999).

SA: *Shadow and Act* (New York: Vintage Books, 1995).

Introduction

Be the voice of night. . . .
Use dusky words and dusky images.
Darken your speech.

—Wallace Stevens[1]

The old generation had certainly pretty well ruined this world
before passing it on to us. They give us this thing, knocked to
pieces, leaky, red-hot, threatening to blow-up; and then they
are surprised that we don't accept it with the same attitude of
pretty, decorous enthusiasm with which they received it.

—F. Scott Fitzgerald[2]

I concede at the outset of this study that the phenomenon we call "soul"
is relentlessly opaque and shadowy, a nebulous thing seen through a
cloud darkly. In spite of the best efforts of reason over centuries of study
and vigorous inquiry, the soul remains a strange property of human life,
something that exists beyond the utmost boundaries of knowledge.
More a source of wonder than an object of reason, soul belongs to a
category dedicated to the art of questioning rather than the science of
knowledge because the study of the soul involves a quest without defin-
itive answers, endlessly deferred and yet endlessly compelling. While the
great classics of art, music, literature, and religion have spoken of soul
with great frequency, the confidence in what can be said and described
eventually falters on the shoals of the deep and inexpressible, which is
why so many works of art resort to the hope that it can be evoked and
felt if not exhaustively described. Music and religion are close companions on this score, as they assume the ability of the human spirit to
reach sublimity with words and sounds that are allusive and elliptical,

that indicate the limits of language as much as its rich possibilities. With this conundrum in mind—speaking of something familiar, but inexorably foreign, something near but as distant as the horizon—I explore the soul's elusive identity and try to add something to these attempts of human speech to name what is fundamentally nameless. And also with this conundrum in mind, I follow Wallace Stevens's admonition to choose dusky words and images, to darken my speech when speaking of the soul's uncanny mysteries.

Other issues this book considers are less conundrums than they are predicaments or crises of the spirit. We live in a time when the values of the soul—beauty, love, justice, compassion, contemplation, and reverence—are frequently replaced by the values of the marketplace—money, power, and pleasure—or in some scientific circles, by materialist accounts of the brain. When modern culture is most hostile to mystery and spiritual meaning, it has a way of diminishing and cheapening the most precious goods of life. Whether the soul is assailed by consumer temptations and indulgences or by an aggressive empiricism intolerant of transcendence, Western culture seems increasingly reluctant to acknowledge depth in the cosmos or human person, fearing that God may continue to lurk in the dark spectral spaces of the unknown. In his "psyche-analytical" approach to this question (a discipline concerned with "soul-analysis"), Jonathan Lear puts the issue in these terms: "Are we to see humans as having depth—as complex psychological organisms who generate layers of meaning which lie beneath the surface of their own understanding, or are we to take ourselves as transparent to ourselves?"[3] His sympathy, as mine, is with the former approach, in which the human soul is seen as a great, deep river with various crosscurrents and frothy vortexes of meaning running through it, forever blocking a clear vision of the bottomless ground of our being.

In my view, the battles fought over these questions are more than speculative questions of philosophy, psychology, or theology; there are more dangerous cultural and political implications. Seen in the context of modern history, for instance, the refusal to concede depth and complexity to non-European peoples often fueled violent imperial projects of conquest and exploitation. In the minds of many Europeans, colonized individuals and communities were named and depicted as they saw fit, regardless of what they thought. Think of the legendary reluctance of Native cultures to bare their bodies and souls to a camera or daguerreotype in this light; perhaps the anxiety was really about the destructive power of the Western gaze as Native American lives and ways were pried open and invaded until everything of value had been plundered. Maybe the reluctance to pose before a white man's camera represented a refusal to be understood on others' terms, a refusal to be turned into a caricature. Perhaps it was a way of guarding the dignity of Native bodies and souls, of keeping their inner selves blurred and impenetrable to Western strategies of representation, knowledge, and power. Perhaps it was a strategy in the same mold of James Brown's expert use of ruses and subterfuges to preserve the inner sanctum of his soul. "He had years of practice," writes James McBride, "covering up, closing down, shutting in, shutting out, locking up, locking out, placing mirrors in rooms, hammering up false doorways and floorboards to trap all comers who inquired about his inner soul."[4] Whether in Native histories or in the life of James Brown, there is a lesson here about the value of concealment and secrecy in the face of Western tendencies, when they lack proper respect for the spirit world, to strip the human condition of soul.

While many of the contemporary artists that I follow in this study recognize the opportunities and prospects made possible by the modern world, they also have profound misgivings for these reasons. These artists are conflicted moderns for whom modern achievements have been impressive in some ways but remarkably thin and shallow when it comes to the development of the human spirit. Lauryn Hill has spoken of a rampant miseducation at work here, a fundamental betrayal of the nobler aspirations of life. The result, she fears, is a generation of "lost ones," big on self-gratification and small on soul. "I'm about to change the focus," she raps, "from the richest to the brokest. I wrote this opus to reverse the hypnosis."[5] I invoke Lauryn Hill because I want to make clear my kinship with her efforts to break the hypnotic spell that has the modern age transfixed by the economy of appetite and avarice and to change the focus from the richest to the brokest.[6] In following the diverse genres of religion, literature, and music in this book, one may expect widely divergent opinions, but I argue that these artists form a unified ensemble of voices when it comes to privileging the jewels of art, wisdom, and compassion over the consumer culture of profit and possession.

MAP OF THE BOOK

This study is concerned with two major streams that have shaped Western ideas of soul: religious and biblical versions of soul (part I), and cultural, musical, and literary interpretations (part II). Though the demarcation here is a diaphanous and porous border, with dimensions of each leaking into the other, these categories allow us to consider soul from different angles, first as a biblical and theological concept and subsequently as a question of style in music, folklore, poetry, and literature. When speaking of this second inflection, I center my attention on African American and Spanish/Latin American traditions for the simple reason that they converge with my own area of expertise and, more personally, touch aspects of my own culturally conditioned soul; this is the music that is nearest and dearest to my own life.[7]

If my study is preoccupied with these traditions, it is not because of any presumption that black and Hispanic peoples naturally possess more "soul" than other groups. Assumptions of this kind are commonly called *essentialisms* in academic circles, meaning that they mistake historically contingent, cultural factors for genetic, racial, and biological factors.[8] In North America the roots of this idea run deep, at least as far back as the nineteenth century, when some writers, influenced by European romanticism, began to see non-European cultures cultures as exotic, tropical alternatives to the cold glaciers of American Puritan culture, on the one hand, and as substitutes for the developing creeds of science, industrial capitalism, and materialism in North American life on the other.[9] In these portraits, black and Hispanic lives were studies in the most vibrant kind of spirituality, bursting with sun-colored pigments: the red hues of emotional intensity, the dark blue pigments of anguish, the rainbows of hope and faith. In contrast to a world of black and white, these cultures gave us iridescent and polychromatic canvases, splashed with colors so variegated that they seemed like newly discovered works of impressionism. In certain ways this attitude—that blacks and Hispanics were aesthetically and spiritually advanced—represented progress over degrading notions of white supremacy and racism, but in other ways it left many of the pillars of prejudice intact, especially the presumption that these groups remained intellectually and morally deficient in spite of their admirable religious and artistic qualities.

I think otherwise, and so if there is sympathy on behalf of African American and Hispanic conceptions of soul in my study, it diverges widely from claims that would turn soul into an innate or ontological quality of certain ethnic groups (*romantic racialism* is another label given this tendency).[10] My interest is, instead, with the grammar of soul in these cultures, in the specific construction of this concept as it relates to the body of beliefs, values, and aesthetics of their traditions. I assume, then, that this concept is historically and socially acquired, and that religion, specifically biblical traditions, played a formative, yeast-like role in helping it rise and ripen. Understood this way, as a grammar or discourse, the concept of soul that developed in the twentieth century was a particular language and argot used by black and brown communities as a means of reclaiming the value and dignity of their embattled traditions. It was a language of dissent and prophecy, a countercultural trope allied with struggles for justice and equality (deeply indebted, in turn, to Jewish, Christian, and Islamic traditions).[11]

Because of the foundational influence of Christianity on these traditions, part I begins with a consideration of the idea of the soul in the Bible, with a special emphasis on literary approaches. Instead of a historical critical approach, I lean on literary and spiritual modes of exegesis, for the simple reason that these approaches are typically more effective in uncovering the contemporary meaning of these texts. While historical criticism assumes an existential distance and is usually more interested in the original purpose of a text than in present-day readings, I am advocating an existential engagement as the best way of approaching the soul of any text, religious or secular. Historical criticism is helpful in probing the skeleton of a text, but not its beating heart and soul, not its flesh and blood. We are better served by an approach that assumes a willingness to open ourselves "to something that deserves to be called their authority, whether we attribute that authority solely to the power of the human imagination or to a transcendent source of illumination."[12] In granting these texts authority in these ways, we acknowledge the possibility that these narratives may influence, challenge, and change us, that they may be, as Franz Kafka said, "ice-axes to break the sea frozen inside us."[13]

If one wonders about the specific logic that governs my choice of themes—from biblical texts to modern literature and hip-hop—I would say that the key characters in this study have a special, often intense, preoccupation with the question of "soul," a fluency with the rules and diction of this concept. Though the flair for "soul" in Federico García Lorca, Ralph Ellison, and hip-hop is a product of contemporary predicaments and themes (especially influenced by cultural nationalisms), these artists remain marked by the Bible's seismic impact. In the quaking and quivering lines of their sketches of "soul"—resembling the trembling effect of the bass on hip-hop speakers—one can still detect numerous aftershocks from the biblical explosion. These mysterious palpitations and yearnings are the subject of part I.

With the ancient roots of this concept excavated and explored, I shift attention to profane views in part II, considering how "soul" picks up modern nuances and becomes synonymous with the elegance of cultural and artistic achievements, especially in music. When turning to Lorca and Ellison, in particular, I consider the place of religion, music, folklore, and the vernacular in their portraits of soul (the subjects of chapters 4–5). For Lorca, gypsy ballads, deep song, and flamenco were the purest stuff of soul, the kind of art that was incubated in the heat of historical struggles among Spain's disenfranchised and hunted populations, especially gypsies, Moors, and Jews. In his poetry one can hear the stirring melodies and rhythms of these soundscapes, the exclamations and cries, the jubilations and ecstasies, all echoing to make it acoustically rich. As one of Lorca's friends once mentioned, he played with words and images as if they were musical instruments, giving the impression that he was always strumming the chords of a guitar or piano while he brought his poetry to life.[14] About Ellison, a trained musician, the same can be said regarding black American culture: the blues and jazz echo in his mind and bounce off the walls and canyons of his novels. They are fundamental to his construction of soul as the tragic-comic attitude toward life.

Finally, running up to the present, I don't think that the soul of our age can be written about without considering the creative influence of the hip-hop generation on the spiritual geography of the twenty-first century. The way Ellison and Lorca once found inspiration in the folk music of their times, countless artists have found inspiration in the street ballads and vernacular eloquence of hip-hop. Whether in circles of literature, music, or cultural studies, hip-hop vibes have become the sound of the contemporary generation, leaving an indelible record of urban problems, conflicts, and innovations on the minds of countless artists and listeners throughout the world. In considering the soul's fundamental kinship with music, hip-hop introduces certain themes and insights on the soul of the modern world that we ignore at our peril (the subject of chapters 6–7).

SOUL AND HIP-HOP

In many ways, the fundamental concerns of this study can be traced back to my earliest fascination with religion and hip-hop. My first introduction to the magic of words came from the profane tongues of rappers. Though I was drawn to a wide variety of musical genres in childhood, from Spanish music to soul and funk, the beats and rhymes of hip-hop had a magnetic appeal more than any other. Though the poetry was usually raw, bitter, and hard, it also had a sweet, smooth, honeyed influence on my ears. It was addictive and made me crave the

taste and melody of words. Maybe it was the swagger of the poetry—
garbled but eloquent—or the ability of the MC to form fluent patterns
out of a bedlam of bass beats and ghetto noises; whatever it was, I was
an early convert.

With this enthusiasm for poetic style and idiomatic verve, mixed with
a curiosity about religious questions, I eventually found myself in graduate school in Chicago, and this was one of the most elevating educational
experiences of my life. Ideas and books nourished my sense of wonder in
these years, swelling and raising it to new heights. At the same time,
though, my education got a jolt from living on Chicago's south side:
Instead of elevating, I would say that it was grounding, as I began to
notice with greater and greater alarm the scope of the poverty and violence only a stone's throw from the University of Chicago's Hyde Park
campus. While my mind burrowed deep in books and libraries, my eyes
and ears started to pick up on many of the battlegrounds on the south
side, and the result was a schooling in ghetto life. When tempted to lose
myself in books (the quixotic temptation that can addle one's brain, as
the case of Don Quixote proves), the pounding bass and gritty realism of
hip-hop brought me back to hard truths and reminded me, á la Sancho
Panza, or Hamlet's dictum to Horatio, that there are more things in
heaven and earth than are dreamt of in intellectual life. In effect, the
music forced me to scrutinize my education for its capacity, and sometimes failure, to spotlight the trials and tribulations of our world.

By some nice happenstance, the years of my graduate education, the
1990s, coincided with rap's most explosive growth and artistic inventiveness. Tupac burst on to the stage of hip-hop wearing multiple
masks—villain and saint, pimp and preacher, street hustler and prophet—
and many others followed suit. As a student of religion, I was particularly intrigued by rappers who would wantonly crisscross the categories
of the sacred and profane, and the list was a long catalog of the most
distinguished rappers: Nas, Lauryn Hill, Public Enemy, Common, Mos
Def, KRS-One, Bone Thugs & Harmony, Wu Tang, and numerous others. In spite of their crucial differences, almost all of these figures created
music that was earthy and raw, but with unmistakable desires and
dreams of transcendence, so that one side of their souls was rooted in the
brute realities of urban life and the other half soared high above the
mundane. The result was often a more mature, if tortured, spirituality
than one would find in many suburban churches, a thug's theology, as
Michael Dyson describes it.[15] Instead of viewing God from the pulpit or
the ivory tower, artists in this vein were rapping about God in a lower

register, out of the baritone depths of the human soul. From these guttural regions, they sometimes reached surprising heights of sublimity, as they wrestled with the crushing weight of suffering, the pits of despair, the darkness of God, and somehow came out kicking and alive like Jacob at the Jabbok stream.

True, there have always been strands of rap that are wack and trifling, but the best of it is a pedagogy in the dungeons of America, served up with juicy beats, guttural moans, and lyrics that, Ali-like, bounce, float, and box the listener's ears. More and more, I wanted to get in the mix and see if these street scriptures had anything to add to my formal studies at the university. If it was the sound and sonorous pleasures of rap that seduced me in my early years, now it was more about the social consciousness and spirituality of the music, how it assaulted the untroubled American conscience for its neglect of the poverty and distress of many American cities. I came to appreciate rap more and more for its ability to psychoanalyze the ills of the body politic, to plunge into the dark labyrinths of the American unconscious, and to force America to confront the traumas of its past and present. I came to value its dissenting heterodoxy when the American civil religion was concerned. Instead of apotheosizing the American dream and turning it into infallible dogma, rap offered a disquieting portrait of American nightmares: burned-out buildings, cities riddled with violence, housing projects that look like prison cells or orphanages, and young black and brown lives that ended prematurely, like fallen fruit that was never allowed to ripen. If nothing else, as I explore in chapter 6, hip-hop has often adopted an apocalyptic mode of utterance—shouts, hollers, screams—as a way of registering the feelings of existential brokenness and urban decay in many of these communities.

But there was something else that I increasingly noticed about the rough and ragged textures of the music: the invocations and appeals to God. Though there is certainly no denying that the music has a very secular, vulgar pitch to it and at times circles the drain in displays of prodigal excess, from hedonistic revelry to swaggering curses, I was also surprised by the frequency and depth of religious language in rap. Even in the thick mud of its wild prodigality, there remains a concurrent flow of the deepest spiritual springs, one that taps into subterranean rivers from black history and adds a mournful, blues-like trickle to the more raging waters of rap's hollers, shouts, and boasts. In these instances, hip-hop can strike a note that is thoroughly immersed and baptized in spiritual waters, in rivers that roll like the Jordan and bleed like the Red Sea. When this happens, hip-hop becomes a testimony, like so much of

American black music, to the brooding depths of great art and to the ability of the human spirit—perishable breath and all—to survive the tyranny of misfortune.

In my reading, the spiritual moments in hip-hop are interrogations of God in the face of confusion and affliction. They give voice to something like a *theologia crucis* or memento mori, reminding us of the bodies and souls left exposed to flames of the underworld. If death is a "beat without a melody," as Lin-Manuel Miranda has poetically called it, hip-hop is a faithful rendition of this bare skeleton beat, the sound of death in banging, tolling, boisterous, and exuberant tones.[16]

Of course, if this all sounds too heavy, I was also drawn to rap music because it was just plain fun, irrespective of the lyrical content. As many modernists have maintained, sometimes poetry can delight in the pure sonic qualities of words shorn of semantic meaning, a celebration of prancing syllables, dancing consonants, stressed syllables, and wailing pitches.[17] In this spirit, even the most frivolous raps appealed to me as long as they contained big, fat, apple-bottom bass and were delivered in a bouncing, uncooked flow, part singing, part talking, part grunting. Only those partial to the music can testify to these delights, the bass vibrating and electrifying the microscopic layers of the soul, making listeners feel that they are made of the same elements of the music, some unseen rhythms and spirits. Such things have a language of their own and can communicate without relying on words, as if the pulses and cadences speak in some ineffable, mystical tongue that calibrates the soul while riding roughshod over it. In such cases, words rarely suffice to explain the delicious beauty of music.

But then again, insofar as rap leans heavily on words and narratives, we must judge it by what it says and doesn't say. And when this becomes our theme, as in this study, my own biased inclination is toward the most artistic forms of rap, in which the lyrics are inventive and meaningful, the song's value is measured by its spiritual weight and ethical volume, and it does so much more than "make the club get crunk." For someone who feels the magnetic pull of transcendence as I do, it shouldn't surprise the reader that I would have a special affinity for the kind of hip-hop that combines dope beats with spiritual and social lessons about life in the hoods of America. Though I can still appreciate the playful party joints, the rap that appears in this study is a stricter diet of poetic, provocative, and thoughtful nourishment, music that is imbued with "moments of truth" as Gang Starr memorably described it, or "moments of clarity" in Jay Z's language.[18]

In my experience, at any rate, rap music has been all of this. It was my compass during my time in Chicago and helped me chart parts of this world, even parts of my own soul, that had once been foreign to this Mexican American kid from Tucson. Looking back on these formative wonder years, I consider some of my experiences inside and outside the University of Chicago to be the building blocks of the study presented here. In the great classics of religion and literature, I explored the tenebrous depths of the soul and learned a lot that shaped the contours of this study. But my years in Chicago also confirmed a truth deep in the American grain of things, that there are wilder truths and more soulful lessons than the classroom can offer, that a whaling ship could be one's Harvard and Yale (Herman Melville), that the slums and tenements of New York could be the finest tutors (Stephen Crane), and that "beyond the walls of intelligence, life is defined" (Nas).[19]

AFRO-LATIN SOUL

At the risk of being repetitive, let me say in clear terms that the main protagonist of my study is the figure of soul. (In this book I speak of "the soul" when referring to the spiritual concept, and "soul" when discussing the cultural, aesthetical understanding, as long as we keep in mind that the latter is distinct but not separate from the former.) Though hip-hop is prominent, my primary focus is on the fate of the soul in our times. Because there are many signs of the soul's retreat or disappearance in modern life, this study digs deep into the underground for signs of the soul's throbbing and vital pulse, especially among African American and Latin cultures. Besides the spiritual value of this effort, studies in Afro-Latin conjunctions have great contemporary significance, especially given the surging waves of Latin American immigrants to the United States and the fact that many of them end up in crowded and pinched quarters, elbow to elbow, if not shackle to shackle, with many blacks in America. Studies on the relationship of blacks and Latinos in the Americas will only grow more urgent and timely, and I hope that this book, with a focus on some of the spiritual, literary, and musical dimensions of this relationship, will join the swelling choruses of black and brown voices.

The seeds of this study lie in the simple desire to add color and culture to a study of the soul. When a study of this sort remains at the level of pure philosophical or theological abstraction, it is almost certain that the embodied nature of soul will be missed, that the wild diversity of human souls in race, culture, and language will be overlooked. And the result is usually an image of the soul that is insipid and pale, resembling very little the idea of soul in living color, the soul as a living, breathing, suffering, dreaming thing. The transition from part I to part II of my study can also be seen, then, as an attempt to provide a thicker description, to sprinkle the soul with the spices and piquancy of human culture. In holding together these two dimensions, the sacred and profane, this study insists on the value of each perspective: the sublime and transcendent qualities of the soul in religious traditions on the one hand, and the brilliant, luminous frescos of soul in culture, art, and music on the other. And this brings us to the ancient view of rap. For the Greeks, the term *rhapsodize (rhapsoidein)* meant "to stitch songs together," so in my study, I hope to be true to ancient and new attempts to stitch together various songs, beats, and human experiences, all in the effort to shed some light on the dark and dusky idea of the soul.

As I explore these different components of soul, I consider Otis Redding's classic album *Complete and Unbelievable: Otis Redding Dictionary of Soul* (1966) as a revealing symbol of the spirit of his age and an intimation of what was to come in hip-hop. Out of the pyrotechnics of Redding's soul, a new tempo was introduced to American life as the meaning of soul was given a new level of intensity, emotional force, and sartorial flair. It would change clothes and take on shades of the night, become blacker and more tender. I am suggesting that a similar ingenuity is apparent in the hip-hop generation, as rappers have added new words and syntaxes, new syncopations and styles to this older lexicon of soul. After ransacking and absorbing the traditional vocabulary (the beats in addition to the dialect), rappers left their own marks on the dictionary of soul, making sure that it would parse and interpret the ghetto conditions of their lives in the late twentieth century. To fully appreciate their modifications, I need to begin with biblical, theological, and literary monuments, then shift focus to the rappers who shook these monuments, Samson-like, to produce new temples of art. In these figures, the acquisition of soul becomes closely related to the search for the perfect beat, rhyme, and style. Rakim describes it this way: "I start to think and then I sink / into the paper like I was ink / When I'm writing, I'm trapped in between the lines / I escape when I finish the rhyme. . . . I got soul."[20] As a tribute to these efforts to escape the traps and confinements of older conventions, or the more treacherous traps of ghetto life, hip-hop has demonstrated mighty powers of soul, combining cool aplomb and sweaty, funky grace to make a combustible form of music that has exploded into many luminous sparks. In the process, something beautiful and resplendent has been fashioned out of an age "knocked to pieces, leaky, red-hot, threatening to blow-up."

PART ONE

Sacred Histories of the Soul

1

In Search of Soul

Let us simmer over our incalculable cauldron, our enthralling
confusion, our hotch-potch of impulses, our perpetual
miracle—for the soul throws up wonders every second.
—Virginia Woolf[1]

Fix every wandering thought upon that quarter where all
thought is done; who can distinguish darkness from the soul?
—W. B. Yeats[2]

Now, my darling Nora, I want you to read over and over all
I've written to you. Some of it is ugly, obscene and bestial,
some of it is pure and holy and spiritual: all of it is myself.
—James Joyce[3]

THE LOSS OF SOUL IN THE MODERN AGE

As so many other ancient pieties are viewed in our times, the concepts
of God and soul have increasingly become objects of suspicion, if not
indifference. Where secularization has been most aggressive in the twentieth century, especially among European and American writers dubbed
the "new atheists," we have seen obituaries written on behalf of both
ideas, as if they are now anachronisms, relics of days of old, when wonder and magic filled the air.[4] In many of these accounts the story of the
modern world is narrated in evolutionary terms, with secularization
greeted as the morning sun, dispersing the murky fog of the night, and
the age of Enlightenment welcomed as the conqueror of the dark ages
of the past. As a corollary of a Eurocentric bias, measuring every corner
of the globe by its own presumptions of cultural superiority, this story

measures and quantifies the development of world cultures by their adherence to Western norms of rationality and finds them crude when they deviate from these norms. It is a story that frequently casts religion in the role of the superstitious and primitive barbarian and reserves the civilizing and colonizing role for science. With a monopoly on truth established by scientific principles, the religious worldview is largely denied and dispossessed of any claim on the truth; this now belongs to the purview of modern rationality, a conception of knowledge stripped of archaic mysteries and primeval beliefs. In this paradigm, little, if any, tolerance is afforded a concept like the "soul." It belongs to an antiquated age whose time is done.

While this narrative of intellectual and cultural evolution has remained an influential model, it has also stirred up swarms of opposition from various artists and intellectuals who dispute its value and credibility. Around the same time that the clouds of disbelief thickened the most (roughly speaking, the nineteenth century to the present), the principles associated with the idea of soul found advocates in numerous modern movements, from romanticism and modernism to African American and Latin American thought. In their own unique ways, these developments resuscitated and breathed new life into the concept of soul, making it stronger and richer, infusing it with the magic elixirs of poetry, myth, melody, and cultural style. In these cases, the various apologists for the idea of the soul revealed a certain degree of misgiving and skepticism about some of the new dogmas that the age of reason sought to enshrine in place of the soul and God. They tended to blame modern secularism for a small and monochromatic view of reason and culture and for a Eurocentric hubris that presumed to judge all that is true, good, and beautiful by its own parochial standards. For those who continued to believe in the power of the soul to claim and raise up a person's life, the Enlightenment's pantheon of new creeds—free enterprise and consumerism, materialism and bureaucratization, science and rationality, and not least, self-assured confidence in European superiority over all other peoples in this brave new world—offered a poor and paltry substitute for the values of old, and many modern artists withheld their devotion.

One might measure the breadth of discontent in modernity by the interest in the soul, by the palpable fear that the soul, once a star, is now in danger of collapsing into a black hole. For Dr. Martin Luther King Jr., for instance, advocacy on behalf of the soul—or what he called "soul force"—revealed a profound sense of discontent and disillusionment with the modern world and tended to act as a spotlight on the numerous cracks and flaws lurking in the foundations of the Western world. His grammar of soul exposed these defects and showed how crushing the forces of modernity have been to many people of color.[5] For millions of colonized and non-European communities, in fact, Enlightenment principles of freedom, rationality, and equality were a burlesque of the facts, so many looked elsewhere for alternative forms of liberation. In spite of pronouncements of the death of God, or the death of the soul, religious traditions remained desirable and meaningful options among African American and Hispanic communities and offered them resources for spiritual and cultural resistance to Western "progress." The idiom and notion of the soul, as a precious fragment of the larger body of Christianity, became a trope of defiance, a prophetic and dangerous weapon of social justice. By tracking the fate of "soul" in this study, therefore, one might not only evaluate the transmutations of the idea at the hands of black and Spanish traditions—specifically, the antimodern and postcolonial gestures in these renditions of the idea of soul—but also assess the state of modernity as the soul increasingly finds itself in a starved and inhospitable landscape.[6]

In this chapter I define "soul"—its sacred and profane manifestations—but at this point I want to invoke Virginia Woolf's reading of Russian literature in the 1920s, because in it she works on the same assumption that guides my study: namely, that the grammar of the soul has increasingly fallen into disuse in the Western world (she singles out the English context), yet it flourishes in other contexts, especially on the edges and margins of the modern world. In this regard, she turns to the raging spirituality of Russian literature to explore regions of the world or regions of her own self where the soul still pulsates with life. If modernity treats the soul as a museum piece, no longer an actor in the drama of modern society, Woolf directs us to places where the soul is still vibrant and alive, where the flicker is more like a furious flame, still leaping and dancing. Perhaps there is something of the exotic in this desire—like the taste of chocolate to a tongue that has only known insipid foods—but more generously, it can be seen as a measure of her discontent with modern European culture, on the one hand, and on the other her genuine willingness to explore the whole circumference of the soul, even parts of her being that her culture did not deem credible any more, parts of her that were inflamed by the Russians.

In England, Woolf argues, the soul is now an alien term and has been replaced by a more staid and rational concept, alone and aloof, flat and emotionless, something that we call the self.[7] In the exchange of the self or the brain for the deep-down caves and grottos of the soul, we have been left with an entity that lacks the numinous density of its older ancestor. If we want to find the soul at its meridian, where it still scorches and blackens, she advises us to look directly into the high-noon sun of Fyodor Dostoyevsky, Lev Tolstoy, and Anton Chekhov. "Indeed," she writes,

> it is the soul that is the chief character of Russian fiction. . . . We are souls, tortured, unhappy souls, whose only business is to talk, to reveal, to confess, to draw up at whatever rending of flesh and nerve those crabbed sins which crawl on the sand at the bottom of us. But as we listen, our confusion slowly settles. A rope is flung to us; we catch hold of a soliloquy; holding us by the skin of our teeth, we are rushed through the water; feverishly, wildly, we rush on and on, now submerged, now in a moment of vision understanding more than we have ever understood before, and receiving such revelations as we are wont to get only from the press of life at its fullest.[8]

In reading Woolf on the Russians, I get the feeling that her pen was dipped in the same feverish ink as her subject matter, because it flies off and rushes through her essays, plunging deep into the seething whirlpools and unfathomable depths of its characters, their beauty and vileness, their saintliness and licentiousness. In her reading, the Russian soul is a maelstrom of astonishing extremes, with its scurrilous sins and unexpected graces, its capacity for perversion as much as mysticism, self-deception as much as enlightenment, baseness as much as nobility. And through it all, there is an unmistakable ethical intensity, a throbbing pulse that alerts the reader to the plight of the distressed in our human, fallen world. She clings to the Russian writers' dramatization of soul—like a rope that drags her through the water gasping for breath—because it seems to buoy her soul with the kind of oxygen lacking in her own modern, bourgeois world. She wants to imbibe deeply the Russian soul, soaking her liver in its alcohol like a Karamazov, because this literature is frequently drunk with surprises and wonders, tragedies and comedies, and yet is perfectly sober when it comes to compassion for our fellow sufferers in the world. "The simplicity, the absence of effort, the assumption that in a world bursting with misery the chief call upon us is to understand our fellow-sufferers, and not with the mind—for it is easy with the mind—but with the heart; this is the cloud which broods above the whole of Russian literature, which lures us from our own parched brilliancy and scorched thoroughfares to expand in its shade."[9]

She summons Western readers to brood over the profound shades of Russian literature for its instinctual, unstudied ability to speak to the heart on the matter of human suffering. If nothing else, it provokes, agitates, and even rubs raw the reader's conscience, calling us to solidarity with others and to a mode of perception and understanding that is more profound than the triumphs of intelligence. On this point, her sentiment is close to the famous line by John Keats: "Do you not see how necessary a world of pains and troubles is to school an intelligence and make it a soul?"[10] Whether in Keats or Woolf, intelligence without soul is a singing voice without lungs behind it, a voice without pathos, pain, or depth.

Keeping in mind Woolf's assessment of Russian soul, this study follows a similar trail, but with African American and Latin American traditions as its guiding spirits. My study operates with an assumption related to the ideas of Woolf and Keats: that there is something wildly quixotic about its endurance in the modern world and something surprisingly revelatory in this foolish passion for the soul, something that can school the modern intelligence on the matters of the human spirit.

As mentioned in the introduction, I suggest we look at these themes and refrains on the soul in two major ways: first, with biblical and theological traditions in mind, and second, in the spirit of the profane, in which "soul" becomes synonymous with exuberant styles, cultures, literatures, and, above all, the powerful currents of music.

ON NAMING SOUL: AT THE CROSSROADS OF THE SACRED AND PROFANE

When reflecting on the idea of the secular in the mid-twentieth century, W. H. Auden made the perceptive claim that it had its origins in "the belief that the Word was made flesh and dwelt among us, and that, in consequence, matter, the natural order, is real and redeemable, not a shadowy appearance or the cause of evil, and historical time is real and significant."[11] In this judgment the idea of the secular was a seed already entrenched in Christian thought, a seed that would mature in the course of Christian history and fully blossom in modern times. Because of the tangled intersections of the sacred and secular in Christianity, where historical time and the natural world are stages for the advent of the divine, the relationship between the sublime Word and the stuff of creation should be seen, Auden contends, in symbiotic rather than clashing terms. In contrast to Gnostic repudiations of time and space, the *saeculum* in Christianity is the womb in which God enters into time and space. In the unity of Christ, the sacred and secular are reconciled.[12] An absolute repudiation of the secular is thus a theological mistake and heresy. It forecloses the infinite possibilities and surprising appearances of God in every facet of the human drama.

My study follows this theological intuition in searching for epiphanies in both sacred and secular guises, but this claim should not be misconstrued to mean that we should conflate or collapse the terms altogether. The distinction between the two is worth defending if only to remind us of the contributions of each domain of human experience. Richard Kearney puts it in these terms: "Only secularization can prevent the sacred from becoming life denying, while only sacralization can prevent the secular from becoming banal. . . . The secular involves the human order of finite time, while the sacred denotes an order of infinity, otherness, and transcendence that promises to come and dwell in our midst."[13] The careful balancing between the two dimensions can avoid the pitfalls of theocracy, holy war, and ecclesial imperialism, on the one hand, and the threat of nihilism, on the other. When an aggressive version of the sacred overwhelms and anathematizes the secular, as in some of the most violent fundamentalist reactions to modernity, the inclination is to bar the revelations that may occur outside the sacred realm, and that may happen unexpectedly in any number of experiences; when the profane is the sole and dominant motif, however, the inclination is to strip the human and natural world of mystery and to replace them with mechanistic and material ideas that are flat, predictable, and soulless.

The main lesson here is that such separations ("soul and body" and "supernatural and natural" can be added to the pairing "sacred and profane") are products of contingent historical genealogies in modern Western Europe and should not predetermine how we understand the meaning of "soul" in Judaism or Christianity or its meaning in African American or Latin American traditions.[14] This is an important point to keep in mind in my study, because conceptions of soul in African American and Latin American traditions, as in premodern Christianity, wantonly trespass across these borders, breaching the barriers that try to keep them apart. I insist, then, on the curious juxtaposition and intermingling of the sacred and profane in these Afro-Latin traditions and hope that the reader can see the redemptive possibilities of both ideas of soul. For this reason, the metaphors of the crossroads and a border are illuminating for my study, insofar as they demarcate regions in between the sacred and profane, somewhere on the transitional boundaries and open plains of these binary oppositions, where contrary and divergent winds breathe life into the idea of the soul.[15]

In this regard there is something richly suggestive about the Yoruba deity Elegua, god of the crossroads, trickster figure, and patron of drumming and rhythm. As the god of the crossroads, he sits at the junction of divergent paths of the sacred and profane, in places where the pious and pompous would never venture, where Robert Johnson once promised his soul to the devil in order to learn how to make his guitar moan and wail. Church folks called a lot of these rhythms and rhymes "devil's music"; so tempting, pleasurable, and ravishing these sounds must have seemed to their priggish ears. And similar aspersions were cast on Afro-Latin music. The term *diablo* was in fact a synonym for the mambo. (The word "mambo" derives from Congo religion, where it referred to the concluding chants of a spirit-possession ceremony.) In its secular incarnations, mambo came to mean the final section of a musical or dance performance, when the artist was given free rein to improvise and let loose with an "anarchy in tempo," *a la diabla*.[16] In these moments the artist was permitted to be unruly, excessive, and profligate in his flow and tempo, as if he, too, were suddenly possessed by wild spirits. Gustavo Perez Firmat writes, "The name connotes excess, outrageousness, lack of decorum. A mambo mouth is a loud mouth, someone with a loose tongue, someone who doesn't abide by rules of propriety. The mambo is nothing if not uncouth, improper, its musical improprieties sometimes even bordering on the *improperio*, the vulgar or offensive outburst."[17]

In the spirit of these uncouth flurries of emotion, I explore some of the creative possibilities of the music of the profane in this study. One might say that the consideration of soul in this book follows the passage from the sanctified soul of gospel music to the devil's music of the blues, R & B, soul, and rap, the route from sacred to profane manifestations. The specific genre "soul music" (a term that originated in the late 1950s along with terms like "soul brother" and "soul food") is an example of the bridge between the two: it was seeded by gospel music but watered and fertilized by the brazen sexual electricity of the blues and R & B.[18] The grooves of Sam Cooke, Ray Charles, Curtis Mayfield, Jackie Wilson, and Otis Redding muddied the stylistic, harmonic, and lyrical distinctions between gospel and R & B, making for soul sermons that were unlike anything heard before. These artists were, in the words of bluesman Big Bill Broonzy, "crying sanctified."[19]

Although I defend this crossroads, it should be clear that I am not arguing that we skirt or run around modernity. While I want to preserve classic Jewish and Christian beliefs on the soul, I also contend that the modern milieu of secularism enabled a degree of creative freedom and artistic inventiveness on this theme, specifically in its forbearing of cultural and musical revelries outside the churches, in the rowdy, disorderly, and bawdy underground of society, in juke joints, chitlin' circuits, and the like. The blues, R & B, funk, and hip-hop all have sacred influences and motifs, but they also challenge the monopoly of grace claimed by the churches and assume, á la Meister Eckhart, that one cannot muffle God and confine him to a church.[20] And the same holds for the literary and cultural creations of Ralph Ellison and Federico García Lorca, both of whom dress up their ideas of soul with a prodigal mixture of the sacred and profane. They surely would have conceded the intuition of John Keats when he defended the poet's freedom in exploring the darkness as much as the light, the mean as much as the elevated: "What shocks the virtuous philosopher, delights the camelion [sic] poet. It does no harm from its relish of the dark side of things any more than from its taste for the bright one. . . . It enjoys light and shade, it lives in gusto, be it foul and fair, high and low, rich or poor, mean or elevated."[21]

On the matter of soul, then, I follow the intuitions of poets and mystics in their daring exploration of the fair and foul, high and low, light and shade, shocking as it might be for the virtuous philosopher or theologian. This Keatsian formulation, it seems to me, has inspired a wide variety of contemporary hip-hop intellectuals, such as Michael Dyson, Cornel West, Anthony Pinn, Imani Perry, Adilifu Nama, Paul Gilroy, and Adam Bradley, as well as numerous others. "Historically," Paul Gilroy writes, "black political culture's most powerful notions of agency have been figured through the sacred. They can also get figured through the profane, and there, a different idea of worldly redemption can be observed. Both of these possibilities come together for me in the traditions of musical performance that culminates in hip hop."[22] Or take another example, from Adilifu Nama: "To hip hop's credit, this sensibility has lessened the artificial and often idealized separations between 'the good, bad, and ugly' aspects of the black and brown experience. Consequently, stringent and bifurcated notions of the sacred and profane have been jettisoned for a messy and fluid assessment of right and wrong."[23] In my exploration of the black and brown conceptions of soul, I thus follow the lead of these scholars but with a special focus on the crossroads between African American and Latin traditions in religion, literature, and music. Since Christianity proved decisive in the understanding of soul in these traditions, the yeast that allowed it to rise, I begin my study with the problem of definition, specifically how the idea of the soul was named and interpreted in Christian thought, before moving on to the profane unfolding of soul.

THEOLOGICAL SOUL: IN PLACE OF THE MODERN SELF

Soul as Imago Dei, *Icon of Divine Presence and Transcendence*

To distinguish theological versions of soul from the modern self, I begin with the fundamental assumption that the human soul is made in the image of God, that it is an icon of both divine presence and transcendence. By virtue of an analogical likeness (similarity in difference), the soul participates in the beauty and goodness of God, though it remains infinitely other than God, weighed down by its heavy mortal coil. By the force of the soul's temporal condition, the soul is divided and dispersed, conflicted and distracted, twisted and distorted (*distentio animi* in Augustine's terms), but it forever remains an image of God, shot through with beauty, wild with divinity, the *imago Dei* distorted but not destroyed. The soul may be, as William Butler Yeats says about the human heart, a "foul rag and bone shop," but it still participates in the splendor of divine infinity and reflects the charged grandeur of God, the deep down otherness of God.[24]

So yes, the soul is an icon of divine *presence,* of the grace that fills and yet exceeds the soul. Insofar as the soul mirrors the divine in its infinite mystery and resplendence, however, it also shares in the nocturnal depths of God; the soul is also an icon of divine *transcendence.* While the soul is holy like God, sacred and precious, of infinite worth and dignity (a fact that was revolutionary for slaves throughout the Americas), it is also shrouded by a cloud of unknowing like the G-d of Exodus. Unlike idolatrous portraits of the self, which leave no room for the Other and crowd out the presence of wonder, the soul is an icon of the Other, a portrait that is filled with light and shade like a chiaroscuro painting of the Renaissance. In the space of a unique singular person, the soul is an aura or trace of the infinite.[25]

In Gregory of Nyssa's portrait of the soul, for example, the metaphor of icon is explicitly invoked: "The icon is perfectly an icon only so long as it is missing nothing of what is known in the archetype. Now, since incomprehensibility of essence is found in what we see in the divine nature, it must necessarily be that every icon keeps in it too a likeness with its archetype."[26] Since the soul is an icon of divine incomprehensibility, the argument goes, the soul shares in this incomprehensibility and formlessness, in that which is without shape or semblance. The soul resembles "nothing"; it is denuded of all graven images, indeterminate and strange. What pertains to God—namelessness—also pertains to humankind. "Man remains unimaginable," writes Jean-Luc Marion, "since formed in the image of He who admits none, incomprehensible because formed in the likeness of He who admits no comprehension."[27]

Augustine's consideration of the conundrum of memory only deepens this *via negativa* of theological anthropology. As he wanders through the hinterlands of the human psyche, his language gropes for metaphors and images that intensify, rather than eliminate, our perplexity and surprise. For Augustine, to put it plainly, the soul is an enigma, and the human person is an "immense abyss."[28] In his winding, circuitous path into the soul, Augustine never discovers an unchanging ground of identity or any essence of subjectivity in the center of the soul's labyrinth. If anything, his discovery entails the dizzying, vertiginous realization of an infinite panorama within, one whose center is everywhere and circumference is nowhere. As for self-knowledge, he can only concede that he knows *that* he is, but not *what* he is; his existence is not in doubt, but his essence confounds him enough for him to say that he has become a great question to himself.[29] When considering the great mysteries of memory in particular, he tells us that he is suddenly lost in astonishment, and a great stupor seizes him.[30] Like any poet addressing an inscrutable question, he reaches for metaphors that describe the wonder of it all: memory is a wide plain, a spacious palace, a storehouse of images, a vast cloister, a cavern and crater, a vast and infinite sanctuary: "Who can plumb its depths? And yet, it is a faculty of my soul."[31]

So as a faculty of the soul, memory poses an insurmountable problem for self-consciousness and makes the search for soul an existential ordeal. "I have become to myself," he confesses, "a land of difficulty over which I toil and sweat."[32] If the terrain of the soul in Augustine is a land of difficulty with numerous caverns and abysses along the way, travel through this territory is like spelunking in subterranean depths, advancing by touch and feel, living by faith not sight. And without a fixed essence at the core, human identity is subject to constant variations, changes, and upheavals, as is evident in so many biblical characters (the subject of the following chapters). The soul is an ever-expanding vessel, one that constantly grows and swells, contracts and stumbles, advances and retreats. For Augustine, though, the keys to the soul's growth and not its ruin are the biblical values of dispossession over possession, *caritas* over the *libido dominandi,* self-renunciation over self-gratification.[33] If the soul is to be true to its divine nature—its fathom-less and shoreless being—it must embody these values with the same wanton generosity as the sun over the desert.

In spite of these apophatic moments in classical theology (the moments of unsaying in theological discourse), however, Gregory of Nyssa and Augustine clearly assumed that we can in fact achieve some wisdom about God and the soul, even if that is a revelation in obscurity, seen through a mirror dimly. Augustine did believe that we encounter God in the labyrinth of the soul, that God graces us with an understanding, how-ever partial, of who we are, who we can be, and who we ought to be. It is obvious, then, that knowledge of God is revelatory and revolutionary for the meaning and purpose of our lives. Even if our grasp of God—and the human soul—is evanescent and imperfect, like Moses's glimpse of God as he passed by, it is enough to stun and transform us (Exod. 33:17–23). And even if the soul is as elusive as a phantom ("Few catch the phan-tom," as Woolf writes; "most have to be content with a scrap of her dress, or a wisp of her hair."), the Christian tradition dresses up the soul in radiant colors and voluptuous profiles, which makes the soul into something a lot more sensual and alluring than a bloodless ghost.[34]

The Aesthetic Contours of Soul: Mysticism, Music, and Festivity

To speak of the soul as an icon—in which God is simultaneously revealed and concealed, present and absent—is to inevitably invite the question of aesthetics. At least in classic Christian theology, especially in the analogical tradition, the experience of beauty is a seductive ruse of God to charm and beguile the soul and hence a confirmation of what is true and good. Nicolas of Cusa said that we can taste eternal wisdom in everything savored, feel eternal pleasure in all things pleasurable, and behold eternal beauty in all that is beautiful.[35] In the myriad forms of creation, everything is saturated with grace, thus compromising the divisions of sacred and profane, spirit and flesh, the transcendent and worldly. God's presence teems and overflows in the cosmos, bathing and penetrating everything, large and small. The human soul, as a result, is indivisible from the elegant tapestry of creation, and a micro-cosm of the larger pattern of the universe. In this world of grace, a "house made of dawn, house made of the dark cloud," the soul walks surrounded and steeped in beauty ("Navajo Night Chant").[36]

In David Bentley Hart's assessment, this classic vision of the soul was eventually forsaken for the modern self:

But before modern subjectivity had fully evolved and emerged from the waters, a person was indeed conceived as a living soul swimming in the deeps, participating in the being of the world, inseparable from the element he or she inhabited and knew; and the soul, rather than the sterile abstraction of an ego was an entire and unified spiritual and corporeal reality; it was the life and form of the body, encompassing every aspect of human existence, from the nous to the animal functions, uniting reason and emotion, spirit and flesh, memory and presence, supernatural longing and natural capacity.[37]

In this enchanted cosmology, the soul is submerged in the being of the world and is related to the whole of creation; it is the brother of the sun, the sister of the moon, and the child of mother earth.[38] And it is of course related to the verbal and musical artistry of the cosmos: When the soul is attuned to and synchronized with grace, it rises into being at the sound of creation's sonata-like summons and moves and dances to the gravitational pull of the heavenly spheres. In fact, as the ancient Pythagoreans, Neoplatonists, and Christian theologians believed, everything is formed with the cadence and rhapsody of poetry and song. God created the universe by the artistry of language like a great orator or musician, filling the silent void of the earth with melody and sonority, producing music from the rotation of the heavenly bodies, so that all of creation became an ode to beauty: the chiming of the planets in their orbits, the splashing voices of the sea, the caroling air, whistling winds, warbling birds, buzzing cicadas, and groaning and pealing thunder.

The concept of the soul in the Middle Ages was a reaping of this Greco-Roman and Jewish-Christian vision, in which music was the food of the soul and a medium of transcendence. Many medieval theologians saw music as both edifying and elevating. They discerned in music a unique mode of perception, one that draws the soul into ethereal spheres of truth. In reference to the musical ear of Gregory of Nyssa, Hart remarks: "According to Gregory of Nyssa, creation is a wonderfully wrought hymn to the power of the Almighty: the order of the universe is a kind of musical harmony, richly and multifariously toned, guided by an inward rhythm and accord, pervaded by an essential symphony."[39] In appealing to this great symphony of creation, Gregory of Nyssa clearly resonated with the rich pedagogical culture of early Christianity, in which the sequence of the liberal arts gradually moved in an ascending pattern through grammar, rhetoric, arithmetic, geometry, music, and astronomy.[40] The liberal arts were spiritual exercises that worked to elevate the mind beyond the bedlam of noises in the world to the perfect consonance of the stars and the beauty beyond them. (Augustine's tract *De musica* is an example of this and culminates in the sixth book with a meditation on the mystical number patterns in music.)[41]

Since music is revelatory of the pattern of the universe, not to mention the divine pattern within the human person, sin might be seen as a note of cacophony and discord that suddenly disturbs the soul's rhythm, pace, and sense of time. Thrown off balance and dazed by sin, the soul is now a dancer without grace, knocked awry and tangled up. As the Lord of the dance, however, Christ enters the world to reform, inform, and transform the soul. Christ recovers the soul's dexterity and converts it from the graceless condition of a will that is curved in upon itself to a condition of charity and self-abandon, lost in the arms of the other—the ecstasy of Teresa of Ávila is nothing else.[42]

While Teresa's ecstasy may be a particularly intense and special case of mysticism and seemingly remote from the experiences of modern man and woman, music has a way of making us all into mystics of sorts, of spreading to us the peace, joy, and knowledge that surpasses all the art and argument of the earth.[43] No wonder that Nietzsche considered the intoxicating appeal of Dionysus to be indistinguishable from music.[44] His own experience of modern music confirmed what the ancient Greeks had understood: that music could seize and shake one's soul in moments of pleasure, and that it is incomparable in its revelatory possibilities. "Compared with music," he wrote, "all communication by words is shameless."[45] Just as Aquinas considered everything he wrote to be like straw compared to what God had revealed to him, Nietzsche considered music in a similar mystical sense, as a spiritual phenomenon with a unique ability to penetrate the secrets of life.[46] Western civilization is filled with testimonies of music's mesmerizing and transporting power, its ability to raise the temperature of the soul to feverish highs. Music can hypnotize, as Biggie says, or it can cause us to lose ourselves in it, as Eminem and T. S. Eliot say, or it can simply make us say "uhhhh," to summon Master P.[47]

In following this stirring signature inherent in music, I want to insist that these kinds of spiritual raptures were not just encased in marble and confined to theological circles during the Middle Ages. One would have witnessed a feast of beauty in myriad rituals, carnivals, festivities, and theatrical performances. Unlike the disembodied forms of Christianity that emerged with the modern world like a late-born heresy, Gnostic in inspiration, premodern Christianity was deeply corporeal. One might say that it had some of the same features as Cervantes's characters in *Don Quixote*: the bodily and sensual sensibilities of Sancho Panza and the magic, marvel, and mysticism of Don Quixote. This Christianity knew the longings of transcendence; the urges of the flesh and *panza;* and the delights of drama, rite, and farce. A rich and round figure, the Catholic baroque soul would increasingly show signs of fragmenting and coming apart, but Cervantes kept it together the way he kept together the bosom friends of his novel: the dreamer and pragmatist, the idealist and realist, the transcendentalist and sensualist.

In other cultures of early modernity, however, the strained ties holding together the "great chain of being" (a vision that integrated divine transcendence and immanence, spirit and flesh, reason and emotions, theory and practice, asceticism and pageantry) increasingly showed signs of rusting and breaking. Under the reforming passion of Protestant Christianity beginning in the sixteenth century, cultures of festivity were gradually replaced by cultures of discipline, leading to forms of Christianity that were more suspicious of ritual, aesthetics, and festivals than the prevailing vision of the Middle Ages.[48] As early as the Reformation, if not earlier, there was a shift in Christianity from corporeal and ritualized practices toward a disembodied and disenchanted form of Christianity, with heavy emphasis on doctrinal propositions, catechisms, and mental states. Though this trend is also evident in the concerns and mandates of the Counter-Reformation, the Puritan variety of these reforms developed a particular concern with discipline and punishment, as it sought to repress the festive, ecstatic, Dionysian expressions of Christianity with a work ethic of self-regulation, restraint, and order. Modern capitalism, as Max Weber famously argued, would be built of such things.

The forms of culture, religion, and custom that did not conform to the new ideals of self-control and restraint became tantamount to indolence, moral torpor, economic debility, and religious barbarism; in North America, Catholic, American Indian, and African behavior and forms of worship were considered cases in point, specifically prone to idolatry, futility, and dereliction of duty.[49] To forge a more perfect union of disciplined, rational, and professional modes of life, cultural and religious traits that did not match Calvinist and neo-Stoic values were to be repressed and colonized into submission; they didn't have a future in a well-ordered society. In the case of Catholics, almost everything they did smacked of unproductive and primitive values: sacramental rites and popular festivals, feasting at cemeteries, dancing around the maypole, the veneration of saints and angels, shrines associated with paganism and the natural world, the aesthetic extravagance of carnival, baroque architecture, and so forth.

Excess and ostentation would fall on hard times in the modern world, leading to a more incorporeal conception of the soul. In someone like René Descartes, this seems clear: his embrace of neo-Stoicism led him to redefine the meaning of "soul," making it resemble the soul of the philosophers more than the soul of Abraham, Isaac, and Jacob, to paraphrase Blaise Pascal. In my reading, this led to a damming of the torrential tributaries of the soul, to a more sedate and staid view. Here is how Descartes described a "great soul": "The greatest souls . . . are those whose reasoning powers are so strong and powerful, that although they also have passions, nonetheless their reason remains sovereign."[50] What would have he said about the holy madness, flaming eroticism, and emotional rapture of Teresa of Ávila or of the black church that W. E. B. Du Bois later described? "A sort of suppressed terror hung in the air and seemed to seize us—a Pythian madness, a demoniac possession, that lent terrible reality to song and word. The people moaned and fluttered, and then the gaunt-checked brown woman beside me suddenly leaped straight into the air and shrieked like a lost soul, while round about came wail and groan and outcry, and scene of human passion such as I had never conceived before."[51] The congregation's sensual, aesthetical drama, described here—the guttural murmurs and shouts, the rushing to and fro, waving and clapping of hands, pounding of feet, weeping and laughing, all the eroticism—surely would have been far too profligate and passionate to suit Descartes's standards. This behavior would have represented the drowning of reason in a deluge of emotion, the rush of blood to the heart that in effect deprives the brain of oxygen. The acquisition of soul demands sobriety, moderation, and reason. For Descartes, black religion, and for that matter the Catholic baroque, would have been quintessential examples of the fall of reason into the undisciplined body of excess and intemperance; they would have been seen as the sudden invasion of a Pythian madness into the sane company of philosophers, or the revenge of Dionysus on the Enlightenment of Descartes's day.

As I consider throughout this study, there is a shared indulgence in the beauty and sensual delights of the human experience in African American Christianity and a Latin baroque Christianity. Though the former tended to be far more auditory (a stress on the spoken Word), while the latter was more visual (a stress on the Logos in visual and ceremonial forms), they converged on a deeply felt incarnational theology, one that electrified the body and aroused the festive, mystical energies of religion. In these instances, the representation of soul was deeply aesthetical and ran afoul of modern attempts to rationalize, bureaucratize, and sanitize the human soul, whether in philosophy, civil society, or the new world order of capitalism.

The Ethical Contours of Soul: What Does It Profit a Man . . .

In the new bourgeois marketplace of the early modern period (especially in Protestant countries from the eighteenth century forward), the integrity of the soul was increasingly endangered. The idea of the soul would have to fight for its livelihood in the face of forces that depreciate its value, that barter and exploit it for its economic worth. Like a parable out of the "prosperity gospel" in North America (the conviction that God rewards enterprising behavior with financial blessings), the new capitalist version of the soul likened the Christian message to the values of free enterprise and effectively consecrated the pursuit of wealth. In severing itself from many of the moral fetters of old—the troublesome injunctions to feed the hungry, clothe the naked, welcome the stranger, and visit the prisoner—the modern self was given free rein to pursue material progress without restriction, to pursue self-gratification with impunity.[52] Classic vices like acquisitive self-interest and greed were magically transformed into benign self-regard, a fundamental right of a modern human person and a guiding principle of the public realm of economics and politics. As Brad Gregory argues, the capitalist society required this new construction of avarice, an ideological about-face that upended the Gospels' negative view of greed and sought to prove Jesus wrong: you can, after all, serve God and money.[53]

Of course the classic Christian position on ethics disavows these principles, this entire alchemical business that would commodify and transform the values of the soul into products of gold. We cannot speak of the soul and not address the exorbitant cost of gaining the whole world: namely, the loss of one's soul (a comment found in all three synoptic Gospels). In assessing this famous adage by Jesus in modern times, it is difficult not to be struck by its relevance and prescience. In contrast to versions of Christianity that hallow the capitalist economy of desire (for fashion, consumer products, fetishes, wealth, etc.), the cultivation of the soul implied in the biblical tradition requires a prophetical, oppositional stand to the sinful drive to possess and dominate the world. It requires a drastic conversion from self-regard to other-regard, a love that is infinite in scope and more lavish and ostentatious than its competitor's values of limitless consumption.[54]

Those who adhered to this classic reading of the concept of the soul and resisted the temptations of the new continued to shepherd many of the grievances brought against the most vulgar and defiling aspects of capitalism. Already at the dawning of modernity, in the early eighteenth century, a figure like Soren Kierkegaard expressed his befuddled dismay at the seeming ease with which Christianity embraced the new bourgeois world. He called this new order "Christendom," a term that signified the betrayal of Christianity and victory for the gods of profit and shameless self-interest (there are no Christians in Christendom, Kierkegaard famously remarked). Christendom represented for him an unmistakable calamity, the parade of glory and power instead of abasement and abnegation, the promotion of sentimentality and mawkishness in lieu of the message of the cross, philanthropy instead of true agape.[55] In these betrayals and others, Christendom was for Kierkegaard a secular order entirely devoid of Christian principles, a civilization now ruled, secretly, by the golden calf or the great beast of Revelation. As the lowly hidden God, a man of sorrows, despised and rejected by all, Jesus is a stranger to Christendom, his teachings discarded, discounted, and unheeded.

In confronting his readers with the strange wisdom of the cross, Kierkegaard reminds us that any Christian rendition of theology begins and ends with the full scope of Jesus's incarnation, born into humble circumstances and fated to die in humiliating and ignominious circumstances. Christendom was a target of so much of Kierkegaard's fury because it recoiled from this difficult message, preferring a theology of triumph to the desolation and absurdity of the cross, aligning itself with the rich and powerful instead of the poor and destitute, preferring Easter over Good Friday. In its glaring discomfort with suffering and death, with human finitude and frailty, Christendom retreated from these realities the way the priest and Levite cringed at the wounded man on the way to Jericho.

The American Self

North America, of course, established its own variety of Christendom, complete with many of the same characteristics identified by Kierkegaard. If we recall, for example, that the early Massachusetts Bay emigrants were largely members of the entrepreneurial and professional middle classes (tradesmen, merchants, lawyers, artisans, and clerics), we can understand Carl Degler's comment that capitalism came to America in the first ships and Max Weber's argument that the capitalist spirit arrived before the capitalist order.[56] It's difficult to dispute the powerful conjunction between Puritanism and capitalism in the American experiment; it was the wind behind the *Mayflower*'s sails. Supported by the divine right of possession and buttressed by the biblical stories of exodus and conquest, this experiment soon achieved combustible, explosive success in the domains of industry and free enterprise. It was not long before this new Israel was designated by John Winthrop "the city on the hill," a light of free enterprise and unlimited material and spiritual progress.[57]

By the nineteenth century the powerful union of Protestantism and capitalism had picked up steam, as many preachers turned the pulpit, in the words of Sacvan Bercovitch, "into a platform for the American Way. The great crusades of Lyman Beecher and Charles Grandson Finney brought 'Gospel tidings'—rugged individualism in business enterprise, laissez-faire in economic theory, and constitutional democracy in political thought."[58] The religious revivalists of the period were fusing Protestantism and American patriotism, Christian morality and capitalist economics, all in the interest of consecrating the Christendom of the New World. With piety and prosperity welded together in this way, every instance of visible success, moral or material, confirmed God's providential designs for America.

For Kierkegaard, as for the classic Protestant reformers, this amounted to a pagan or secular morality, nothing remotely close to the dark wisdom of the cross, where God appeared incognito in the distressed face of the beggar and vagabond.[59] As a betrayal of Christianity's difficult message, Christendom seemed to insist on the opposite: God's presence in the gilded facades of worldly success. In this scenario, the poor and powerless were abject instances of moral bankruptcy and spiritual failure. In fact, throughout the nineteenth and twentieth centuries the poor and unemployed, vagabonds and prostitutes, orphans and delinquents were depicted in such terms, examples of failed values and failed lives. But more ominously, as Michel Foucault has argued, these groups—especially those of a darker shade of brown—were turned into pathological subjects and in many cases criminalized.[60]

Because of new legislation directed at poor, vagabond, and colonized subjects in both Europe and North America, in the nineteenth century a whole new class of illegalities was created, and prison populations began to swell as a result.[61] This repressive climate, in Foucault's reading, "increased the occasions of offenses, and threw to the other side of the law many individuals who, in other conditions, would not have gone over to specialized criminality."[62] Whether through travel restrictions, greater demands for productivity in the workplace, discrimination in the judicial system, or vicious practices of displacement, exclusion, and incarceration, many new laws and regulations gave free rein to practices of ruthless injustice, the hand of naked power held out in gestures of benevolence.[63] An example is the benign-sounding California Act of 1850 (An Act for the Government and Protection of Indians), which permitted officials to arrest and sell to the highest bidder Indians who were found intoxicated or vagrant or were accused of crimes. The act even gave whites the power to purchase Indian children by making available certificates for the custody of these children. (Over the next approximately thirteen years, an estimated twenty thousand American Indian children were held in bondage.)[64]

Bourgeois ideals of freedom, in short, coexisted with violent measures that denied liberty to many. Republican ideals were plainly mocked by the existence of chattel slavery, wage slavery, and other methods of punishment and abuse. It was culture well practiced in the sophistry of freedom, but with a sanctimonious eloquence that rang hollow for many Americans. For those who lived in the underground of American society, such as blacks, American Indians, and Mexicans, life remained confining and restricted, as if, to invoke Foucault once again, they were "the lepers of old."[65]

For the reader curious about the relevance of this discussion to the sublime matter of the soul, I recall the devil's offer of world dominion to Jesus: "All this I will give to you, he said, if you will bow down and worship me. Jesus said to him, away from me, Satan" (Matt. 4:8–10). In the Christian mind, the matter of worldly dominion has everything to do with the well-being of the soul. When power and wealth become the ruling principle of one's life, the soul is dethroned and replaced by something unworthy of its name, something that dons a crown of self-aggrandizing vanity instead of a crown of thorns. By considering the shadowy opposite of the soul, its rival and alter ego, we hope to deepen our understanding of the terms and implications involved in this regime change.

The shifting connotations of pride are further evidence of this altered state of affairs in the modern world. In Andrew Delbanco's reading, the American self—self-made, calculating, overweening—became increasingly heedless of traditional warnings of pride until it became a god in its own right (the promise of the serpent in Genesis). "Pride of self, once the mark of the devil," writes Delbanco, "was now not just a legitimate emotion but America's uncontested god. And since everyone had his own self, everyone had his own god."[66] Just as avarice, once a mark of sin, became a legitimate and vital force in modern economics, pride of self was cleansed of the devil's shadow and made into a staple of American individualism. The American self thus came into its own in the nineteenth century. By fiercely asserting itself against all odds, dangers, and aboriginal rights, pride of self grew to monstrous proportions and validated the expansionist urges of land-grabbers, settlers, businessmen, whalers, and forty-niners. As S. C. Gwynne puts it in his powerful narrative of the westward push of Americans, the main players in North America, in contrast to the presidio soldiers and missionaries of the Spanish New World, were rugged and obdurate pioneers; the "vanguard was not federal troops and federal forts, but simple farmers imbued with a fierce Calvinist work ethic, steely optimism, and a cold-eyed aggressiveness that made them refuse to yield even in the face of extreme danger. . . . They habitually declined to honor government treaties with Native Americans, believing in their hearts that the land belonged to them. They hated Indians with a particular passion, considering them something less than fully human, and thus blessed with inalienable rights to absolutely nothing."[67] Needless to say, the compulsive belief in manifest destiny, reinforced by the American civil religion of exceptionalism and triumphalism, led to numerous calamities, if not outright genocide, for American Indians.[68]

In a Christian assessment, these attitudes smack of idolatry: an anthropomorphic god fashioned out of the material of the human ego, and driven by an insatiable appetite for the world's goods. Those in previous ages had names for this behavior—blasphemy, sin, idolatry—but Americans gave a new spin to this approach, labeling it enterprising, pioneering, and dauntless. This was a conceit so brazen that not only would this expansionist behavior annex Texas, swallow parts of Mexico, seize American Indian lands, and enslave Africans, but even the heavens seemed vulnerable to its oversized willfulness. Captain Ahab in *Moby Dick* sized up the attitude perfectly: "Talk not to me of blasphemy, man. I'd strike the sun if it insulted me."[69] If that century of extraordinary economic and territorial growth apotheosized the self in this way, the principles associated with the classic soul were at risk of going the way of the bison on the Great Plains.

One may choose to embrace the concept of the modern self over the old creed of the soul (this choice itself is one of the hallmarks of modernity), but I am interested in the growing feeling of alarm and foreboding, even outrage, about this decision in favor of the modern self. In nineteenth-century America, dissenting voices—warning of vanity like the preacher of Ecclesiastes—were heard from a host of American isolatoes, from Nathaniel Hawthorne and Herman Melville to Ralph Waldo Emerson, Walt Whitman, Henry David Thoreau, and Mark Twain. Whether or not they were "voluptuaries of the soul"—Theodore Parker's description of Transcendentalists—there was a palpable concern among all of them about the survival of the soul in an age of positivism and "gilded" dreams.[70] In some cases, showing a clear sympathy for Christian socialism, writers sketched grand capitalists as swindlers, confidence men, and vampire-like creatures, thirsty for the blood of the innocent. In Melville's novel *Redburn*, for example, a man of this sort appears in all of his deformed and grotesque glory: "He was an abominable looking old fellow, with cold, fat, jelly-like eyes; and avarice, heartlessness, and sensuality stamped all over him. He seemed all the time going through some process of mental arithmetic; doing sums with dollars and cents; his very mouth, wrinkled and drawn up at the corners, looked like a purse."[71] There is something about this figure that conjures the image of Satan, with his deformed body mirroring his deformed soul. The spell of money has become a trance in the man's life, and his soul is now comatose, dead to any higher values. If this grim apostle of money is a representative capitalist, Melville's sketch is a cautionary tale of capitalism gone terribly wrong, a system without humaneness, without beauty. He registers the same concern that his mentor, Nathaniel Hawthorne, had about the United States: "a country where there is no shadow, no antiquity, no mystery, no picturesque and gloomy wrong, not anything but a commonplace prosperity in broad and simple daylight."[72]

Though evident in most of his novels, the aspersions Melville cast upon capitalism achieve their finest formulation in *Moby Dick*, especially, in my view, when the author makes an explicit connection between slavery and the business of moneymaking. When Pip, the black cabin boy, is thrown overboard, Stubb can only think of the financial forfeiture if the whale is lost: "We can't afford to lose whales by the likes of you; a whale would sell for thirty times what you would, Pip, in Alabama." Ishmael's response captures the species of being that Stubb represents: "Though man loves his fellow, yet man is a money-making animal, which propensity too often interferes with his benevolence."[73] In recognizing human ambiguity—the capacity for both love and greed—Melville pays some attention here to the noble nature of humankind, but the stronger strain is the animal-like impulses that degrade the human spirit and transform our nature into that of a predatory shark or wolf: *homo homini lupus*. In business and politics, as in life, these latter propensities have a way of shipwrecking the higher aspirations of the soul.

As the twentieth century set in, the climate for the soul became even more inclement and severe, leading many writers of the age to warn of the soul's wizening or disappearance altogether. F. Scott Fitzgerald's novel *The Great Gatsby* can be read in this vein, as a cautionary tale about the high price that the pursuit of fortune exacts from one's moral character and spiritual integrity. Jay Gatsby has been consumed by the romance of money, and his life has been given to the service of a "vast, vulgar, meretricious beauty."[74] However dazzling and magnificent this dream of wealth appears in his eyes, the novel shows how specious and cheap this mirage of beauty is, how much it can entice and ruin at the same time. Though Fitzgerald never displayed "the conviction of a revolutionary" in his work, he certainly channeled the "smoldering hatred of a peasant" toward the moneyed, leisured classes in America—the beautiful and the damned—in much of his fiction.[75] Marius Bewley sums up *The Great Gatsby* thus: "In the end, *The Great Gatsby* is a dramatic affirmation in fictional terms of the American spirit in the midst of an American world that denies the soul."[76]

This denial of the soul is by no means a temptation of the secular realm alone; for Fitzgerald, the malady had a long reach and spread like contagion into the heart of the church. The words of Beatrice Blaine in *This Side of Paradise* have much of Fitzgerald in them: "Often she deplored the bourgeois quality of the American Catholic clergy, and was quite sure that had she lived in the shadow of the great Continental cathedrals her soul would still be a thin flame on the mighty altar of Rome."[77]

This character wants the warmth, incandescence, radiance, and burning colors of a darker, more mysterious variety of Catholicism. Thus the novelist pines for alternatives to American middle-class values (the cheery optimism, the family values, the worship of financial success, the triumphant God) and at one point declares an attraction to the "Mexican God," who would be something strangely different, more like a baroque God from a land of "sad, haunting music and many odors . . . where the shades of night skies and sunsets would seem to reflect only moods of passion: the color of lips and poppies."[78] In this exotic mood—describing a dream of the pageantry of the soul—the novel closes with the protagonist throwing his pen and soul to the side of socialism, that most frightening idea for the bourgeois American. The implication is plain in Fitzgerald's first novel: the soul flickers and falters in America, and he dreams of other fields and meadows in which his soul can grow, roam, and rebel.

If it is not obvious, I am arguing that the idea of the soul in the classic Christian tradition is bathed in sunsets and twilights of this sort, and many of the artists discussed here sought to preserve this vintage, dusk-like representation. In fearing the betrayal of the soul in America—where the soul is confused with commonplace prosperity without shadow, antiquity, mystery, or the cross—they raised their voices in foreboding and forewarning.

Many black and Hispanic writers would join this chorus of discontent. In Latin America the budding movement *modernismo* arose as a critical reaction to scientific positivism and economic materialism. (José Enrique Rodó's *Ariel* and Rubén Darío's poetry are classic examples, later followed by the avant-garde and so-called magical realism.) In North America African American writers cried out against assaults on the bodies and souls of their community in the nineteenth and twentieth centuries. In both cases, Latin Americans and African Americans largely embraced Christian ideas, adding their own signatures and styles to classic views of the soul and consequently fashioning fresh iterations of the "moods of passion"—haunting music, ostentatious pageantry, existential burdens— that are the stuff of the soul. Though often buried under the landslides of economic and political success in America, their perspectives are fresh riffs on the priceless value of soul in our modern or postmodern world. W. E. B. Du Bois held one such perspective; I begin with him because he is a powerful example of the kind of soul that burns brighter than a thin flame, more like a conflagration that swept across the plains and hills of America: the soul of black folks. Though Du Bois's understanding of the soul was deeply informed by the black religious experience in America, it was also indebted to the romantic tradition, and for that reason I consider him in the second part of this chapter, with an emphasis on the cultural, stylistic, and profane understandings of the soul.

PROFANE INTERPRETATIONS OF THE SOUL

Romantic Soul: Herder and Du Bois

Du Bois's life echoes many of the themes we have explored thus far, especially the construction of the soul as antibourgeois, a weapon of protest against the vulgar drive for material fortune. This theme emerges most explicitly from Du Bois's notorious arguments with Booker T. Washington. As is well known, their relationship became strained and sour over fundamental definitions of success in America. In Du Bois's estimation, Washington's vision for education, in its concrete manifestation at the Tuskegee Institute, was far too conciliatory to the American idioms of triumphant commercialism and material prosperity and disappointingly silent when it came to black civil rights. To Du Bois and others like him, the model of industrial training at Tuskegee implied that black liberation would hinge on blacks' success in the marketplace and adoption of the American dream, with all of its glittering promises and fantasies, its cornucopia of goods. The success of the black community would be assessed by how it capitalized on its opportunities and on its diligence, thrift, and industry in the American economy.[79] For Du Bois, sounding like a classic biblical prophet, this particular dream smacked of fanaticism and misplaced reverence, as it reduced the purpose of education to economic advancement and worldly success. Du Bois of course withheld his allegiance to such a vision, arguing that the examined life had an infinite worth beyond its cash value.

Even when black folks baptized themselves in the rivers of commerce, Du Bois complained, it did not end blatant violations of human rights, the systematic acts of terror and violence against the black community. The black man had often cried "amen" to the principles of commerce and duly done obeisance to them, "but before that nameless prejudice that leaps beyond all this he stands helpless, dismayed, and well-nigh speechless; before that personal disrespect and mockery, the ridicule and systematic humiliation, the distortion of fact and wanton license of fancy, the all-pervading desire to inculcate disdain for everything black. . . . Before this there rises a sickening despair that would disarm and discourage any nation save that black host to whom 'discouragement' is an unwritten word."[80] In these eloquent lines and others, Du Bois left no doubt where the fault lay. Even while navigating the tempestuous waters of American life, black Americans were subject to vicious undercurrents and tides that sank many of their endeavors and hopes. For America to advance on this matter, laws would have to change, rights would have to be defended, and justice would have to be reinforced. As the years went on, Du Bois only strengthened his prophetic commitment to these things, and he always believed that the stuff of liberal education—the training of the mind, heart, and soul—was imperative in the struggle for equality and justice. The ideals of good, beauty, and spirituality were anything but idle, metaphysical matters; they would enliven the search for human dignity and inspire prophetic denunciations of the "dusty desert of dollars" in America.[81] He claimed Socrates, Jesus, and St. Francis of Assisi as allies.[82]

Besides echoing religious and philosophical themes, Du Bois's depiction of the soul no doubt expressed the worldview of many romantics. His years of graduate study in Berlin (1892–1894) affected him deeply. Besides having the opportunity to learn from thinkers like Friedrich Schiller and Wilhelm von Humboldt, the imposing ghosts of Johann Goethe, Karl Marx, and Johann Herder were everywhere, and they haunted and instructed him on the matter of soul. During those years he swam in deep rivers of romanticism, and this clearly saturated his thinking. Considering the widespread discontent that many romantics felt with the Enlightenment—especially over its instrumental, syllogistic uses of reason and its alliance with market values and industrial capitalism—the influence is obvious. Almost all romantics took aim at the soul-deforming impact of modern culture, especially in its most sordid incarnation in the industrial world, and sought to recover the value of art, music, poetry, and religion. In a sense, God's grandeur was at stake in a world where, to quote Gerard Manley Hopkins, "all is seared with trade; bleared, smeared with toil."[83] Du Bois certainly fit into this pantheon of renegade dissidents who raised their pens and paintbrushes in protest against the financier and capitalist, the man who "feels no poetry and hears no song."[84]

But there were other romantic innovations surrounding the question of soul that left their imprint on Du Bois, in particular the concept of soul as *Volkgeist,* or the spirit/soul of a people. In this reading, "soul" belongs to an entire culture and is synonymous with the spiritual life of a nation. Kwame Anthony Appiah describes it thus: "We can think of the soul here not as an individual's unique possession, but rather as something she shares with the folk to which she belongs."[85] As a communal possession, soul is a product of the finest achievements of a culture, especially its folklore, poetry, myth, and music. By taking aim at the arid rationalism, elitism, and materialism of the Enlightenment, the romantics saw themselves as protecting the endangered life of the spirit, especially its full-bodied, aromatic richness in the culture of a people.

Just as Du Bois imbibed this spirit as a protest against U.S. expansionism and capitalism, a host of Latin American writers and artists would follow suit and embrace the language of soul in opposition to the most base and ignoble of North American ambitions. Hispanic literati came to consider themselves priests of the eternal imagination or, in José Enrique

Rodó's words, "keeper of souls" at war with the spiritual philistines of modern mass society and capitalism. (Besides Rodó, others in this camp include José Vasconcelos, Antonio Caso, Francisco Calderón, Alejandro Korn, and Rubén Darío.)[86] For both African Americans and Latin Americans, the romantic vision of "soul" proved elastic and malleable enough to reconfigure in light of each distinct ethnicity and noble enough to confer dignity on each of their traditions. When denied political or economic power, the cultures on the edges of Western modernity adopted "soul"—and its spiritual manifestations in dance, music, folklore, and myth—as an idiom in their struggle for equality and justice.

In seeking to resuscitate the ailing, bedridden notion of myth and soul in this way, the romantics of various stripes, in Europe and beyond, saw themselves as physicians of national well-being (the eighteenth and nineteenth centuries were an era of nationalism, after all). By recovering the lost stories, legends, epics, vernacular languages, and songs of a *Volk*, they would infuse a feeling of pride in cultures and traditions that had been devalued, exploited, and dismissed. "Mythic poetry," writes Bruce Lincoln, "which the Enlightenment disparaged as a form of primitive irrationality, had been re-theorized under the signs of authenticity, tradition, and national identity."[87] What was trampled upon by the Enlightenment became something like buried treasure for romantics, and every effort was made to excavate and preserve such precious relics. Romantic artists thus hunted for these folk treasures in an effort to shore up cultural nationalism: James MacPherson (1736–1796) published poetry that was purported to be the ancient voice of the Scots; epics like the *Nibelungenlied, Kalevala, El Cid,* and *Chanson de Roland* were released as testaments to the greatness of their respective cultures; and later, as the twentieth century arrived, many poets and modernists turned to the cultural reserves of their national traditions. Yeats turned to Celtic legends and myths, Miguel Ángel Asturias looked to Mayan myths, Alejo Carpentier recovered Afro-Latin religions, Gerard Manley Hopkins focused on the Anglo-Saxon vernacular, Lorca celebrated Spanish ballads and "deep song," Du Bois turned to black spirituals, and the list goes on. Recall in this vein James Joyce's definition of his literary purpose: "I go to encounter for the millionth time the reality of experience and to forge in the smithy of my soul the uncreated conscience of my race."[88]

For the romantics, the "uncreated conscience" of each unique culture was at stake in the war with the defilers of soul. Though their dispute with the Enlightenment was unmistakably modern and new, we can also trace the issues involved here back to the ancient Greeks. As early as Heraclitus and Plato, poets were often slighted by philosophers, such as when Heraclitus heaped scorn on the *hoi polloi* (common people) for their intellectual shortcomings and affection for poetry: "What understanding or intellect have they? They trust in poets of the common people and treat the mob as their teacher, not knowing that 'the masses are bad, the good are few.'"[89] And Plato followed the basic outline of this model, thinking that *mythoi* and music appealed to the basest part of the human soul (the emotions more than reason) and to the baser forms of humanity, like women, children, and the lower classes.[90] If he conceded the value of poetry, myth, and music, it was largely for those who were unable to follow the subtleties of philosophical argumentation or, more interestingly, on occasions when philosophical certainty could not be established, such as in the fate of the soul after death or on the nature of the gods. (This is obvious in *The Timaeus*, in which he resorts to myth to make sense of the creation of the universe.)

Whatever the case, it is clear that the romantics wanted to recover the Greek poets (Homer, Hesiod, the tragedians) more than the philosophers and to disturb the hierarchical privileging of prose over poetry, logos over mythos, analytical reason over eros, theory over music, and propositional argumentation over narrative. They were challenging the disembodiment of language from oral inflections, rhythms, and timbres, and they were challenging the rupture and bifurcation of language and music, reason and emotion, form and content, and theory and practice. By reuniting these dimensions—a search for the other half in this dualism, in the manner of the myth of Aristophanes in the *Symposium*— they would nurse the fractured soul back to health, restore humanity's original nature, and return people to a time when wordsmiths were singers and mythmakers, rhymers, and signifying poets.

Du Bois's deeply felt identification with the folk songs and spirituals of African Americans can be seen as a note in this larger cultural score. In choosing to adopt Herder's popular understanding of folk-soul, he placed his work in the romantic context of *Sturm und Drang*: "So dawned the time of *Sturm und Drang*: storm and stress today rocks our little boat on the mad waters of the world-sea; there is within and without the sound of conflict, the burning of body and rending of soul."[91] Here Du Bois clearly catches the wave of romanticism's emotional unrest and turmoil—storm and stress—but he also gives it a distinct meaning, fraught with the stress of being black in America. Rocked on all sides by violent waters, he says, the black soul is torn in two and unreconciled, striving, on the one hand, for participation in America, and on the other, for the preservation of African identity in a nation that smells of burning black flesh.[92] Besides implying that one can belong to two different *Volkgeists*, an African and an Anglo-American (a significant point itself), the most striking element of these ruminations has to be the glaring portrait of the psychic torment and physical rupture of black lives. Du Bois's reflections on black soul are always close to a threnody, dirge, or jeremiad, and they translate the raw forms of racism and terrorism into the idioms of high culture, converting the screams and sobs of slave ships, auction blocks, and cotton fields into the stuff of literature. Similar to the way the writers of the American Renaissance sourced and refined native preaching styles in the nineteenth century, Du Bois transformed the popular sentiments and idioms of black America into a more polished literary art.[93] This is nowhere more evident than in his powerful analysis of the "sorrow songs" of Afro-America; it is in their melodies, born of the dust of toil, he remarked, that the soul finds its most articulate and exuberant expression.

Du Bois considered the spirituals—"the rhythmic cry of the slave"—the most beautiful expression of human experience born on this side of the sea.[94] For him, these folk songs were eloquent proof that slaves had an undeniable capacity for grandeur in ideas and emotions. They were evidence of artistic genius among the oppressed and despised in America, proof of black folks' deep well of spirituality, their hidden springs of magnanimity. Sometimes muted and weary, then ecstatic and effervescent, sometimes broken with trouble but still dogged in hope, they were almost always live wires of emotion that burned through pain and despair. With pitches and pulses that caused the mercury of the soul to rise to its summit, this musical folk poetry poured over the listener in tides of emotion, spilling light and harmony into a world of darkness and dissonance, breathing grace and fire into every nook and cranny of the soul. Where blacks had to "roll through an unfriendly world," Du Bois saw these songs as something like the crooning of a mother's alto voice: "Mary, don't you moan, don't you weep."[95]

As many writers have noted (Albert Raboteau, James Cone, Eddie Glaude, and others), Du Bois may have overstated the otherworldly emphasis of the spirituals (claiming that they could be religiously fatalist and escapist), but he saw with great insight their aesthetic value, that they were fundamentally ennobling of black dignity and transformed the Babel of suffering into a liturgy of song, dance, and ecstasy.[96] Like a religious incantation and ritual, these canticles beseeched God with body and soul, wail and moan, complaint and supplication, and gave the human spirit a chance to catch the Holy Ghost, to be seized and baptized by fire. Whatever else would happen, for Du Bois this music was a tangible example—in contradiction to the Enlightenment's disdain for the masses—of the rich poetry of the humble slaves, the embodiment of their most primal instincts, desires, affections, fears, dreams, and hopes.[97]

The key to Du Bois's analysis of black folk-soul is the simple yet radical claim that these cultural liturgies were the equal of any other artistic achievement in Europe or elsewhere. On this point he followed Herder's refusal to rank the *Volkgeist* of various nations. (Terry Eagleton refers to Herder, accordingly, as the father of cultural studies.)[98] In contrast to some other German thinkers, including Heinrich von Treitschke, a teacher of Du Bois in Berlin, Herder championed a tolerant cultural and linguistic pluralism, without any presumption of cultural inferiority on the part of these national spiritualities; for Herder, cultural differences were incommensurable, not tiered.[99] He viewed cultural and linguistic variety as something like a great orchestra of humanity, with each culture contributing different sounds and instruments, each gifted and worthy of a seat in this ensemble of musicians, none better than the other.

In spite of Herder's pluralistic vision, however, the concept of soul was later desecrated by the German Nazis, South African Afrikaners, and other racist regimes of the twentieth century. In their hands, as George Fredrickson has demonstrated, folk-soul became indistinguishable from an obsession with the purity of bloodlines and thus was synonymous with a version of cultural identity cleansed of all foreign contaminants.[100] Used as an ideological ruse in the battle with all "inferior" races and cultures, folk-soul was increasingly stained by fantasies of racial essentialism and cultural dominance. Since the history of "soul" includes this vicious legacy of racism, these facts should give us pause. Racism was born out of an impulse similar to, though wildly perverted from, that which led to the formation of folk-soul: namely, the desire to create cohesion, belonging, and national identity. In the case of racism, however, essentialist categories of race and identity led the proponents of folk-soul to create pyramids of domination, with their own racial group at the peak.[101]

As I see it, this leap into the mire of modern racism represented an idolatrous caricature and misrepresentation of soul. When the soul is dragged through the dirty waters of racism, we end up with a perversion of the concept, a notion that shares hardly anything with the classic view of the soul in Christianity and very little with the views of soul among the best of the romantics and modernists. In these latter instances, as in the work of Du Bois, Lorca, or Ellison, folk-soul is the scourge of materialism, possessive individualism, cultural elitism, and discrimination.[102] It is a communal value that seeks to preserve the spiritual treasures of culture even as it invokes a radical and transformative future.

The Power of Blackness

In the best understandings, the vision of soul avoided the crude disfigurements of racism and instilled a healthy sense of pride in cultural traditions that had been relegated to the dungeons of history. It tapped into subterranean rivers to water the roots of one's cultural traditions, turning something once uprooted into a healthy family tree. As Yeats put it, this sort of work amounted to the "calling of the Muses home."[103] When invoking the Muses (daughters of Zeus and the goddess Mnemosyne, or "Memory"), the epic poet was recalling and preserving the stories of old; and when the bard sang his poetry with a lyre—the particular instrument associated with Apollo—the poet effectively joined knowledge of the past (a gift of the Muses) with a seer-like knowledge of the future (associated with Apollo).[104] In this construction, words and odes, melodies, and stories all play a key role in defining a people's past and future: where they have come from and where they are going.

It was a "homecoming" of this sort that motivated Du Bois—and later cultural nationalists—to write essays paying homage to what black folks had endured and overcome in America. Resisting attempts to silence and bury black memories in an unmarked grave of dishonor, he exhumed the memory of the dead not only to rewrite the American past, but also to prophesy a more just future. Through this reconstruction of American identity—now with the souls of black folks haunting any portrait of life in the United States—Du Bois gave the American experiment a new element to test: the "power of blackness." Though this was Melville's expression—spoken in tribute to Hawthorne's tragic sensibility—Du Bois called this element "home" and made it epitomize the plight of African peoples throughout the globe. In so doing, Du Bois rebaptized the "power of blackness," plunging it into dark waters and branding it with the mark of the runaway slave, exploited sharecropper, or urban indigent. The meaning of "soul" was transfigured, not in dazzling lightness, but in darker shades, as if it had been suddenly pulled through the mud and dirt like the face of the blind beggar when Jesus smeared mud on him (John 9:1–7) or when Jacob wrestled with God in the dirt by the river Jabbok (Gen. 32:24–32).

Whereas in Hawthorne's and Melville's writings "the power of blackness" was synonymous with a seer-like vision of evil, passed on to them by their sin-obsessed Puritan ancestors, for Du Bois it was the power of actual black lives to scale mountains of injustice and oppression. Du Bois did not deny the existential account; he simply broadened it to include the untold stories of those on the dark side of the veil; in effect, he added a "thick description" to Melville's vision. Through his eyes this concept became a trope of artistic and cultural achievement in the face of centuries of abuse and enslavement. Black soul was the rising phoenix out of the ashes of conquest and affliction, the strange fruit that bloomed in the most blighted of conditions. By fleshing out the meaning of "soul" and "blackness" in relation to the specific experiences and achievements of black folks in America, Du Bois added a certain depth and richness to these terms that was lacking in even the best American Gothic writers.

At the same time, there is something more to this portrait of blackness that takes us beyond the urbane and highbrow genius of Du Bois, deeper into the heart of the profane. In honor of Leslie Fiedler or Melville, we might call this the Faustian path of soul, or in honor of Lorca, the way of *duende,* or for hip-hop, the raw, vernacular version of soul.[105] In each case, the path of soul requires us to swerve from piety and polished erudition to travel into more dangerous and forbidden domains of human experience. In straying from orthodox paths in this way, we open ourselves to the wilder, funkier, and more eccentric possibilities of soul, something closer to the streetwise imagination of Jean-Michel Basquiat than the classic mind of a Michelangelo, closer to the gritty, vulgar insights of hip-hop than a Ludwig van Beethoven, Wolfgang Amadeus Mozart, or Richard Wagner. In confining our search for soul to conventional piety or classical music and art, we risk lulling the creative imagination to sleep and consequently neglecting the moments of clarity and beauty that happen in surprising and unexpected locations: in the boisterous and crowded realities of urban life, in riotous and insolent music, in forbidden dances, and in strange and raucous thoughts. It could be that the blasts of noise in orthodox traditions—dreary dogmatics, hypocritical piety, and repressive righteousness—drone on and prevent us from hearing new sounds or from seeing the pied beauty in "all things counter, original, spare, strange."[106]

In the modern era the legacy of spiritual, aesthetic, and moral revolt—inspired by the example of Jesus in his agitation with religious

authorities—finds many disciples in America, including figures as disparate as Melville and Du Bois, Howlin' Wolf and Tupac. In their flirta-
tions with blackness, the traditional patterns of soul are battered and
smashed, then suddenly reconstituted again to make something truly
original and unforeseen. Based on their examples, exile from society
and conventional institutions is not only a handicap; it may lead to
unique possibilities in perception, vision, or experience. Melville's Ishmael describes these possibilities thus—"a long exile from Christendom
and civilization inevitably restores a man to that condition in which
God placed him, i.e. what is called savagery"—and then adds, "I myself
am a savage."[107] By identifying a dimension of savagery within his own
being, he essentially establishes his likeness to everyone beyond the pale
of the civilized world. Like his namesake in the Bible (the biblical Ishmael is exiled along with his African mother, Hagar), Melville's Ishmael
will wander the earth with other exiles and savages and come to the
realization that they all share the same humanity. In the course of his
unlikely relationship with Queequeg (the tattooed heathen called "Son
of Darkness" by Captain Bildad), Ishmael reaches the conclusion that
this "wild idolater," worshipper of a black god, is nothing less than his
fellow man, to whom his respect and love are owed: "Consequently,"
he concludes, "I must unite with him in his (religion); ergo, I must turn
idolater."[108] Rebellious syllogisms of this kind—a mutiny against the
legal and moral laws of his day and an embrace of outcast lives and
estranged sensibilities—are the basis for Melville's own judgment that
he had written a wicked book.[109]

In this reading, if one attained the power of soul, it would be achieved
by mirroring the human cargo of Melville's ship, freighted as it was with
the meanest sailors and savages, renegades and castaways, maroons and
rogues (including an American Indian, a Zoroastrian, a Polynesian, an
African, black Americans, Quakers, etc.). Soul in Melville would thus
contain the whole cosmos; it would be one of the roughs and have its
helm and rudder steered by tattooed heathens and sons of darkness. In
archetypal American fashion, the soul would become a melting pot for
the lives of many people, refined and coarse, graceful and rowdy, with
this legion of styles gelling into one, while still allowing space for each
one's unique flavor.

In rummaging through the nether parts of the human soul in these
ways and allowing ourselves to be schooled by the renegades and castaways of social and religious life, we naturally enter a battleground on
which a life and death struggle ensues with the problem of evil, or in

Job-like fashion, with God; this, too, is part of the power of blackness. In this case, the most profound quests of the soul depend on the spirit's capacity to scrutinize the wreckage of history and to face God in the style of the biblical patriarchs who defied him, moments of the deepest spiritual sublimity, when grace drips into the deepest basins of the soul, only, it seems, in the midnight hours of anguish.

And now, in our own modern context, these examples have multiplied in direct proportion to the troubles of our age, so that such ordeals have become the signs of the most credible kind of soulfulness. In American musical traditions, whether the blues, jazz, R & B, soul, funk, deep song, son, or salsa, the power of blackness surely includes refrains of agony and quarrels with God. As American musicians found their voice, they channeled their experiences of marginalization through their music and directed some of their "blues" against the guardians of the sacred. In many cases their art appeared to many as a delicious but dangerous, demonic power, a dark enemy of societal and ecclesiastical norms. As if to feed this judgment, many of these artists channeled the trickster or "bad man" temperament by bringing the noise to genteel society, wreaking havoc in their lyrics and dances and in general playing their music for the demonized others of society. Considered vulgar and coarse, many of these artists would be accused of making deals with the devil at the crossroads or ghettos of American society.

Worship as Defiance

In weighing the nature of "soul" in this study, I devote considerable space to black humors, the products of untamed and raw power, prophecies that unsettle the prevailing rules of society. If it's true, as music critic Jon Pareles writes, that most music "implies that a set of rules is in effect, governing where notes can be placed in pitch and time, and what the acceptable timbres might be,"[110] then we can say that the most memorable of American musical styles have challenged these rules, allowing the right amount of anarchy and dissonance to make something unexpected and new, for example, the introduction of an Otis Redding rasp, a Billie Holiday quiver, a flamenco's piercing cry. In the scarred, trembling timbres of these voices, a surfeit of pain seeps into the music and interrupts the orthodox rules of music or society, making for the perfect, dissonant music of the soul. To the ears of genteel society, this is all some kind of black magic, but for those who can appreciate a broader range of creativity, there is a blessed rage for order in these howls of the human voice.

If anything, black musicians in this vein have only proliferated in the post–civil rights generation. The hip-hop generation has brought together a host of trickster figures and organized a coup of civil rights etiquette and propriety. In its mutinous postures, hip-hop took the soul and funk music of earlier generations and made it harder and edgier, deep-fried the funk, so to speak. In "funkifying" this older tradition, hip-hop introduced the speech patterns of street hustlers, thugs, and pimps to the smooth grooves of R & B. With the street vernacular as its medium, hip-hop picked up the scraps of language that other, more refined styles had discarded and disdained; tattered and frayed words seemed more fitting symbols of the lives they lived in the alleyways and projects of the ghetto. So rap music culled the "shunned expressions of disposable people," as one critic put it, and made beats and rhymes out of these castaway vocabularies.[111] By using prohibited idioms in a revolutionary manner, hip-hop sought to break free of the prison of language. (Adam Bradley reminds us, after all, that "vernacular" originates from the Greek word for a slave born of his master's house, *verna,* so hip-hop represents the liberating energy of the vernacular, breaking free of incarcerating conventions and realities.)[112]

And if hip-hop is not always revolutionary, it is almost always crafty, astute, and wily. It uses logos—reason, speech—in both modern and ancient ways. As Bruce Lincoln points out, long before the word became synonymous with reason in the age of the Socrates and his disciples, logos was primarily a speech of cunning and guile, employed by the weak and the young against the strong. Homer and Hesiod associated the term with the ruses of deception and duplicity used by trickster figures to compensate for their relative powerlessness (e.g., Hermes, called master of guiles, used his "seductive *logoi*" to trick his older, stronger brother, Apollo; Odysseus is given the epithet "clever" or "cunning" throughout *The Odyssey* as he is shown outwitting stronger opponents).[113] In the case of hip-hop, whether rappers are conjuring Greek or African tricksters, their sly skills can be considered a rendition of this ancient view of logoi, in which subversive slang, outlaw expressions, and irreverent counternarratives are employed by the poor and young to outwit the enemy. In these instances, the playfulness of the trickster, or the Faustian pact as I have described it, is a symbol of defiance, a prophetic disturbance of the repressive aspects of the Puritan American sociopolitical order.[114]

I think of J. Cole's description in "Dead Presidents 2" as a combination of the kind of profane cunning and sacred inspiration I have been discussing here: "my flow like a devil spit it, and heaven sent it."[115] In this compact sentence, J. Cole encapsulates many of these disparate experiences in black music. His lyrics, he suggests, are gritty and slick like the devil's language or perhaps twisted like a serpent's tongue, but finally inspired by God. At its best, the genre of rap is a forked tongue in this way, sometimes venomous and poisonous, biting hard at social decorum and political perfidy, but then, in the same breath, spitting faith and hope, transforming the poisons of ghetto life into a cure. With traces of both poison and potion, hip-hop turns music and lyrics into a wily form of speech (logoi), against the black holes of the bourgeois capitalist order that suck light from the lives of the poor and disenfranchised. "I pay the toll fighting for my own soul," Lauryn Hill remarks, "'cause the bourgeois type of mental sucks like a black hole."[116]

In these examples the meaning of "soul" swings back and forth between the sacred and profane, high and low culture; it can signify spiritual complexity as well as a culture's street wisdom and cool aplomb, especially in music, dance, and verbal virtuosity. In her reflections on soul and hip-hop, Imani Perry clarifies the issues: "By soul I mean that which has some spiritual depth and deep cultural and historical resonances to be felt through the kind of music and sounds made by the vocalists. . . . Soulful music is music of joy and pain, unself-consciously wedding melody and moaning, the sound of the dual terror and exultation of being black in America."[117] In this reading soul gives voice to many layers of style and substance—struggle and suffering, terror and jubilation, vulgarity and sublimity—and stitches them together like an auditory collage or mix-tape of various sentiments, beliefs, and values.[118] The product, as Nas once said about his own style, is a wild arrangement of poetry, preaching, and straight-up hustlin'.[119]

Ultimately, then, I view the power of blackness through the eyes of these spiritual and cultural styles, in which flirtation with the profane, vulgar, and foul is an instrument of salvation and a disguised form of love and justice. One might say that this construction of blackness contains a heavy amount of irony, in which blasphemous and forbidden thoughts conceal a virtuous interior and saintly soul. In other words, as Kierkegaard and Melville tried to warn us, looks can be deceiving: Beneath the glitter and glamor of Christendom, beneath all of its moral rectitude and sanctimoniousness, there may be hidden sin, a charnel house underneath clean white sepulchers (Melville's image). Conversely, it could be that true goodness remains unrecognized by the rulers of the world or the guardians of holiness, so that if we want to search for God, or search for soul, we need to turn to the parts of our world where poverty and desperation are rampant: in the trials of the streets, in the crowded despair of prisons, and in the crosses of the hood. This is to say that the path to redemption in Judaism or Christianity is never a straight line but rather something more rambling and unpredictable, like the trail of a vagabond, or the shuffling, whirling, and winding of a break-dancer, or the sly contrivances of a rapper. Yeats was right, in this sense, to call good and evil "crude analogies," because sometimes the path of soulfulness requires the intrepid and bold daring of a soul rebel in the mold of Bob Marley, Dr. King, or Cesar Chavez, and sometimes it requires the impiety of a blues or rap artist in the mold of Billie Holiday, Jelly Roll Morton, or Tupac Shakur.[120] It seems to me that this is what Emerson meant when he said that the soul *becomes* when the saint is confounded with the rogue, or what Melville meant when he channeled Job's defiant roar: "I now know that thy right worship is defiance."[121]

Sometimes right worship is indeed defiance, and sometimes, to cite Melville again, it is to kneel and revere. If anything, this study explores the ideas, sounds, and styles that include moments of both, that know when it is fitting to negate and defy and when we must affirm in a loving embrace. If there are moments when we must deviate from the crudest versions of "good," when we must, as Simone Weil says, turn away from God, it will not be long before we fall back into his arms.[122] The jazz great Louis Armstrong expressed his own version of this sentiment. When accused of turning away from God and embracing the devilish delights of blues and jazz, he would respond in words penned by W. C. Handy (though in his own rasping, gravelly voice): "Just hear Aunt Hagar's children harmonizin' to that old mournful tune. It's like a choir from on high broke loose, amen. If the devil brought it, the good Lord sent it right on down to me."[123] In generations to come, Aunt Hagar's children will find new mournful occasions to sing and rap about, and the products of their efforts, however infused with hellfire, will remain a gift that has broken loose from the heavens.

2

On Hebrew Soul

De Eloquentia Vulgaria

And I tell you that you should open yourselves to hearing an authentic poet, of the kind whose bodily senses were shaped in a world that is not our own and few people are able to perceive. A poet closer to death than to philosophy, closer to pain than to intelligence, closer to blood than to ink.

—Federico García Lorca[1]

Oh! Rabbi, rabbi, fend my soul for me
And true savant of this dark nature be.

—Wallace Stevens

At the end of Socrates's *Symposium,* late in the night when all the revelers at the party have succumbed to sleep except for Agathon and Aristophanes, Socrates shares a prophecy of a poet yet to come. He dreams of a poet who will combine tragic and comic styles in a new, comprehensive manner. Presumably this artist will make poetry out of the wild discord and contradictions of human life—out of grief and laughter, violence and love, the sublime and the ordinary—adding bits and pieces of each to make a rich brew. If one is persuaded by Eric Auerbach's argument in *Mimesis,* however, this prophecy never materialized in ancient Greece. While the Greeks mastered tragedy and comedy, high and low styles, they generally kept the two apart, rarely allowing the experiences and characters of ordinary, everyday life to play a significant role in anything but comedy. For the marriage of these disparate styles another kind of genius had to emerge, outside of the aristocratic culture of the Greeks, and it did so at the hands of barbarians at the farthest edges of the Greco-Roman world, nomads and tribes that came together to produce the sacred writ of the Bible.[2]

By joining together the incongruent themes of tragedy and comedy, the Bible turned the spectacle of lowly, poor lives—shepherds and wanderers, exiles and refugees, the conquered and colonized—into the stuff of sublimity. For the first time in Western history the lives of the ordinary, poor, and rude were the subject of lofty narratives, with themes that were as sublime as anything found in Greek tragedy or philosophy. In contrast to the emphasis on the ruling classes in Greek tragedy, nothing was too humble or too coarse for biblical texts. They inscribed everything in their pages and made the long treks of exiles and slaves sacred history. Access to the Bible's tree of knowledge, to its soul, is only possible if we have the eyes and ears to recognize the unlikely wisdom that comes from the experiences of the dispossessed, that oozes from the Bible's lowest branches like thick sap.

I begin this chapter with a consideration of the terminology of *nephesh* in the Hebrew Bible, but I also explore the meaning of this concept from a more elevated, bird's-eye perspective, one that surveys the dense, tangled forest of the soul from a literary and narrative perspective, in the last part of this chapter. Because the concept of the soul is the product of a story—a "living book" as Teresa of Ávila said—I do my best to unspool the narrative threads of this story, with a specific focus on the way the Bible commingles tragedy and comedy and hence weaves together its drama with high and low strands of thought. As I discuss later in the chapter, the result is a pattern that features, in bold color, the sensibilities of the outcast, the outsider, and the downtrodden, so that if one can speak of the heart and soul of the Bible, it will be found in the Bible's predilection for these themes. Later interpretations of "soul" in Western history—say in African American or Latin American Christianity—addressed many of these themes when they spoke of "soul," even when it was transfigured in a newer, more modern light. But here I begin with a discussion of some of the basic qualities, tones, and inflections of *nephesh* in the Bible.

NEPHESH AND THE BREATH OF LIFE

As an entry point, I begin with *nephesh*'s association with the life force of a living being: the soul is related to the needs and respirations of the human body, to the blood and oxygen coursing through one's veins (Gen. 9:4; Lev. 17:11) or to the throat, where life is maintained by the absorption of food and respiration of air (Ps. 107:5; Eccles. 6:7; Isa. 29:8; Prov. 6:30). *Nephesh* is a source of life, the secret power that enlivens the body and spirit of a person, the gush of life vivifying and quickening the substance of man and woman, bringing it into being. More encompassing than corporeal or spiritual needs alone, the soul is a shrine or reservoir for a variety of passions and hopes, both sensual and intangible.

Because *nephesh* is connected to the breath of life (in its verb form, it can mean "to respire or breathe"), it also suggests something deeply intimate and interior to the human person and thus can be used in the Bible with a personal pronoun, as in "my *nephesh*" (Gen. 19:19; Judg. 16:30; Ps. 54:6). In this form the term seems to indicate the sanctity of personal identity, that which constitutes the unseen fabric of a singular human being. With this nuance added, *nephesh* is the life or spirit that defines and distinguishes one person's existence from others, the quintessence that makes one unique and peculiar. As a product of God's maternal care in the womb, the soul is irreplaceable and inimitable: "You formed my inmost being; you knit me in my mother's womb" (Ps. 139:13). In this vein, Robert Alter notes that *nephesh* can mean a person's essential self, in addition to "life force" or "vital spirit."[3]

Notwithstanding this intimacy between God and the human soul, however, the Hebrew soul remains a creature of flesh and blood; it is not inherently divine. The Torah leaves no doubt on this point: Like the grass of the earth and flowers of the field, the human person will wither and drop its leaves, fade, and return to the dust, says the poet and prophet Isaiah (Isa. 40:6–7). The human soul is fragile and impermanent, vulnerable to events outside its control and always vexed by the burden of the grave (Josh. 2:13; 1 Sam. 19:11; Ps. 34:23). Given the omnipresence of death and destruction in ancient Jewish history (individually and collectively), it is only natural that *nephesh* would be marked by the heavy and at times awful destiny of Israel. If biblical authors speak of Israel as often tottering on the edge of ruin, it is scarcely different when they consider the human soul: it is human-all-too-human. Consider the distressed effusions of the soul in the following psalm:

> For my soul is sated with troubles,
> my life's reached the brink of Sheol.
> I'm counted with those who go down to the Pit,
> in darkness, in the depths.
> Your wrath lies hard upon me,
> With all your breakers you afflict me. (Ps. 88:3–8)

The image here of descent into the Pit (similar to the "Pit" of lions into which Daniel is thrown or the "Pit" of the whale in the Book of Jonah) is of course a confrontation with the underworld. The psalmist here is in an existential struggle, fighting for his life, doing what he can to keep the breakers from submerging his soul. With troubles all around and God's displeasure upon him, the poet seems to be dying many small deaths: "We consume our years like a sigh" (Ps. 90:10).

Although the author of the psalm directs his blackest emotions at the heavens here, we cannot overlook the fact that he (apparently miraculously) continues to live and write. It is impossible to read the scriptures and not notice the myriad forces that menace and threaten one's personal identity, but at the same time, the Torah is a tribute to the remarkable capacity of the human soul to survive to tell the tale, an achievement of both grit and grace. Snatched from the grip of Sheol, these moments of survival suddenly become the occasion for praise by the psalmist. It is natural, then, that the Psalms pair, in almost exactly equal quantities, psalms of supplication with psalms of praise. (These two types comprise two-thirds of the Psalms.)[4] While the psalms of supplication give voice to the crushing weight of sorrow and suffering, the psalms of praise are jubilant, celebratory, and restorative; the former describe the downward slope into the depths of anguish, and the latter record the capacity of the soul to ascend from the pits of life (Psalm 121 is specifically called "a song of ascents" in this regard). The Psalms represent the soul in rich, polyphonic notes, both high and low, exultant and downhearted, a rowdy mixture of fears and torments on the one hand and undaunted spiritual aspirations on the other.

NEPHESH AND TRANSCENDENT LONGINGS

Besides suggesting respiration, personal identity, and life force, *nephesh* is also associated with immeasurable and sublime longings. Derived from the root *wh* (to desire) and the verb *ns* (to rise), *nephesh* is related to hopes and cravings that would elevate the mundane existence of humanity. In this sense, while *nephesh* is as vulnerable as a naked body in the desert and as susceptible to decomposition as any other creature of earth, it also embodies the ethereal and transcendent desires of man and woman, their ferocious appetite for God. However brief and transient our lives are, human beings have inexhaustible desires that distinguish us from all other animals, and *nephesh* is the source of these emotions, the restless energy that makes us long and hanker for impossible things: love, righteousness, God. "As a deer yearning for streams of water, so my soul yearns for you, God. / My soul thirsts for God, for the living God. / O when shall I come to appear before God?" (Ps. 42:1–2; see also Ps. 25:1; 130:5; Song of Songs 1:7).

The *nephesh* represents the far-reaching and untethered desires of humankind, the Abrahamic drive to seek, to strive, to reach for the unknown. Insatiable and infinite in its hunger, the soul is forever wanting, forever roaming in search of new worlds and new possibilities. The soul stretches out and follows "knowledge like a sinking star, beyond the utmost bound of human thought."[5] It is endlessly drawn toward God, a moth to the flame.

Because it is sealed with the *imago Dei,* the *nephesh* also participates in the divine nature of God and shares with him the uncanny powers of creation. Endowed with the ability to name the things of creation, human beings have been given the art of language, with the potential to make something out of nothing, life out of death, order out of chaos, and beauty out of a blank canvas. Lest this blessing become a curse, however, biblical thought is relentless in rebuking man for his vanity and actions that disdain mortal limits. The children of Adam are constantly reminded of their origins in the earth, that they are made of dust and ashes. (The name "Adam" is, after all, derived from the Hebrew *adamah,* or soil.) Recall this solemn moment in Genesis: "The Lord God fashioned the human from the soil, and blew into his nostrils the breath of life, and the human became a living creature" (Gen. 2:4–47). Working with earth and clay, God infused this organism with his own spirit and thus imbued it with dignity and divine properties. The soul is thus bifurcated, a curious mixture of both chthonic and transcendent qualities.

NEPHESH AND THE HEART

Since the Bible often pairs soul and heart, we should consider the points of contact between these two, as in the great commandment in Deuteronomy, "You shall love the Lord your God with all your heart and with all of your soul and with all of your might" (Deut. 6:5), and Josiah's determination to follow the Lord's decrees with "all his heart and soul" (2 Kings 23:3). This injunction is of supreme significance and is to be fixed on one's arm and forehead, inscribed on one's doorposts, engraved on one's heart, and recited to one's children. Everything that one is, everything that one can be, is contained in these words and implies a total, comprehensive dedication to the covenant with YHWH. "Heart" and "soul" bleed into each other; both can be seen as repositories of the transcendent, spiritual qualities of human beings, and both are centers of love and reverence. Together, they are the intimate sanctuaries of human nature, in which God confers life, wisdom, and understanding, "where individuals face themselves with their feelings, their reason, and their conscience, and where they assume their responsibilities by making decisive choices for themselves, whether those are open to God or not."[6] To retreat into the deep caverns of the heart and soul is thus to find the real "me," the oldest and nearest and truest "me." Somewhere deeper than our public personas lie heart and soul, where God will suddenly confront us with the most momentous and vital of decisions, will undress and strip away our egos, leaving something of greater value, something made of dust, debris, and sublimity.

It can be assumed that every atom of one's being is summoned in these moments of crisis and revelation, so that all of one's emotions are roused: sadness and anguish, love and joy, bitterness and confusion, delight and praise (Jer. 13:17; 1 Sam. 1:10; Ps. 31:8, 35:9; Song of Songs 1:7). The Bible makes prodigal use of human sentiments, preferring the idioms of pathos, poetry, song, and prayer to philosophical discourse. By gathering together the untidy array of human desires, it employs a volcanically emotive manner of speech, combining spontaneous, heart-felt effusions with moments of carefully scripted artifice. The balance between artlessness and artifice gives many of these texts a vitality and throbbing pulse that separates this stormier art from other more polished, cerebral styles.

Though there are numerous cases in which heart and soul touch and melt into one another, there are also boundaries drawn in the Bible. It seems, for example, that biblical writers assigned a special place to knowledge when speaking of the geography of heart: the heart, not the mind, is the dwelling place of human reason. Hence the author of the Psalms can pray that "the words of my mouth and the *meditation* of my heart" will be acceptable to God (Ps. 19:14). If reason operates from the terrain of the heart, as this text implies, we can assume that human knowledge, in the biblical view, is undivided from the emotions and shares a kinship with them.

The Melodians's classic song the "Rivers of Babylon" ruminates on this exact sentiment. When they pray that God will receive the words of their mouths and the meditation of their hearts, the song beautifully explores the tangled threads of knowledge and emotions in the Bible.

Better than many academic exegetes, they capture the desolation of the Psalms, as well as their impossible dreams and hopes. In a wistful, plaintive key, the song pleads for justice and redemption in a world far away from home, somewhere in exile on the lonely shores of the river of Babylon, believing that the musings and ponderings of the heart will guide those in bondage to a land of freedom and truth. In the magic of such art, affect is subtly transformed into knowledge and knowledge into affect:

> By the rivers of Babylon, where we sat down
> And there we wept when we remembered Zion
> Cause the wicked carried us away, captivity
> Requiring of us a song
> How shall we sing King Alpha's song
> In a strange land?[7]

Indeed, how shall we sing God's song in a strange land? This is the question that has been the provocation and inspiration for a lot of black music in the Americas. In drawing on the biblical text, The Melodians saw themselves and their peoples through the predicament of the ancient Israelites, and they joined their melodies and prayers with the black Israelites in captivity and diaspora. By summoning the spirit of Moses and using the narratives of the Bible to confront the oppressive pharaohs of their age, reggae artists were faithful to Hebrew conceptions of redemption and justice. And they were faithful to the rebellious and melodious understanding of *nephesh* in the Psalms, its curious ability to achieve wisdom through the right ingredients of protest, passion, affection, melody, and cadence. What Bob Marley called a "soul rebel" (the title of Bob Marley's 1970 studio album) belongs to this Hebrew bloodline of *nephesh*.[8]

In this world of the Psalms, then, the heart is capable of penetrating insights, so that human reason is never estranged from the passions and sentiments. A crucial biblical insight follows on the heels of this understanding, one that is key to my study: namely, that knowledge of the heart is accessible to all, educated or illiterate, lowly or highborn. In the biblical vision God makes wisdom lavishly open to everyone (and flagrantly, too, when it threatens the official scribes and priests). Since the Sinai covenant was established with all the Israelites, both the lettered and the unlettered, knowledge and obedience are enjoined on all; it is not a covenant made only with a philosophical or aristocratic elite. "And these words, which I command thee this day, shall be in thy heart; and thou shall teach them diligently to thy children" (Deut. 6:6–7).

Since it makes no discriminations between rank, class, or wealth, divine wisdom is widely disseminated in this tradition. If anything, the Hebrew God seeks out those barren of such distinctions and rescues them from oblivion and disregard (cf. Hannah's prayer, 1 Sam. 2:7–8). In the biblical vision the heart of the humble person is more likely to be the bearer of wisdom than the puffed-up heart of the proud and powerful one. The heart is a conduit of a special kind of knowledge unlike anything the eye can see or ear can hear, a custodian of an ironical wisdom, as in this pivotal text when Samuel goes against convention to anoint Jesse's youngest son, David: "And the Lord said to Samuel, 'Look not to his appearance and to his lofty stature, for I have cast him aside [Jesse's oldest son, Eliab]. For not as man sees does the Lord see. For man sees with the eyes and the Lord sees with the heart'" (1 Sam. 16:7). In the ways of the corrupt world, the firstborn will always inherit position and power, but the biblical God casts this preference aside and exalts the lowly, a transformation of great historic significance. In the prophetic tradition (as in this case of Samuel's choice of David), the eyes of the seer—clouded over and blind to the world's values—follow this intuitive vision of the heart, in which truth and justice are revolutionary and subversive of the status quo.

Isaiah puts it this way: "I dwell in a high and holy place, say the Lord, but with those who are contrite and humble in spirit, to revive the spirit of the humble and to revive the heart of the contrite" (Isa. 57:15). Though God comes from on high, he appears on the stage of human history among the simple and lowborn. And this message is central to the story of Exodus, in which God appears to Moses as a God of the oppressed slave. Though Moses was summoned to mountainous heights, he was assured that the God of his ancestors had seen the Israelites' afflictions and heard their cries, and "therefore I have come down to rescue them from the power of the Egyptians" (Exod. 3:7–8).

In branding this memory of slavery on the soul of the Torah, the biblical authors demanded that its hearers and readers constantly revisit this sacred theophany, never allowing comfort or success to induce the stupor of forgetfulness. For our purposes, this means that the matter of soul in the Bible is represented in earthly shades and colors, in black and brown hues that are indicative of the struggles of the lowly. Any search for soul in the Bible must accordingly travel with the Israelites through these narratives of captivity and exile, cross the river Jordan, and always welcome the Other who comes in the form of the poor and enslaved. These circumstances and injunctions alone place the Hebrew concept of the soul at an infinite distance from Greek, aristocratic conceptions of the soul (whether the aristocracy of the hero, as in Homer, or the aristocracy of the philosopher, as in Socrates, Plato, and Aristotle).

NEPHESH IN ITS NARRATIVE CONTEXT

The Inscrutability of God and Man in the Bible: The Shadows of Nephesh

Auerbach opens *Mimesis,* his extraordinary journey through Western literature, with a contrast between Homer and the Bible, the Greeks and the Jews. Though his subject is the story of literature from antiquity to the twentieth century, one of its key themes is the formative influence of biblical narrative on the entire scope of Western literature. In considering biblical narrative with such care and insight, Auerbach was something of a rare fish in literary circles of the early twentieth century, swimming against the stream of interpretation that regarded the Bible with enlightened condescension, ranking it far below the Greek imagination.[9] As an exile himself—a German Jew forced into exile by the Nazis in 1935—he regarded the urgent realism of the Bible, especially the narratives of expulsion and bondage, as a key to his own self-understanding and more generally as a key that might unlock the hermetic codes of modern literature.

By concentrating on the form and style of these sacred texts and contrasting them with Homer, Auerbach made various discoveries. One in particular has to do with the laconic and rough tongue of biblical narratives. In Auerbach's reading, biblical narrative is far more restrained than Homer's epic poetry: it holds much back and does not explain everything; it leaves things and characters partially unsaid, unknown, and unexplained; and it controls language with an ascetic discipline. His primary example is the command to Abraham in the matter of his son, Isaac (Gen. 22:1). From out of nowhere, from some mysterious height or undetermined depth, God suddenly appears to Abraham and demands obedience. In contrast to Homer's narratives, very little is said about the setting in which this happens, the characters, or their motives, and even less is said about the nature of this unpredictable, unfathomable God. The contrast with Homer is illustrative: "Whence does he come, whence does he call to Abraham? We are not told. He does not come like Zeus or Poseidon from the Aethiopians, where he has been enjoying a sacrificial feast. Nor are we told anything of his reasons for tempting Abraham so terribly. He has not, like Zeus, discussed them in set speeches with other gods gathered in council; nor have the deliberations of his own heart been presented to us."[10] In contrast to Homer's depiction of the gods, the Bible veils God with profiles of indeterminacy; he is devoid of anthropomorphic features, totally Other. In painting pictures of the divine with words instead of images, Israel deconstructed the common representations of pagan gods, choosing to envision God in impalpable, imponderable forms, without a vast array of visualizations. As a fitting illustration of this perspective, the symbol of emptiness became a rich allegory for the Jews, a signifier of the desert-like barrenness of YHWH. Legend has it, for example, that when Pompey conquered Israel and approached the Holy of Holies, he was startled to find an empty room. According to Tacitus, he remarked: "The shrine had nothing to reveal." Pompey, it seems, expected something tangible, some effigy in burnished gold or bejeweled silver, but he found nothing of the sort. The significance of emptiness was lost on him; it was a blank and meaningless sign to him and his legions, but for the Jews there was splendor in emptiness. YHWH was an anagram of the desert landscape itself, a luminous void, making all images of G-d evaporate in the sun like puddles of water on the burning desert soil, turning them into a fleeting mirage that forever recedes before one's eyes.[11]

Similar mirages or shadows are apparent in the Bible's representation of its key characters. Though we clearly learn about biblical characters in the Hebrew Bible, there is nonetheless a shroud of secrecy, a penumbra of obscurity, and a subtle haziness that keeps them hidden from human knowledge. In considering these characters, we are faced with an impossible question like the one Moses poses to God: What is your name? The response, "I am who I am, YHWH," is an answer with gaps and fissures, lacking in vowels, a reminder of divine ineffability. When Isaac is introduced, for example, we are only told that Abraham loves him, not whether he is handsome or ugly, intelligent or stupid, tall or short, kind or cruel. Details are scant. In fragmentary speech and resounding silences, the narrative simply instructs Abraham to take Isaac and "go forth" (in the same spirit of Abraham's first summons to leave his homeland and migrate to a new land in Gen. 12:1–3, a model for all intrepid explorers).[12] In the space of this terse narrative, we are introduced to the riddling and puzzling richness of the Bible. By leaving so much in a cloud of indeterminacy or secrecy, this narrative arouses in its readers a taste for mysteries that exist beyond the borders of what can be said and thought. The story pulses with hidden meanings and challenges the reader's imagination to compensate for what is missing.[13] In the silences, gaps, and missing vowels, biblical stories refrain from telling us what to think about each and every episode or character and subsequently invite us—or confront and cajole us—to supply our own meaning. As economical and austere as the narratives may be, there is untold treasure hiding here, gold mines under the dry desert soil.[14]

Thus the reader journeys through the course of biblical narrative, as through the course of life, a lot like Abraham does, mystified and bewildered but beguiled and allured by the unthinkable. Homer's narrative, by contrast, is a paean to what can be expressed and thought. (The Greek philosophers, of course, extended this confidence even further.) He gives us a feeling that almost everything can be described and understood: the passions of gods and men; the delights of physical existence; the adventures and dangers of life; the fears, cruelties, and valor of human beings; and even the awful and ennobling reality of death. Whereas Homer seeks to diminish the mystery of life, the Bible extends the obscurity and envelopes us in that mystery, placing human beings within its vast canopy. The Bible abhors transparency.

In consequence, *nephesh* is a foil to transparency and a metaphor for the strange, opaque, twilight regions of the human person, for what is shadowy and slippery about human identity, for what only God can see (1 Sam. 16:7, 25:37; Ps. 44:22, 64:7). Though the soul is as intimate as one's own breath, it remains a trace of the sacred Otherness that resides within us all, a mark of the unknown, as if it were engraved with a hieroglyph that stubbornly defeats decryption, like the tattoos on the body of Queequeg in *Moby Dick* (undecipherable "mystical treatises," in Melville's words).[15]

While much of modern thought has sought to shrink the scope of the unknown, I agree with Emerson that artists—he singles out preachers, poets, and musicians—pay homage to the enigmas of life. "After the most exhausting census has been made . . . this is that which the preacher and poet and the musician speak to: the region of destiny, of aspiration, of the unknown."[16] Perhaps intuitively, poets, preachers, and musicians build their works of art out of the dark materials of wonder and sublimity. They recognize the persistent presence of foreignness in the shadows of our being, even after the most careful and exhaustive census is performed. They are the best exegetes of the Bible.

The Mutability and Eccentricity of Nephesh: A Center of Surprise

Since the obscurity of the divine also extends to biblical characters, these souls are resistant to explanations that presume to offer absolute clarity. The shadows of the narratives cling to all of the characters like a spider's web that has them—and us—in its clutch. One might say that the most intriguing characters of the Bible are the most entangled, the most scrambled and confused, the most human. There are so many layers to their mysterious souls because they undergo many surprising and dramatic changes, and they are never static. These characters advance and retreat, develop and regress, and are always subject to the wayward misfortunes and humiliations of life. Though freedom is a crucial attribute of these creatures, the narratives also show them bandied about and dragged along by events, leaves carried by the wind. No one epithet adequately summarizes these characters, because they have undergone too many changes for one designation to stick. Jacob *(Ya'aqov)* is a "heel-grabber," but this label reveals nothing about the actual changes and revolutions in the course of his life. At the most, this label characterizes the genius of "Israel" (Jacob's new name after wrestling with God) as a tradition of art and spirituality that confronts God with the wiles of a trickster, the combativeness of a wrestler, and the agony of a wounded warrior. It epitomizes the kind of wounded wisdom that is central to the painful history of Israel.

With an eye trained on the surprises, agonies, and eccentricities in biblical art, we learn something valuable about the soul: it is a "center of surprise," in Robert Alter's nice choice of words.[17] Though awakened and infused with the divine breath of life, the soul of biblical characters is also made of the stuff of earth: dust, mud, and funk. What else can account for the imperfections and follies of people as seen in biblical narrative; what else explains their astonishing array of beauty and vileness? The highest aptitudes and possibilities of human beings are surely celebrated and extolled in the Bible, but rarely without digging into the lows, nadirs, and dregs of their lives. Rabbi Hillel caught this play of irony in the Bible in his aphorism, "My humiliation is my exaltation; my exaltation is my humiliation."[18] And the same irony appears in biblical narrative: the exaltation of biblical characters is menaced by failures, humiliations, and shameful deeds.

Indeed, almost all of the biblical patriarchs rise and fall, the way Skip James's famous blues voice much later would rise on soaring, falsetto notes, then suddenly fall into hot and dirty wails.[19] Though chosen and blessed by God, Abraham, Isaac, and Jacob each has his moment of slithering in the dust, creeping as a matter of survival, getting by the fly way. Each experiences life as a refugee or slave, for example. Moses is no different; he survives a murder conspiracy, endures exile, and then dies in the middle of the desert. The ebbs and flows of David's life may surpass them all, though. Robert Alter sizes him up well:

> David, in the many decades through which we follow his career, is first a provincial *ingénu* and public charmer, then a shrewd political manipulator and a tough guerilla leader, later a helpless father floundering in the entanglements of his sons' intrigues and rebellion, a refugee suddenly and astoundingly abasing himself before the scathing curses of Shimei, then a doddering old man bamboozled or at least directed by Bathsheeba and Nathan, and, in still another surprise on his very deathbed, an implacable seeker of vengeance against Joab and against the same Shimei whom he had ostensibly forgiven after the defeat of Absalom's insurrection.[20]

David's volatile life is given theatrical exuberance in the Bible. He changes costumes, masks, and performances like an itinerant actor, flipping and flying like a circus acrobat. It's almost impossible to ascribe a single essence to his character because it is constructed of many personas and personalities: shepherd, soldier, king, poet, musician, lover, father, and through it all, a man with an extraordinary divine destiny. And even this latter role, with its related heroism, doesn't exempt him from the tribulations of life: the violence and turmoil in his kingdom; the heartbreaking deaths of Jonathan, Absalom, and his son by Bathsheba; the iniquities and mutinies of his children; the humiliating experiences of life as a refugee; and so forth. In old age he ends up disheveled and doddering, after spending a life fraught with unrest and turmoil. We imagine him at this point with a dazed and confused look, reeling from the mercurial fluctuations in his life, from everything added and subtracted to his days on earth. His biographers charge his persona with the same friable ephemerality and floundering fallibility that any other human being has, showing us flashes of his eventful life in his sallies and sorties, his conniving and scheming, his victories and defeats. There is not one life story in David, but multiple histories, multiple acts, and multiple dramas.

In these episodes of David's life the Bible is concerned with the whole arc of David's life, not his individual psychology. Unlike a modern novel, the Bible generally does not give us access to the inner life of David's soul. We may get glimpses of his psyche through his prayers—especially if we give him credit for the Psalms—but his innermost being remains opaque to everyone save God.[21] His actions are often surprising and unpredictable for this exact reason: we are not privy to his motives and subjective consciousness. When he acts, we don't know what to expect, such as when he weeps and fasts for his son while he is still alive, but when the son dies, he washes, changes his clothes, worships the Lord, and eats. His behavior provokes dismay and curiosity in his servants, as in the reader. We expect acts of penance and abstinence after his death, but his explanation is convincing and eloquent. "Now that he is dead, why should I fast?" David remarks. "Can I bring him back again? I shall go to him, but he will not return to me" (2 Sam. 12:23). David's whole life is made up of similar surprises.

Consider the somersaults of the life of Joseph as well. He goes through numerous meteoric ascents and precipitous plunges. As a child, Joseph has grandiose dreams of success and power; in one he sees bowing before him his brothers' sheaves of grain, and in another the sun, moon, and eleven stars (Gen. 37:5–9). Apparently naïve about the envy and enmity such presumptuous dreams might provoke, he tells his brothers about them and becomes the object of their jealousy and anger. They first plot his death and then, after reconsidering, sell him as a slave. Later, in Egypt, Joseph's destiny will ebb and flow even more: no sooner does he become the household servant of the captain of pharaoh's guard (Potifar) than he is falsely accused of seducing Potifar's wife and ends up imprisoned. Despite being the chosen and beloved son of Jacob and being blessed by God, Joseph suffers more degradation and loss than any other brother. First thrown into a pit (and the language of the pit, *bor*, is related to the depths of Sheol in the Psalms), then sold as a slave, and then kept prisoner, Joseph's character is measured by extraordinary adversities. Eventually, though, after gaining the trust of the pharaoh through his dream-interpreting skills, he is released from prison and given a powerful position. Now the story seems to bear out his exalted dreams in childhood—but with one major caveat.

By the time Joseph rises to the heights of his career (as prime minister to the king of Egypt), he has undergone a lifetime of painful lessons and has clearly become humbled. Now in his glory, he seems to wear his pride more like sackcloth than a flamboyant, ostentatious tunic of many colors. And it is this new, chastened wisdom that clothes him with grace and a capacity for forgiveness and compassion. Now, with his brothers in danger of starving, he acts with pure altruism and affection, drained of any resentment or bitterness. When his brothers throw themselves at his feet, Joseph responds, "Have no fear! Can I take the place of God? . . . I will provide for you and for your children" (Gen. 50:19–21). Only now is Joseph's chosen status validated; only in this tearful and compassionate embrace of his desperate brothers does Joseph justify his youthful dreams of greatness. In the words of Jon Levenson: "That which legitimates

Joseph's authority is the critical element of which his dreams betrayed no premonition whatsoever: his service for those he would rule, his deliverance from dire affliction of those who would do him obeisance."[22]

The soul of Joseph's character, then, seems to emerge from these pages as a lot more tender and benevolent for having endured the various trials of his life, including imprisonment and slavery. Exposed to the tempests of history, like a pendulum his soul swings up and down, erratically and unpredictably, but then finds a wise equilibrium. In this way the Bible creates Joseph, and every other actor on the biblical stage, with the same stuff of which history is composed: variability, surprise, and idiosyncrasy.

In both examples discussed here, we can say that the Bible captures something vital about the dark and knotted human soul, giving us a map of human nature that guides us through the undiscovered countries of the soul. By maintaining a degree of reticence and reverence when exploring the topography of God and man, the Bible designs the narratives with clouds of unknowing enveloping and veiling the major characters, not excluding the character of God.

The Makings of Realistic Prose: The Historical Context of Nephesh

In narrating the history of the Israelites, biblical writing was pioneering in other ways, too, especially in rendering divine truth in historical terms. In the Hebrew imagination, history is the mother of truth, as Cervantes suggested in *Don Quixote:* "witness of the past, example and lesson to the present, and warning to the future."[23] In accord with this vision, the Torah is witness to the revelations of God that unfold in human history; it is witness to the past, example to the present, and warning to the future. Instead of a rational conception of truth—where reason is the chief source of knowledge and determines what is true— truth in the Bible is an event, manifestation, or epiphany that materializes in the raucous episodes of history and that happens outside the predictable boundaries of reason alone.[24] This is evident in the form of the Torah itself: instead of the epic genre, popular in the ancient world of pagan myth, it adopted a form of prose narration that would record the events and trials of Israel in the course of its historical life. Using natural and ordinary dialect, biblical prose captured the involvement of God in human experience and turned this testimony into a centerpiece of the Jewish religious universe. By orbiting the constellations of language and privileging the spoken and written word, Israel relegated images, shrines, and priesthoods to positions of secondary importance, dislodging them to the outer limits of its cosmos.[25] Especially in the wake of the destruction the second Temple (70 C.E.), Israel turned more definitively to its sacred books as a substitute for cataclysmic interruptions of its cultic life. In consequence, literature became the privileged medium of God's unveiling in time and space, and this made the meaning of truth, including the meaning of *nephesh,* a time-bound concept.

The fact that sacred books became the privileged traces of God's actions in history—icons of the word—led to both complications and blessings. Though the writers of the sacred books surely regarded the voice of God in these texts as eternal and perfect, they also knew that God's revelations occurred in the messy and untidy conditions of history, through flawed and fallible human hands. Unlike the creators of flawless portraits of heroes in classic myth, these writers of prose accepted the ambiguities and contradictions of human affairs; their heroes are bungling creatures, and their narratives are equally bungling and unsystematic. Jewish and Christian apologists frequently had to defend these writings—which appeared so human, so desultory, coarse, and uncouth—against the derisive accusations of classic pagan authors.

By viewing the snags, blind corners, and dangerous reefs of human experience as possible sites for divine visitation, these authors navigated the courses of history in the way that Mark Twain later wrote of the riverboat pilots of the Mississippi: steering by feel alone, without the benefit of sight or map. Human experience was pressed and wrung for every possible drop of wisdom as these authors articulated lofty, sublime truths through the earthen vessels of real-life struggles: in domestic affairs; political turmoil and warfare; and the terrors of diaspora, expulsion, and captivity. Their subjects were not fixed, timeless, one-dimensional beings, but men and women who experienced change and loss. The characters were seen to grow and develop, succeed and fail, all in relation to the vicissitudes of life. Alter describes this literary revolution as an expression of Israel's conception of God:

> The monotheistic revolution of biblical Israel was a disquieting one. It left little margin for neat and confident views about God, the created world, history and man as political animal or moral agent, for it repeatedly had to make sense of the intersection of incompatibles—the relative and the absolute, human imperfection and divine perfection, the brawling chaos of historical experience and God's promise to fulfill a design in history. The biblical outlook is informed, I think, by a sense of stubborn contradiction, of a profound and ineradicable untidiness in the nature of things, and it is toward the expression of such a sense of moral and historical reality that the composite artistry of the Bible is directed.[26]

As Alter suggests, the monotheistic revolution in the Bible led to a complicated and unsettling view of the world. By not evading the stubborn turmoil of human affairs—the rank and gross things in the unweeded garden of the world, to quote Hamlet—biblical writers captured parts of human experience that eluded more rational or mythical treatments of human behavior. Their prowess in literature proved effective in recording the throbbing pains and exhilarations of history without sweating inconsistencies. They preferred their musings on life to be rough and turbulent, a better match for their lives in the difficult and testing settings of the ancient Near East.

Thus, in lieu of syllogisms and arguments that would resolve the aporias of human experience or myths that would provide simple resolutions to human conundrums, biblical authors aimed at fidelity in recording God's presence in and through the melees and struggles of time, situating their characters in their natural and social-political contexts—a style that we have come to know as literary realism.[27] Though extreme attention to visual details is missing in the Bible—a staple of modern realism—the illuminations in its pages occur through specific historical trials and social contexts, features that are frequently invisible in myth. By using prose instead of epic poetry, the Bible shifted the focus from the timeless events of myth to the "wayward paths of human freedom, the quirks and contradictions of men and women" and created in the process a rough and fledgling form of realism.[28] "Israel perceived the suffering and dangers of life in a highly realistic fashion," remarks Gerhard von Rad, "and saw itself defenselessly and vulnerably exposed to them, and showed little talent for taking refuge in any sort of ideology. . . . Rather, it possessed an uncommon power to stand its ground before negative realities, to acknowledge and not repress them even when they could not be coped with spiritually or intellectually."[29] While myth was by no means expunged from biblical writing, the authors nonetheless anchored their narratives in the nitty-gritty exigencies of life, even as these untidy conditions proved unnerving and disquieting, incapable of logical clarity.

Nephesh in Exile and Diaspora

In many ways the preference of Israel for sacred literature over myths, shrines, and sanctuaries makes sense for these nomadic desert dwellers: their images of God reflected the necessity of flight and movement in the face of disastrous threats to their existence. (Notice, for example, the makeshift shelters and ambulatory tents of worship described in the biblical texts.) Even when the Jews eventually established a dynastic monarchy and built the first Temple, their memories were haunted by exile, migration, and diaspora; the texts preserved a feeling of estrangement from sedentary life. Notwithstanding the importance of the settlement in Israel, therefore, there is a clear preference in the Bible for narratives of exodus and dispossession over those of conquest and possession, for the prophets over the kings (Elijah, for example, is certainly preferred to the Israelite kings in 1 and 2 Kings). The prophet Samuel eventually gives his support to the monarchy, but it is a grudging support with a caveat the size of Mount Sinai (1 Sam. 8:10–18). And if we follow the Deuteronomic depiction of abuse, immorality, and violence in the house of David and his children (riddled as it is with rebellion, incest, adultery, and exploitation), we will notice the prophetic argument in favor of dispossession and alienation over dynasties and cities.

I like Herbert Schneidau's description of this aspect of Hebrew narrative; he reads it as an ethos of alienation: "In philosophic terms, what the Bible offers culture is neither an ecclesiastical structure nor a moral code, but an unceasing critique of itself. For this critique a certain cost must be paid: we habitually call this cost 'objectivity' but its original name was alienation. . . . It evolved from deliberately chosen and painfully intense experience of alienation: as the prophet's sense of Yahweh weighs down on him, he sees man as dust, man's strivings as futility, and he feels chosen, set apart, estranged."[30] The Hebrews cherished, in contrast to the settlements of high civilizations, a seminomadic self-image that imbued their prophetic imagination with a distrust of cities and all pleasures associated with them: the comforts and decadence, the injustices and moral decay. In this vision, every great and powerful civilization turns gluttonous and cruel with its success; all of them have seeds of Sodom and Gomorrah in them, just waiting to be watered by the temptations of wealth and power. (Although the most common image of Sodom and Gomorrah is a city rife with sexual impropriety, the sin identified by Isaiah is injustice and mistreatment of the poor; for Ezekiel, it is an excess of food and "not aiding the poor and needy" [Isa. 1:9–10, 3:9; Ezek. 16:49].) And if the corrupted civilization is not Sodom and Gomorrah, then it is Babylon or Nineveh or Tyre: sin crouches at the gates of these cities like a ravenous tiger ready to pounce, and only the prophets seem to notice the extent of the ferocity and injustice.[31]

When a civilization turns savage and unfeeling in this way, the most vulnerable groups have little choice but to journey elsewhere. In the Pentateuch, the plain fact of hunger is a vital part of the drama; Abraham, Isaac, and Jacob are each forced to migrate to Egypt or Gerar because of famine in the land. This is the description of Isaac's migration: "Now there was a famine in the land, besides the former famine that had occurred in the days of Abraham. And Isaac went to Gerar, to King Abimelech of the Philistines. The Lord appeared to Isaac and said, 'Do not go down to Egypt; settle in the land that I shall show you. Reside in this land as an alien and I will be with you'" (Gen. 26:1–3).[32] Famine drives many of the patriarchs into exile: first Abraham to Egypt, then Isaac to Gerar, and later Jacob and his children back to Egypt, all as a matter of life and death (recall that Joseph's success in Egypt is due to his prophetic awareness of the impending famine). In each story, the setting and plot are unmistakably influenced by the constraints of life in the desert. The threat of famine looms large and compels the characters to plan an escape to where water and food can be had (and, not surprisingly, disputes over water rights play an important role in these stories, such as in Isaac's disagreements with the Philistines in Gen. 26:17–23). In this way, the natural environment of these deserts—unforgiving, implacable, virtually uninhabitable—encroaches on the narratives like a sudden dust devil and hurls everything into a violent twister.

In their struggles with this deadly terrain, the patriarchs' experiences adumbrate the plight of Israel throughout the Tanakh. The oscillations of their lives—humiliation and exaltation, enslavement and liberation, exile and homeland—are representative of the plight of Israel as a whole.[33] Israel wanders through biblical literature in the same spirit of the patriarchs, searching for God in the most desolate of conditions. It is after all in the wilderness, at Mount Horeb, that God appears to Moses in a burning bush; in the wilderness where God sends manna to the Israelites, who are on the cusp of starvation; in the wilderness, during a time of severe drought, that God rescues the dying Hagar and Ishmael and sends ravens to feed the thirsty and starved Elijah; and in the wilderness, according to Hosea, that God first betrothed himself to Israel and fed her with grain, wine, and oil (Exod. 3:1–6, 16:13; Gen. 21:15–19; 1 Kings 17:6; Hosea 9:10). In these accounts and others, the desert is a place of menacing emptiness, but also, in keeping with the stark hiddenness of G-d in Judaism, a symbol of the naked sublimity of the divine, the vast void that is ironically always ready to burst, monsoon-like, onto the parched landscapes of human life. In the words of Hosea 14:5–6:

I will be like the dew to Israel, and he shall blossom like the lily.
He shall strike root like the forests of Lebanon.
His shoots shall spread out.
His beauty shall be like the olive tree and his fragrance like that
   of Lebanon.

In the Bible, God's fragrant presence in history breeds life where the geography is withered and dew and blossoms where the soil is hard and fallow. Israel shall spread out and flower, mirroring the lilies of the field, the forests of Lebanon, and the whole splendor of creation. In Hosea, in fact, the immense arc of the desert sky is seemingly transformed into a canopy under which promises and vows are exchanged, where God appears out of the heart of darkness like a surreptitious lover and seduces Israel (Hosea 2:14ff.; Jer. 2:1–3; Isa. 1:21–26, 54:1–8). Betrothed to God in the wastelands, Israel becomes a bride of the desert and will come to know both the giddy exhilaration and heartrending agony entailed in this marriage.

If we learn anything about the soul in these texts, then, it is that the soul is made of the earth and has material needs and weaknesses; plain hunger drives this fact home. Famine causes people, places, and things to dry up and wither; turns gardens into wastelands; and makes communities into rolling stones. The desert has the power to disorient or even level the human soul. The desert "bewilders human vanity," to invoke Richard Rodriguez, and reminds us of our "insignificance—lessons of mortality, lessons of austerity, lessons of depletion."[34] The desert has wide, gaping jaws that can swallow like quicksand even the highest achievements of man and woman. One of Isaiah's powerful visions states:

Why, the nations are a drop from the bucket,
Like the balance's dust they're accounted. . . .
All nations are as naught before him,
He accounts them as empty and nothing. . . .
He's enthroned on the rim of the earth,
And its dwellers are like grasshoppers. . . .
He turns princes into nothing,
The rulers of the earth he makes naught. (Isa. 40:14–16–20)

In all of his pride and glory, says the prophet, man builds towers into the sky, ostentatious palaces, and nations with immortal pretense and forgets his Maker. In targeting the overweening pride of man, the prophet spits lyrics like roaring thunderstorms, battering and annulling all delusions of grandeur, reminding the rulers of the earth that no one can run a hustle on mortality.

Implicit in these texts is an understanding of a soul—a pilgrim soul—that is on a long journey, a soul with a past, present, and future. The human person is always in process, impermanent and changing, a river Jordan that is murky and muddy, raging in parts and trickling in others, venturing into the wilderness, and not always sure where it's headed. Human identity is defined as much by its rambling as by its stability or constancy, drifting through the ancient Near East the way blues artists would much later drift through the South.[35] If one can speak of the architecture of the soul in Israel, it resembles the mobile shelter of a *sukkah*, or the ark of the covenant, or the *merkavah* of Ezekiel's vision. The soul, too, partakes of the exile of Israel; it, too, is displaced and estranged, expelled from its previous glory in the garden of Eden and cast into the maelstrom of desert life; it, too, wanders and advances, develops and regresses like Abraham, Isaac, and Jacob; it, too, experiences the disorientation and panic of Hagar in the desert, terrified of watching her child die; and it, too, knows the tears of Mother Rachel, weeping for her lost children. And yet like the Holy of Holies, the soul carries within it a sacred presence or transcendence that buoys it and prevents it from being buried by the desert sandstorms. The soul also knows vast plains of hope and that new things are coming; it knows that old men, once broken and beaten, will dream new dreams, and that the sons and daughters of Jerusalem will once again prophesy (Isa. 41:18, 52:11–12; Joel 2:28).

Lessons for the soul are thus evident in much of the bittersweet beauty of the Bible. The Bible, differing so much from Plato or Aristotle, turns the themes of exodus and migration, slavery, and famine into parables of the human condition and thus depicts the whole scope of human affairs from the perspective of a conquered and hungry people, desperate and fragile in their fleshly constitutions but still indomitable and spirited in their purpose. Because so much of this story is shrouded in darkness and expressed in simple, self-effacing language, however, the characters are always prone to misunderstandings and failures. Few of them see far enough ahead to be able to avoid traps and deceptions. They are always unfinished products, slipping and falling while doing their best to press on to the end, where God beckons. The characters of these stories enter their pages like actors who have not been told the ending to the story—they know about the director's vision and goodness, but they must use their own talents and creativity, must improvise and invent, must know when to add their own verses to the play.

Soul under Duress: The Groans and Protests of Nephesh

Yet before reaching the denouement of the drama, the soul of man in the Bible is caught in the middle. If we follow the sweep of the biblical story carefully, the promises made to the patriarchs are endlessly deferred; the reality of exile postpones settlement in the promised land and continues to be the main theme running throughout the body of the text.[36] In fact, the narrative from the ancestral history in the Pentateuch (ending with the death of Moses in exile) up through the Deuteronomic history (Joshua, Judges, 1 and 2 Samuel, 1 and 2 Kings) follows a trajectory that is a constant peregrination among residence in Israel, exile, and return.[37] In the course of Deuteronomic history, there is a steady march toward the terrible destruction of the Northern kingdom (722 B.C.E.) and ultimately the fall of Jerusalem in 2 Kings 25 (587 B.C.E.). From the expulsion of Adam and Eve in the Pentateuch through further expulsions and catastrophes in the Deuteronomic history, the theme of exile is a constant presence, the string that connects the various episodes and shards of the Tanakh.

If we consider the suggestions of historical critics that much of this material was edited or written just before, during, and just after the Babylonian exile, we might begin to appreciate the scope of this theme and the importance of the tragedies of the sixth century. Richard Elliott Friedman tries to capture these terrible circumstances: "Religious leaders of our community are executed. The national leader's children are butchered in front of him, then his eyes are put out, and then he is led away in manacles. We are carried away in a group of thousands, probably never to see our country again. And then we live as outsiders in our conquerors' county. It is a horror."[38] Needless to say, these events proved decisive for Hebrew existence: Nebuchadnezzar had created a wasteland west of the Jordan River, and the land of Judah was in ruins.[39] Annual days of fasting were instituted to commemorate the misfortune, and the literature of the period increasingly reads like a dirge, full of lament and mourning, smarting with the wounds of war.

The books of Jeremiah, Second Isaiah, Lamentations, and parts of the Deuteronomic history all bear the scars of the period of exile like an iron yoke. The book of Deuteronomy includes numerous references to these tribulations (implied here as a prophesy): "You will perish quickly from the land" (Deut. 4:26); "Yahweh will scatter you among the nations" (Deut. 4:27); "Yahweh will drive you and your king . . . to a nation that you have not known" (Deut. 28:36); "You will be lifted off the land" (Deut 28:63); "Yahweh will scatter you among all the peoples from one end of the earth to the other" (Deut. 28:64); "You will not lengthen days on the land" (Deut. 30:18); "I shall cut off Israel from the face of the land that I gave them" (1 Kings 9:7).

It is important to recognize that many books of the Bible were written with these existential millstones around the neck of Israel.[40] If nothing else, these contextual details have a way of adding flesh (lacerated flesh, let's say) to the skeleton that I am trying to sketch. If these books were edited and written with the wolves of exile howling at the gates of Jerusalem, then we need to read them with the sound of alarm and distress ringing in our ears. We need to consider them with the appropriate sensitivity for the momentous tragedies of the era. As barometers of the intense pressures of oppression and violence faced by Israel, many of these books—the Deuteronomic history, Jeremiah, Second Isaiah, Ezekiel, Habbakuk, Lamentations, and the rest—give "the very age and body of the time its form and pressure" (*Hamlet* 3.2.23–24).

The book of Jeremiah is an example of what happens to the soul of man living in tortured times. In the book bearing his name, Jeremiah enters the long line of Hebrew prophets as one of the last of his kind, a man belonging to a virtually extinct office (Jer. 7:25, 44:4–5). Jeremiah is cast in the same mold as Moses, but with enough idiosyncrasies to break the mold and make him an "inscrutable oddity," to quote Walter Breuggemann.[41] This man is a speaker of parables and is himself the strangest of parables.[42] Everyone within earshot of his message seems baffled by this riddle in human clothing. He is misunderstood, distrusted, mocked, persecuted, and altogether despised. He lives as a fugitive, endures imprisonment, and suffers the dreadful consequences of the prophetic calling.

Jeremiah's soul is in effect a cauldron of distraught emotions, blackened by the conflagrations of the day. With the "sword at our very souls/ throats," Jeremiah speaks on behalf of a nation that is threatened by annihilation (Jer. 4:10). With this image of a sharp sword up against the *nephesh* of Israel (here associated with the throat), Jeremiah makes us feel the blade cutting and tearing at Israel's soul, ready to steal the lifeblood of his people. Stunned and terrified by these ordeals, he has a hard time containing himself, carried away as he is by passions that well up in him and threaten the retaining walls of his heart. Consider the bitter poetry of these lines:

My anguish, my anguish! I writhe in pain!
Oh the walls of my heart!
My heart is beating wildly;
I cannot keep silent,
For my *nephesh* hears the sound of the trumpet and the alarm of war.
  (Jer. 4:19)

The insistence here of the repeated words—"anguish," "anguish," "heart," "heart"—escalates the intensity of emotions in the poetry, as if his sorrow is picking up weight and force like an avalanche, causing a breach in his innermost being that makes his heart tremble and quake. Facing the impending destruction of his homeland, Jeremiah speaks with the visceral, gut-deep passion of a poet and prophet as he lets loose what the Sioux have called the "tremolo," a high-pitched, ululating cry of grief and dismay. There is no repose here.

One can discern all these troubles even on the surface of Jeremiah's text, in the style itself. Compared to other prophetic books, Jeremiah's text is made up of discontinuous speech patterns; they break up and dissolve into less structured discourses.[43] In classic prophetic books there is often a progression of poetic oracles: first prophecies of doom for Israel, then prophecies of doom for other nations, followed by prophecies of restoration. In Jeremiah, instead of steady and systematic development, we find "continual reversals, deadlocks, setbacks, and resurgences. The restlessness and apparent aimlessness of the prophet's career is thus captured in a unique and profound way."[44] Jeremiah's book is organized in the currents of a Heraclitean swirl of change, as if he is prophesying on a boat battered by tsunami-like waves or prophesying on the run or in exile (as, of course, he was). The book incarnates the disjunctive and erratic mobility of the prophet's life, as Joel Rosenberg puts it: "The relativity of the historical hour, the alteration of preaching to context and circumstance, are stressed as the prophet is shown churning about in relentless movement—adapting, clashing, revising, retrenching, threatening, pleading, promising."[45] So the prophet must always adapt, revise, and plead because the hours and days of his life have been so wildly unpredictable and bewildering. History is more like a labyrinthine trail of tears to Jeremiah than an evolving continuity, and he scripts his book accordingly, with the appropriate degree of disarray to match an age that seems so out of joint, so "illmatic," as Nas might put it.

Suffering the unrest of his age, Jeremiah tosses and turns to make sense of it all. He directs wild cries of grief at God, or is it at an inscrutable fate? Either way, the man is in crisis. The most famous cry is in Jeremiah 20:14–17:

> Cursed be the day on which I was born!
> The day when my mother bore me, let it not be blessed!
> Cursed be the man who brought the news to my father, saying,
> "A child is born to you, a son," making him very glad.
> Let that man be like the cities that the Lord overthrew without pity;
> Let him hear a cry in the morning and an alarm at noon,
> Because he did not kill me in the womb;
> So my mother would have been my grave, and her womb forever great.

On the brink of despair, Jeremiah allows his most bleak and forlorn thoughts to stream into an ocean of protest. Though the preceding passage concentrates on his own personal plight, his prophecies chronicle the grim fate of Israel as a whole, decimated without pity. Reminiscent of Job, Jeremiah's personal experiences of unmerited suffering seem to have opened his eyes to the misfortune of his age at large, an age fattened on war and human flesh. As a result, the Deuteronomic explanation for the problem of evil—that suffering is a result of human sin and idolatry—undergoes a shock and disruption that leaves it and any dogmatic explanation for the problem of evil less certain, more equivocal. Indeterminacy is introduced on this matter when Jeremiah, this sensitive diagnostician of the ills of his world, seriously begins to brood about the grand scale of human suffering. Suddenly cracks and holes begin to show in theodicy's great edifice, and this has a way of making Jeremiah seem more confused and unhinged, like a mother who has buried her only child. Now he will suggest images that reveal his sympathy with the afflicted—lambs led to slaughter—and even bring charges against God (Jer. 11:19, 12:1). He adapts and revises his theory on the problem of suffering to better mirror his heartrending personal experiences.

Instead of exonerating God with sentimental and pious platitudes (the "windy words" of Job's friends), Jeremiah uses his tongue to lash out at God in the style of Job (Job 16:3–16). The book of Lamentations—traditionally attributed to Jeremiah—hits the same note:

> Cry out to the Lord from the heart, wall of Daughter Zion.
> Shed tears like a torrent, day and night!
> Give yourself no rest, and do not let your eyes be still.
> Arise! Wail in the night, at the beginning of every watch.
> Pour out your heart like water in front of the Lord.
> Lift your hands to him for the lives of your children,
> Who collapse from hunger in the middle of the street. (Lam. 2:18–20)

This choice to dwell on the fate of children, in their innocence and blamelessness, makes the poet's charges against God more stinging and convincing. Throughout Lamentations the author thrashes about with God, turning to and against YHWH, accusing, pleading, beseeching, wailing, and loving. At times Lamentations singles out God for violence, even malevolence, against God's daughter Zion; then, when the hour is the darkest and despair the fiercest, the poet returns to God in an effort to shore up the fragments of his life against total ruin (Lam. 1:13, 2:21, 3:32). It seems abundantly clear that the author has relinquished any attempt at logical consistency. With Zion left alone in a city once full of people, with princes impaled and bound by their hands, with virgin daughters raped and enslaved, and with famine claiming so many innocent lives, there can be no theological systems, no theories of distributive justice (4:10–12). Even music is in exile, gone from the forsaken city (4:14). Lamentations ends with the agonizing question that haunts much of the Hebrew Bible: "Why have you forgotten us completely? Why have you forsaken us these many days?" (4:20).[46]

Blood-curdling cries of this sort are startling and daring, but it seems to me that they belong to a long biblical tradition on the question of theodicy that prefers the existential struggle with God—in shrilling notes of protest and supplication—to philosophy's business of detached, logical argument. It is in these dirge-like voices, wailing and wrestling with God, that we catch the sounds of Jewish soul.

Thus, instead of a rational doctrine of evil, the book of Jeremiah—like Lamentations, Job, Second Isaiah, the Psalms, and others—grapples with suffering in a way that abjures facile explanations and consolations; it might best be compared to the way that music handles human suffering. Instead of moralistic and didactic rationalizations of suffering, the poetry of the Bible gets at the question of human suffering without explaining or solving it; the response to theodicy is more rhapsodic than discursive, more lyrical than logical, more oracular than speculative, more pragmatic than theoretical. As Ralph Ellison would later say about the blues, the jagged grain of pain is kept alive in Jeremiah's oracles, gripped and caressed until the pain is transcended, not by the consolations of philosophy but by a tragic and comic lyricism.[47] In this ballad-like approach to suffering, I see Jeremiah battling the problem of evil as a blues artist or rapper would: signifying, protesting, moaning, slurring, and even dogging his opponents. In his unique staccato style, disjointed and fragmented, Jeremiah's speech cries out and barks the way Charlie Patton would later bark, growl, and attack the strings of the guitar until it begged for respite, "shouting out his blind defiance at the unyielding elements."[48] Like so much of biblical poetry—intended for oral recitation—Jeremiah's words have a sonorous, musical quality to them, and they pluck at the heart's strings, tear at a person's guts, and cauterize the wounds of the spirit to prevent a widespread lesion. The only thing missing for Jeremiah to be a bluesman or rapper is the guitar or some fat, funky bass.

I mean this quite literally: in the book of Jeremiah, the prophetic oracles maintain a flow and cadence, and this fact suggests to the careful reader that God's revelation comes to Jeremiah in a craggy blues voice, rich in "worried notes" and trance-like rhythms, with a certain musical groove sounding in his ears, flooding and shaking his soul. In his exchange with God, a call-and-response pattern, Jeremiah riffs on God's melodic revelation and adds his own voice to the session. The result is an artful combination of chants, shouts, prayers, poems, and dreams, all vented in notes that are at times plaintive and mournful, then suddenly merry and hopeful, such as when he revels in the thought of the young and the old, the blind and the lame, picking up the tambourine and dancing to the beat of gladness. His words betray ebullience at such moments and are the more remarkable for being uttered in times of distress. His prophecies thus stretch themselves in several directions, from the "the whole valley of the dead bodies and ashes" to the rising of the sun in the east, where the sun shall come crashing through the darkness (Jer. 31:40).

Tragic-Comic Soul in the Prophets

By capturing the highs and lows of his experience, Jeremiah gives us bits and pieces from both tragedy and comedy. Ignoring rules of noncontradiction, he offends expectations that would separate the thorny problem of suffering from belief in God's goodness and justice. As dark and distressing as Jeremiah's oracles are, they convey an overwhelming conviction that God will gather Israel from the ends of the earth—the blind and the lame, the pregnant and the laboring, the immense throng—and lead them to refreshing streams of water (Jer. 31:8). Now everyone, from the least to the greatest, shall know God, and the covenant will be inscribed not on tablets of stone, but on the hearts of man and woman (Jer. 31:34).

As proponents of these dreams, the prophets frequently made themselves enemies of the status quo. Since the Jewish prophet frequently courted the support of the people—not primarily of the king and the aristocracy—it is not surprising that the prophet played the role of detractor, sometimes even jester, in Israel. After all, he spoke on behalf of a God whom Israel had represented as a defender of the poor and needy, and this frequently led the prophet into confrontation and conflict with the ruling classes. In summoning the prophet out of an unpredictable variety of backgrounds—sometimes coarse and lowly, sometimes refined and lofty—the call often sabotaged class distinctions, showing little respect for official pedigrees. Unlike kings and priests, usually members of the ruling class, the prophet was drawn from every social stratum; his was a calling, not an office.

Needless to say, callings of this sort can be subversive and unruly, unpredictable gusts of magnetism suddenly turned tornado, as when God's spirit was poured out on the rowdy and rude variety of people at the camp in the wilderness. The reaction of the establishment was reminiscent of what Joshua, son of Nun, said to Moses, "'My lord, Moses, stop them.' But Moses said to him, 'Are you jealous for my sake? Would that all the Lord's people were prophets and that the Lord would put his spirit on them'" (Num. 11:28–29). In Moses's defense of unauthorized prophecy, we are given the paradigmatic vision of prophecy in Israel in all of its explosive and democratic potential (see also Ezek. 39:29 and Joel 2:28).

The crux of the matter is that classic prophecy in Israel hearkens back to the charismatic style of leadership in Israelite history, especially during the time of Moses. Though the classic prophets emerged alongside the monarchy, long after the age of Moses, these new generations of prophets refused to become part of the royal court and thus kept themselves beyond the reach of the king's coercion. (Apparently king Ahab, before the emergence of the classic prophet, had over four hundred professional prophets in his pocket; see 1 Kings 22:6.) If there is compulsion pressing on the prophets' hearts and souls, it is coming from God, not the king; they are the voice of the Other. Michael Walzer writes that by the time of the classic prophets, "the prophets left the royal court and moved into the public spaces of Israel's cities and towns." And on the significance of this new social location, he notes: "Shrine and city, the streets, the gates, even the temple courtyard: the importance of these new locations cannot be overemphasized. When the prophet spoke only to the king, he was working, presumably, on the assumption that the king's decision was the only one that mattered. . . . But when the prophet speaks in public, the working assumption shifts. Now it appears to matter that ordinary men and women think this way or that way, live or don't live in accordance with the law."[49] Once advisers to kings and principalities, the prophets now move their residences from the palace to the streets, which changes everything. "Run ye to and fro through the streets of Jerusalem," cries Jeremiah (5:1). In this new context on the street corners and margins of the city, the prophets cast their lot with ordinary folk, with the poor and vulnerable, the needy and abused. They are now beholden to a higher authority than the royal court or temple. And from this vantage point, with fresh and alert eyes, they see things that cry out for attention and remedy. They see the world with the unstudied virtuosity of a young rapper or street poet, someone who speaks of life in the hood from firsthand experience, without the affected condescension of an upper-class philanthropist or intellectual.

Without the authority of the monarchy, priesthood, or professional post, the prophet converts his displaced and exiled location into a mobile platform.[50] From his street pulpit he musters every scrap of eloquence he has to convince and exhort the people that he is speaking on their behalf and, of course, on behalf of God. When he succeeds in this task, he does it by giving his oracles an aesthetic value, making them stirring, articulate, and compelling to his supporters but vexing to his foes. He imbues his words with a pictographic quality and makes them radiate with energy and propulsive power as they leave his mouth, words suddenly flying off his tongue and detonating when they reach their target. Though the prophets' oracles give us the impression of having been rushed and extemporized, it is a mistake to overlook the craft involved, the way they adorned and garnished their words with rhetorical skill. For fear that their frenzied words would end up on rocky soil, to be trampled and forgotten, they would use poetic strategies to make their language plough deep into the hearts of their listeners.

But of course the prophets' rhetorical genius was also ethically motivated and clearly expounded on the duties of love, justice, and compassion, especially for the weakest and weariest. In speaking on behalf of the Other, the prophet would single out the rich and mighty for shirking their responsibilities to the poor. ("Shirking" is the exact word; in Arabic, *shirk* is idolatry, and for the prophets the seductions of greed, power, and violence were forms of idolatry.) Amos, for example, denounces the rich for innumerable sins, from an overindulgent lifestyle (he singles out their opulent houses, fine wines, and perfumes) to selling the poor into slavery (Amos 2–3). Isaiah says that his *nephesh* hates sacrifices; he desires, instead, acts of justice: rescuing the oppressed, defending the orphan, and pleading for the widow (Isa. 14–17). Jeremiah, too, burns with furor on the matter of justice; he seems to have been involved at one time in negotiating a release of slaves prior to the Babylonian invasion. When slave owners renege on their promises, Jeremiah takes the opportunity to blame their deeds for the captivity of Israel (not unlike the way Abraham Lincoln would later connect the American Civil War to the sins of the nation): "You have not obeyed me by granting a release to your neighbors and friends; I am going to grant a release to you, says the Lord—a release to the sword, to pestilence, and to famine" (Jer. 34:17).[51]

In these cases and others, the prophets give us the impression of largeness in the matter of soul; all other commitments and pieties are small by comparison, diversions from the love owed to God and neighbor. In the interests of the poor and vulnerable, the classic prophets indict the ruling classes for debauching the soul. In their hoarse, scathing voices, they warn their listeners and readers about counterfeit forms of holiness. With the eloquence of a street poet, a prophet "uses language in a way that engages the minds and touches the hearts of his listeners; he has to remind them of what they know, evoke their historical memories, play on the nerves of their commitment, their guilt, their hopes for the future."[52]

Based on the narrative framework of the entire Hebrew Bible, it is clear that the writers give voice to a counterintuitive and countercultural vision of the divine: God's power is manifested in powerlessness, sublimity in poverty, strength in humility, and splendor in weakness. If I insist on anything throughout this book, it is that this outlook touches on the soul of biblical narratives. It is nothing short of remarkable that the humble writers of this oppressed and deprived nation charted literary and religious territories never explored by others, including the Greeks. I have repeatedly referred to the blues in this chapter because something similar happened with that music and later with rap. Using the crudest musical tools available to them, a paltry assortment of harmonies, and a compositional structure based on repetition, these "musicians of a despised race and class," writes Ted Gioia, "offered their contemporaries a vivid world of new tone colors . . . like painters whose magical palettes conveyed hitherto unknown shades of the spectrum."[53] However crude and unrefined the Bible may appear to many critics, I contend that it also discovered unknown shades of the artistic and religious spectrum, shades that represented not only the authors' views of God, but also nuanced and enigmatic views of human identity. These narratives were also an achievement of soul.

If this is true for the soul of the narratives, it is also true for the *nephesh* of the individual Israelite: if it were to find its purpose, it had to be modulated and aligned with this vision, had to find its meaning through the love of God and the love of the poor and needy. When in harmony with this larger symphony of soul in the Bible, the *nephesh* would fully realize its potential as a creature made in the image and likeness of God. This was a lesson that another Jewish figure, a lowly Nazarene woodworker, enjoined on his followers. In the Christian vision the figure of Jesus came to represent all of God's resplendent power in a whisper-like form, empty of stateliness and pomp, a man who did not grasp at Godly power but instead emptied himself and took the form of a servant (Phil. 2:6–7). Like the Hebrew prophets, this man, too, had mad soul.

3

Christian Soul and the Revolt of the Slave

It is in flesh, with flesh, and by flesh that the soul contemplates all that the heart contemplates.

—Tertullian

But love has pitched his mansion in the place of excrement; for nothing can be sole or whole that has not been rent.

—W. B. Yeats[1]

Unless we become as rogues, we cannot enter the kingdom of heaven.

—Emily Dickinson

Perhaps better than anyone else, one of the loudest critics of Christianity, Friedrich Nietzsche, seized on a fundamental fact about this Jewish movement: that it bears the ignoble mark of a slave. In Nietzsche's view, Christianity represents a slave revolt against all the noble principles of antiquity and the introduction of base and grotesque values into Western civilization. "Modern men, obtuse to all Christian nomenclature," he writes, "no longer feel the gruesome superlative that struck a classic taste in the paradoxical formula 'god on the cross.' Never yet and nowhere has there been an equal boldness in inversion, anything as horrible, questioning and questionable as this formula: it promised a revaluation of all the values of antiquity. It is the oriental slave who in this fashion took vengeance on Rome and its noble and playful tolerance."[2] As an affront to classic aristocratic taste, Christianity took vengeance on Rome by adopting the ghetto tongue and style of its Jewish brothers and sisters and used it to curse and subvert the patrician values of Greco-Roman culture. Aided and abetted by the vulgar and rude narratives of the Bible, blueprints for this revolution, this ragtag army of Christians besieged Rome with a countercultural ethos and struck a blow at the Roman Empire's values of slavery, patriarchy, hierarchy, and military dominance.[3] For Nietzsche, these "oriental slaves" upended the cherished achievements of Greco-Roman culture and instigated a carnival-like subversion of Roman hierarchies, a world turned upside down. The chickens had come home to roost.

And Nietzsche doesn't pull any punches when he claims, correctly, that Christianity inherited this slave's morality from the Jews: "It was the Jews," he writes in *On the Genealogy of Morals,* "who in opposition to the aristocratic equation (good=aristocratic=beautiful=happy =loved by the gods), ventured with an awesome consistency, to suggest the contrary equation, namely, the wretched are alone the good; the poor, the weak, the lowly are alone the good; the suffering, the needy, the sick, the loathsome are the only ones who are pious. . . . It is with the Jews that the slaves' revolt in morality begins."[4] Though there is plenty of Nietzsche's customary hyperbole in these lines, it is also an argument that he makes consistently. It was in fact gospel for Nietzsche, the gospel of Dionysus or Zarathustra against the gospel of Christ. In this chapter on the Christian "soul," I begin with Nietzsche because he had a rare gift for getting at the heart of things, for exposing the naked truth of his subject like a great sculptor with a block of stone, chiseling, hammering, and blasting away until the core is laid bare.

Although I find myself greatly at odds with his judgments, Nietzsche captured well the volcanic impact of Christianity in history (a volcano of mud, he called it).[5] Others certainly noticed the disturbances in the terra firma of the pagan world and may have called attention to their implications, but for Nietzsche the introduction of Christianity was epoch-making, a tectonic shift that dislodged everything he admired about the Greeks and Romans and corroded their dignified souls with volcanic ash. Nietzsche's perspective has great value for analyzing the changes and upheavals in Western conceptions of soul. We would do well to listen to his judgments, if only to better understand the "soul revolution" that began with the introduction of Judaism and Christianity into the world.

GENERAL REMARKS

The Christian Revolution of Soul

As original as he was, Nietzsche's scathing voice brings to mind early pagan critics of Christianity, those who saw Christianity as an uncouth superstition carted into Greco-Roman civilization by wild and marauding hordes. In fear and trepidation, these critics heard the rowdy, barbaric yawps of Christian tribes escalating in tone and tenor, and this roused their disdain, like a conservative American of the twentieth century at the first sounds of the blues or rock 'n' roll. Celsus, for instance, spewed venom at the Christian message for appealing to slaves and pickpockets, thugs and prostitutes, and gullible women and children. He expected Christians to march to the same drummer as every other Roman religion, and when they stepped out of line and introduced cacophonous and riotous beats into the stately symphony of the empire's values, he charged them with crudity. Who other than these reprobates, he sarcastically asked, would believe their vulgar story about a crucified Jew whom they adore as god?[6] Celsus mocked Christian views of grace and agapic love in ways that anticipated Nietzsche: "But let us hear what folk these Christians summon. Whoever is a sinner, they say, whoever is unwise, whoever is a child, and, in a word, whoever is a wretch, the kingdom of God will receive him."[7] Apuleius, too, author of *Metamorphoses,* despised Christians for welcoming the dregs of the empire, the illiterate and poor, the beggars and slaves. Although Apuleius was famously tolerant of a variety of religious devotions, his liberalism had clear limits when Christianity was involved. He had nothing but contempt for cults that rejected Roman culture and specifically for the rabble who "worship Jesus as a god."[8]

Before challenging these appraisals, I want to acknowledge the valuable insight that they unexpectedly provide. As outsiders to the tribe of Christians, these critics had a way of identifying the distinctive nature of the Christian message better than many apologists and thereby got to the carotid artery of its soul quickly and thoroughly.[9] While some apologists would try to convince the empire that Christianity was neither dangerous nor sinister, pagan critics in the mold of Celsus and Apuleius read the books and creeds of Christianity as though they concealed a gunpowder plot hidden beneath their parchments and practices, ready to raze pagan civilization. For a figure like Tertullian, these critics hit the target with their analysis, and instead of denying and dodging their conclusions, he embraced them—without, naturally, endorsing their overall verdict. If it was barbarism that they imputed to the Christian hordes, Tertullian did not spurn the accusation. "Deliberately outraging the sensibilities of his literate audience," Elaine Pagels writes, "he addressed his own subversive messages directly—even preferentially—to the 'rabble.'"[10] Tertullian's *De Testimonio Animae* is a case in point, in which the question of soul, he insists, is best considered not in a symposium of educated elites, but in the company of the "simple, rude, uncultured, uneducated," with those who inhabit the fringes of the empire, the souls who "belong entirely to the road, to the street, to the workshop."[11] In this deliberate reversal of the world's proclivities, Tertullian offended the Greco-Roman status quo and developed something like a theology of the streets, one that shifted allegiance from the emperor and his gods to disaffected and ordinary people, a preferential option for the rabble, so to speak. As happened with the classic prophets of Israel, discussed in chapter 2, there was a sudden paradigm shift from owing loyalty to the king and his royal court to owing loyalty to God and his court of paupers and plebeians.

In this transfer of allegiances from the kingdom of Rome to the kingdom of God, Tertullian's understanding of soul is governed by the assumption that every Christian, made in the image of God, is capable of understanding the most sublime truths. In one instance, speaking to his uneducated audience, he encourages them to trust their intuitions: "Have faith in your soul; thus you will believe in yourself. . . . Every Christian workingman finds God and manifests God."[12] By appealing to the gut-level intuition of workers and slaves, Tertullian insisted that Christian truth was readily available to everyone, irrespective of level of education or place in the social hierarchy. As I dig into the narratives of the New Testament in this chapter, especially the Gospel of Mark, keep in mind this wild acrobatics of the Christian creed, in which everything is overturned. Only those who saw it for the dizzying revolution that it was—again, we need to give Nietzsche credit here—seemed to penetrate into its deepest core.

But I want to circle back to examine some of stories in the New Testament related to the idea of the soul, with a special concentration, as seen in chapter 2, on the literary contours of these texts. As I have asserted, the concept of soul in Judaism and Christianity was shaped and produced by stories; it was bred, fed, and fattened by stories from the Bible, with seasonings from the Greeks and numerous others. By concentrating on the literary and theological guises of the soul in the Bible, we might better appreciate one major branch of its "Jew-Greek" family tree and be able to judge the merit of Nietzsche's accusation: "That one [Christ] taught men to despise the very first instincts of life; that one mendaciously invented a 'soul,' a 'spirit' to ruin the body."[13] I take a very different route than Nietzsche when venturing through the chambers of the soul. I do, however, concede this one fundamental fact: that the Christian vision of life, of soul, and of everything else is largely shaped by a slave's values. In this sense, at least, Christianity represents the revolt of the mob against its masters.

Psukhe

The Greek version of the Hebrew bible, *The Septuagint,* translated *nephesh* as *psukhe,* and the New Testament followed suit. *Psukhe* inherited the principles and conceptions of Hebrew soul examined in the previous chapter; it connotes respiration, life force, vital spirit, or essential self, the whole human person in his or her unity, both animal and spiritual qualities.[14] *Psukhe* is the "form of the body," says Aquinas; or the "boundary" between material and spiritual reality, says Maximus the Confessor; or the vital power and immensity that "animates and exercises all the organs," says Emerson. "It is not the intellect or will," Emerson continues, "but the master of the intellect and will, an immensity not possessed and that cannot be possessed."[15] By unifying the diverse influences and experiences of a person's life, the Jewish and Christian version of soul is a swollen river of many histories and voices, converging in the human person to demarcate and define a person's identity.

By encompassing the stories, myths, prophecies, wisdom traditions, and laws of Israel, the Christian idea of soul remains yoked to the Jewish tradition. Evidence of this is everywhere, but it is particularly clear when one considers the fleshly constitution of the soul. William Faulkner had this dimension in mind when he considered the power of human touch to cut into the soul: "There is something in the touch of flesh with flesh that abrogates, cuts sharp and straight across the devious intricate channels of decorous ordering . . . touch and touch of that which is the citadel of the central I-Am's private own: not spirit, soul."[16] Not spirit, but soul; for Faulkner, the soul is distinct from the spirit because of the former's bond with the "earthly tenement" of the flesh, a tenement of brittle bones and tired flesh. The soul is a "private citadel" of God's presence and a vessel of transcendence, but it is also a creature of time and consequently is vulnerable to decay, death, and the assaults of evil, as well as prone to mishaps and misapprehensions. In the course of the sacred drama in biblical texts, the human soul is stretching and groaning to realize its highest possibilities, but it must do so while wracked by sin, suffering, and agony. Even the soul of Jesus, free of sin, will know agony, know the terror of death. In the garden of Gethsemane Jesus responds with fear and trembling as he faces the prospect of crucifixion: "My *psukhe* is in agony unto death" (Mark 14:34). And later, just before Jesus takes his last breath and darkness covers the whole land, he quotes Psalm 22: "My God, my God, why have you forsaken me?" (Mark 15:34).

When considering these tormented, unadorned lines, we know right away that we are in a world far removed from impassible souls, from a conception of human life that is cold on the matter of emotions and distant from the sensual passions of human nature. Mark's characters are not spectral or wraith-like: they are fragile, wounded, and desiring souls, and they use their emotions with vitality. In the age of Jesus, the idiom of emotion is the lingua franca of all Israelites and the means of understanding the distinctive patterns and impulses of soul. The systoles and diastoles of the soul are always related to the burning desires of the heart, the needs of the human body, the cries and outrages of the spirit. As concentrated allegories of these human emotions, and distillations of intense sorrow, the laments placed in the mouth of Jesus illuminate the Israelite conception of soul in all of its passionate, convulsive vigor. Intense and gnomic, Jesus's outcries are summations of the aches and wails of many centuries and many marred lives. We can say that there is something like an "identity of passions"—in Ralph Ellison's sense of a common struggle—that joins the death of Jesus with the history of Israel, in this regard.[17] Judaism and Christianity are made up of similar exclamations, exhortations, and dogged decrees, such as when Luke speaks of the achievement of soul through one's capacity to endure hostility and persecution: "By your endurance you will gain your *psukhe*" (Luke 21:19).

The soul of the Gospels is built of such appeals and injunctions, of gaining one's soul through fortitude and suffering. The Gospels' refusal to wax philosophic means that nothing in the abstract, no theory or generality, is advocated if it does not entail the daily bread of human experience and human struggle. Even biblical laws will be judged wanting unless they enflame the passions, embolden the spirit, and concentrate one's attention on what averts or repulses the gaze of others: disfigured bodies, famished flesh, and broken spirits. The care of the body (not its ruin, pace Nietzsche) is thus synonymous with care of the soul in the Christian vision; anything else amounts to a disincarnate spirituality, a heretical form of Christian thought.

Any conversation about the nature of the soul must follow the central doctrine of incarnation. Followers of Christ are summoned by the example of the Word who pitched his tent in the excrement of the world, emptying himself of majesty and taking the form of a slave (as Yeats said; Phil. 2:7). Disciples of this humble and humiliated Messiah must be willing to follow suit and respond to Jesus's relentless pleas to care for the hungry and thirsty, the naked and sick, the imprisoned and mad, and the blind and deaf. In making sensual contact with human flesh in this way, the Christian version of soul is constituted of a thousand sordid images, to borrow T. S. Eliot's words.[18] Instead of confining our conversation on soul to general theological assumptions, however, I suggest that we place the concept of soul in the narrative context of the Gospels; in Mark, for instance, the constitution of the soul—its sordidness and sublimity—jumps off the pages and comes alive. I begin with Mark and then wander across the borders of various Gospels as this chapter unfolds.

LITERARY SKETCHES

Setting and Style: The Case of Mark

The story of Mark is set during the time of Roman rule and occupation of Israel. In an ironic twist to the tragic circumstances that resulted in the destruction of the temple and city, the author came to consider this story "good news," the *euaggelion*. Numerous scholars have alerted us to the fact that similar language was used to describe the birth of Caesar Augustus: "he who put an end to war and will order peace, Caesar, who by his epiphany exceeded the hopes of those who prophesied good news *(euaggelia)*."[19] By raiding the language of the empire and using it to describe a radically different sort of *euaggelia*, and a radically different sort of savior, the early Christians revolutionized the idiom and ideology of empire. If the "epiphany" of Caesar Augustus signaled a new era of the Pax Romana—a peace by conquest and domination—the Christian savior signaled a new era governed by mercy and compassion for the wretched of the earth. In the New Testament's transliteration of the empire's "good news," the word acquired an entirely different meaning, one that contradicted the gospel according to Caesar Augustus. The differences in the philosophies of governance are dramatic: God's reign begins from the margins and dregs of the empire, while Rome rules from the center; God's reign privileges the poor and vulnerable, while Rome privileges the strong; and God's reign advocates renunciation and dispossession, while Rome rules by force and violence.

Evidence of Mark's sympathy for the former values is clear if the reader notices how frequently Jesus and his followers are compelled to work on the edges of Israel, as if there is a centrifugal force at work in the gospel. Consider, then, that Jesus begins his ministry in the wilderness at the Jordan River, not in Jerusalem, and continues to work in the peripheries and shadows throughout his life. "From the point of view of the Judean authorities in Mark's story," one scholar writes, "God works from the established center in Jerusalem. By contrast, for Mark, God's rule begins from the periphery, from the edges. The pardon of sins that took place in the temple now appears in Galilee. The interpretation of the law that emanated from Jerusalem now occurs in the village of Capernaum. The authority of the high priest and the Sanhedrin council is now assumed by a woodworker from Nazareth."[20] Mark's Jesus drifts through the text on the fringes of the civilized world, and he engenders hostility for threatening and essentially decentering the centers of authority in Jerusalem and Rome. Mark's Jesus is a stray itinerant, leaving his traces in the rural villages of Galilee (Mark 6:6), in deserted places (Mark 6:33–34), by the sea, or in Gentile territory like Tyre and Sidon (Mark 3:7–12). By seeing the world through the eyes of this unassuming and peripheral prophet and situating him in the context of the written and oral traditions of Israel, Mark created an unprecedented style, part biography, part history, part apocalypse, part tragedy and comedy. He assimilated a variety of genres and made something that did not fit any of the known registers of ancient literature: "It is too serious for comedy," writes Erich Auerbach, "too contemporary and common for tragedy, politically too insignificant for history."[21] By dramatizing God's epiphany as a human being of the humblest social station, without political majesty or highborn distinction, Mark trespassed across many literary and class borders.[22]

Other factors distinguish Mark's gospel from classical literature: notably, the way it swaddles its wisdom in common and rough, yet dignified and grave, forms of speech, thus making for a "barbaric grandeur" (to use Richard Wright's description of the slave spirituals).[23] As I suggested in chapter 2, this simple, dry bones style is somehow fitting of the geography of the biblical world. The story survives, even thrives, on the simple alms of bread and water, like a desert ascetic. In stripping down language to its barest forms, where nouns are often unchaperoned and lacking in unnecessary adjectives, Mark captures not only the sparseness and severity of desert life, but also the depth of human suffering. If it's true, as Virginia Woolf put it, that "there is a stage of suffering where any expression save the barest is intolerable," then Mark's literary barrenness, close as it is to silence, is somehow the best form of thought for handling crisis and affliction.[24] Since Mark has a laconic style (consistent with parts of the Torah, as we've seen), the episodes are usually more suggestive than descriptive: he renounces elaborate explanations; he speaks and then withdraws, like a good servant. Mark's gospel often leaves things unstated and implied, in the shadows, because the world, and certainly God, is awe-inspiring and unknowable. More like a summons and invitation than a disengaged dogma or theoretical proposition, then, the narrative requires contemplation and devotion to apprehend what cannot be said in plain terms. And so the reader, if faithful to this awareness, will participate in the drama, take a place in the action as if we, too, are characters in the story.

Something of this challenge is dramatized in almost every riddle/parable told by Jesus, if only the reader can unlock its closely guarded secrets. Depending on who hears them, riddles may reveal or obscure. In Mark, Jesus uses riddles as a way of eluding and mystifying authority figures, but they also mystify his inner circle.[25] While there is no doubt that Mark's Jesus wants to scatter his teachings to the winds and have them take root among every follower, like the seeds of his parable, the disciples consistently misread and distort the message of this peculiar prophet. In this ironic Gospel, it turns out that the outsiders and outcasts of Israel are frequently the most successful in deciphering the riddles. They succeed where the insiders fail, which indicates to the reader that the keys to the kingdom, and the wisdom of this story, cannot be contained or controlled by any one group. Wisdom is now offered to an unrestricted parade of individuals: lepers and laborers, beggars and prostitutes, the righteous and sinful, people in all shapes and sizes, colors and textures, a patchwork variety.[26]

Major Characters in Mark

When considering the major characters in Mark, it is most striking how often Jesus's disciples fail to grasp his message. True, they leave their homes and rush off to follow Jesus as if he were the answer to the riddle of their lives, but they consistently overlook and trip over the fundamental message, a blindness that seems surprising for those so close to Jesus. Often tongue-twisted and confused, his disciples are all too human, drawn by the author with a black brush that veils their minds in darkness, weakens their capacity for courage, and makes their hearts susceptible to vanity and self-deceit. Jesus tries time and again to be a compass for their wayward souls, but the disciples seem hell-bent on going their own way. When Jesus is trying to school them in the lesson of the cross and the demands of self-denying service, the disciples argue over which one is the greatest (Mark 9:34); when Jesus feeds the crowd of four thousand, the disciples remain clueless about the messianic significance of this festive abundance (Mark 8:17–18); and when Jesus is transfigured and speaks to Moses and Elijah about the new Exodus (a liberation of those in bondage), Peter responds in ignorance and fear (Mark 9:6). Even when Peter seems to make sudden progress in correctly identifying Jesus's messianic nature, he is quickly rebuked for misunderstanding what this entails (Mark 8:33).

As the narrative reaches a crescendo in Jerusalem, the failures do not cease; if anything, they become more egregious. In the garden of Gethsemane, with Jesus's life hanging in the balance, his disciples succumb to a somnolence that is metaphorically important in Mark, suggesting something like moral lethargy, spiritual inertia, or plain ignorance (Mark 14:37–41). In fact, at this moment of truth, when Jesus is arrested and tried, all of his disciples forsake him and flee in fear (Mark 14:50–51). Mark ends with the female followers (the only ones who remained with Jesus when he was executed) fleeing the scene of the empty tomb "in trembling and astonishment, and saying nothing to anyone for they were afraid" (Mark 16:8). The disciples are shown to have dark spots in their vision, occlusions in their souls, and lacunae in their fortitude. They grope for the truths of the story, but their aims and observations frequently miss the target. The light of Jesus beckons them, like drifting boats, from the shore, but the fog makes it difficult to locate the exact harbor where they will anchor their souls. Mark's narrative is covered in such fog, a billowing, tantalizing obscurity.

In spite of all of these botched moments in the lives of the disciples, though, they remain remarkable creatures, if only for asking the right questions and for following the right teacher. These individuals rarely have the right answers, but they pick up their nets and leave their homes because they are compelled by the right questions, possessed by the search.[27] However much they misunderstand Jesus's instructions, they have intuitively sensed something divine in him, something that has angled their souls in the right direction. Even if it takes frequent attempts by Jesus to cure their blindness (like the blind man cured by Jesus after the second attempt), the secrets of the kingdom gradually unfold to them, truly a radiant truth (Mark 8:22–26). Like someone staring into an eclipse of the sun, eventually their eyes, after experiencing blindness, begin to see spots of light that look like shooting stars, streaking toward a miraculous horizon. As Rakim would say years later, as you stare into the darkness "soon you suddenly see a star / you better follow."[28] The disciples glimpse enough of the star of Bethlehem to follow in his footsteps, and they hear and comprehend just enough to keep them longing and pining for the whole truth of this parable in the flesh. The manifestations of truth in the figure of Jesus drive the disciples forward in amazement and awe, hoping and believing that the scales will gradually fall from their eyes. None of this would have been possible without their initial willingness to embark on this extraordinary journey, to break with their immediate surroundings and go forth into unknown lands like their father, Abraham.

Minor Characters

Something similar could be said about the minor characters in Mark and the other Gospels: they are possessed by the search and bewitched by this mysterious prophet. In fact, in contrast to the disciples, the minor characters are far more perceptive; it is the poor and blind, the unclean and foreign, women, and widows who exemplify the values of the Gospel more than the inner circle of Mark's disciples. Like Hester Prynne, the outcast and sinner in Hawthorne's *The Scarlet Letter,* these figures have "moral X-ray vision": they possess a clairvoyant ability to spot sin among the pious and powerful and are the quickest to recognize the Messiah in the humble woodworker. They possess a sightless form of seeing, a blindness that is true vision. As outsiders to the powers of the world, their minds are not darkened by the lures of mammon or the narcissism of entitlement. As the Spanish word for outsider connotes—loner, renegade, or iconoclast—the plight of an outsider, however unenviable, can engender iconoclastic inventiveness and refreshing insight. The minor characters that people Mark's gospel, not to mention the figure of Jesus himself, are renegades of this kind.[29]

It's fair to say that these lowly characters have the most insight in the story because their needs are so dire and grave. Trapped by diseased conditions, conniving authorities, and evil powers, they grasp Jesus's significance with their whole being: aching flesh, tormented souls, and intuitive minds. While others see Jesus in a restricted way (as a miracle worker, political leader, or blasphemer), these individuals recognize the persecuted Jesus as a brother in their own affliction. In Mark, many of these characters are women: the persistent and humbly faithful Syro-Phoenician woman; the desperately faithful woman with the unstoppable flow of blood; the selfless, poor widow; the anonymous woman who anoints Jesus for burial; and finally, the three women (Mary Magdalene, Mary the mother of James, and Salome) who have an important and ongoing role in the narrative, daringly accompanying Jesus to his death and then afterward returning to his burial site to anoint him. In some ways these characters are marginal to the story, but in other ways they are essential, and they are far more discerning and courageous than the male disciples.

Other minor characters with this penchant for discernment include Simon the leper, who receives Jesus in his house; Simon of Cyrene, who carries Jesus's cross as he is led to his death at Golgotha; Joseph of Arimathea, who wraps and prepares Jesus's body for burial; Bartimaeus, a blind beggar (Mark 10:47); Simon the leper (Mark 14:3–9); the mad and unclean Gerasene man (Mark 5:1–13); and the centurion, the only one in the Mark's gospel to confess Jesus's identity in such a direct manner, "Truly this man was God's Son" (Mark 15:39). Using their "third eye" more than any other faculty, these characters demonstrate a capacity for seeing beauty beneath suffering, glory beneath ignominy, and divine love in the guise of an outlaw and rogue. As representatives of all afflicted souls, they are able to comprehend the difficult truth of the Bible; it is the banished and troubled ones who turn their faces toward this nomadic Nazarene, instinctively, like a flower toward the sun or birds toward the south.

Jesus has come to lift the yoke from these people's shoulders, to ransom their burdened lives: "The Son of Man came not to be served but to serve, and to give his life as a ransom for many" (Mark 10:45). When reading these words, keep in mind that the understanding of "ransom" in Mark is synonymous with the liberation of a slave or hostage or someone in debt. More specifically, according to Adela Collins, the Greek word *lytron* includes the price of freedom for a slave (Lev. 25:51–52; Exod. 6:6), the money paid to redeem prisoners of war (Isa. 45:13), compensation for damages (Exod. 21:28–32), deliverance from the distress of hunger and thirst (Ps. 107), or more generally, buying back what belongs to God (Lev. 27:30–33; Num. 3:11–13). The prophet Hosea uses the term in a more metaphorical way: it is the redemptive action of God from the rule of Hades and the power of death (Hosea 13:14).[30]

Mark's understanding of "ransom" echoes these various interpretations; they converge in his hands and become a powerful force that joins together the literal dream of deliverance, bodily and material, with a spiritual and theological interpretation, two hands joined together in prayer. His narrative defines the rule of God's kingdom by this inclusive, all-encompassing mission: freedom from subjugation and inhumanity on earth, in the here and now, as well as freedom from the rule of Hades, and life everlasting, where death will be no more and the righteous will shine like the stars (Dan. 12:2).

Sordid Souls

Is there any doubt that many of these characters are in need of "ransom"? They live in close proximity to people and places that have been polluted by blood, mud, and earth, and to many in society, this virtually buries them in oblivion. They inhabit places and circumstances of grinding poverty, in which contact with filth and waste, blood, and death have made them unclean in the eyes of the ruling classes (Herodians, Romans, Pharisees, priests, scribes). Like the millions of slum-dwellers in our world today, there is no soul here that is unsullied, that is not touched and smeared by the heat of the desert, the cruelty of disease, the pangs of hunger, the squalor of poverty, or the toxicity of death.

The case of the Gerasene man stands out because he is unclean many times over: as a Gentile, a pig herder, a possessed man, and a man who lives in a graveyard. Given to fits, rages, and uncontrollable violence, he has been given by Mark the perfectly fitting name of Legion, for the Roman military units of his day (also given to wild fits of violence and destruction). While the man is dirty and repulsive to others, Jesus dares to enter his estranged, banished world and treat him like a proper human being. In this act alone, Jesus brings down the walls of caste, nationality, and holiness that bar the man from communal life. And of course he brings him peace, as the man is essentially lifted out of the graveyard that has been his home, redeemed from death, and reborn to a new life. Mark makes him a model for the Christian life: "Then the man went off and began to proclaim in the Decapolis what Jesus had done for him, and all were amazed" (Mark 5:20).

Jesus's assault on the purity laws of his time follows this mold: it defies social and religious laws that marginalize and degrade those individuals forced to dwell in the gutters of the social order. For the temple and its authorities, the preservation of cleanliness and purity amounts to the preservation of holiness; for Jesus, however, the holiness of the soul is a messier matter, a summons to put oneself in the worn, haggard shoes of the poor and unclean, even if it means violating the rules that were created to advance piety. One approach excludes and alienates, the other gathers in wanton and lavish affection; the former is wholesome and sterile, the latter is dirty and hot; the former protects the sacred from the incursions of the profane, and the latter breaks down the borders that separate the two, so that grace is seen as coursing and raging through squalid regions of human experience.[31] In story after story, Jesus's understanding of holiness offends the official account by unmasking the sins hiding under the cloak of respectability and righteousness, on the one hand, and by highlighting the potential for goodness among the pariahs of his time, on the other. By jolting and unsettling the "morticed metaphors" of dead convention (in Gerard Manley Hopkins's words), Jesus revives the humane spirit of religious laws and decrees. Jesus is following the provocative, incendiary truths of the prophets in these ways, stripping religious observances of all extraneous matters until he reaches the raw core of the Torah: love of God and love of neighbor.

In judiciously criticizing the harmful effects of some religious laws, Jesus demonstrates how much these marks of impurity—physical deformities and blemishes, blood and disease, earth and muck, being foreigners and outsiders—stain the soul of both victim and observer. Uncleanliness estranges the victim from the human community; it demeans and subjugates, confines one to a slum or reservation, makes one into a criminal or brutish thing. Like scarlet letters or the branded marks of a slave, these aspersions slight and reduce the victims; they have the power to abase and isolate, to beget feelings of shame and unworthiness.[32] Recall the harsh words of Leviticus concerning the treatment of lepers: "The person who has the leprous disease shall wear torn clothes and let the hair of his head be disheveled; and he shall cover his upper lip and cry out, 'Unclean, unclean.' He shall live alone; his dwelling shall be outside the camp" (Lev. 13:45–46).

In the annals of history there have been countless instances of such exclusion, in which torn clothing, disheveled hair, and dark skin have been emblems of one's uncleanliness. In the modern world, racism and colonialism have operated with similar understandings; modern prejudice has called out "unclean, unclean" to a host of non-European cultures and communities. When General George Crook (1830–1890) spoke of American Indians, for example, the first adjectives that rolled from his tongue concerned the impurity and offensive smell of Native peoples: "They are filthy, odiferous, treacherous, pitiless, cruel and lazy."[33] And according to Thomas Powers, this was not an unusual impression; white soldiers and pioneers of the American West were quick to trace their repulsion against the Indians to smell—"an odor resembling a mixture of smoked beef, muskrat and polecat"—and this only exacerbated the inclination to corral and displace them to somewhere in the wilderness, beyond the olfactory range of white civilization.[34]

If offensive smells were not indicative of savagery and inferiority, color and caste have put communities "outside the camp" of the modern world as well. Saidiya Hartman's work on the Atlantic slave route illustrates how pervasive this mentality was in the making of the modern world. She describes the building by the British of Cape Coast Castle in 1674 on the Gold Coast of Africa, headquarters of the Royal Africa Company. The castle was designed with a massive underground cellar for securing slaves. Here in this dungeon and infernal prison, thousands of slaves were kept before they were branded, chained, and shipped. Hartman notes that the British called these cellars "factories," for reasons that should be obvious: treated like raw material or, worst, waste products, slaves' bodies were regarded as fetid and seedy, only good when exploited as a labor source or commodity.[35]

In this intestinal labyrinth of dungeons, Hartman continues, one would find mounds of feces, bones, and blood. When describing these horrors, the emotional pitch of Hartman's voice is raised to soprano highs, as she speaks as though with the authority of someone who has witnessed these events firsthand:

> Human waste covered the floor of the dungeon. To the naked eye it looked like soot. For a century and a half after the abolition of the slave trade, the waste remained. . . . Waste is the interface of life and death. It incarnates all that has been rendered invisible, peripheral, or expendable to history writ large, that is, history as the tale of great men, empire, and nation. It evokes the dull ordinary horror of what is vile, worthless and contemptible—a pile of shit. Waste is the remnant of all the lives that are outside of history and dissolved in utter amnesia.[36]

If I wander here from the pages of the New Testament, it is to better understand the nature of the Christian revolt. The figure of Jesus emerges in the pages of the New Testament as a startling figure, someone who disturbs the standard "tale of great men" and tells a different tale, one dedicated to individuals mired in filth and expendable to history. If these lives are contaminated and disgraced by dirtiness—dirt, recall, is matter out of place, misplaced or displaced—Jesus seeks to right the wrong and give them their rightful place in the kingdom of God. His mission is described in no uncertain terms: to ransom slaves, proclaim liberty to captives, proclaim good news to the poor, give sight to the blind, and bring freedom to the oppressed (Luke 4:18). This is why Christianity, as Simone Weil emphatically insisted, is a creed for slaves.[37] This is why lepers and beggars, slaves and untouchables, the godforsaken and the hopeless found in Christ a defender and liberator.

In seeking to embody and exemplify these directives, Jesus surely befouled his own soul; in these narratives, Jesus is clearly taken for one of the unclean himself. For coming from a despised town and region (John 1:26); for welcoming women of ill repute (Luke 7:37); for touching women with hemorrhaging disorders (Luke 8:43); for calling to him prostitutes, tax collectors, and despised groups like Samaritans (Mark 2:15; Luke 17:16); for eating with drunks and whores (Luke 7:34); for consorting with lepers and cripples, beggars, and outlaws (Mark 10:36); for healing those living among graves and pigs (Mark 5:1–13); and for embracing children (Matt. 19:14)—in short, for summoning the untouchable groups of society—Jesus was considered one of the defiled and was in constant danger of being killed.

When considering the significance of this context for our understanding of the soul, we would have to say that it colors that understanding with the unmistakable shade of brown, in Richard Rodriguez's portrait: the color of migrants and laborers, the color of decomposing and aging bodies, impure mixtures, and adulterated blood. (Jesus himself, in John 8:48, is accused of being a Samaritan, a member of one of these impure minority groups.)[38] The Christian depiction of "soul" is khaki-like, a Persian word meaning "dust" and related to the Latin *cacus,* excrement. Reading the episodes and stories of the Gospels with this in mind, we might say that the form of love enjoined on us is not only sweet like jasmine, but also rank and bitter, and always willing to risk contact with all specimens of humanity.

Fugitive Souls

By showing such concern for the outcasts of his time, Jesus also came to know the plight of an outlaw and fugitive—a fact evident in each of the Gospels. Threats came at him from many directions: he escaped a plot to throw him off a cliff (Luke 4:29); attempts to stone him (John 8:59); Herod's efforts to kill him (Luke 13:31); and even the designs of his own family to restrain him (Mark 3:21). In John's gospel, the author captures Jesus's evasive movements with the perfectly applicable Greek word *krypto* (secret, hidden, cryptic). Encoded in this term is the whole furtive mystery of the Messiah's identity and destiny, his divinity buried beneath a harried human existence. For all of John's high Christology (a stress on the divinity of Christ), he also describes, in realistic terms, the dangers that Jesus must circumnavigate. On Jesus's journey to Jerusalem, in particular, the threats build to intense levels, as the narrative tries to keep pace, breathlessly, with Jesus's tortuous, convoluted movements. Richard Cassidy describes it this way: "First Jesus appears, controverts, escapes arrest (7:30), reappears, proclaims, escapes arrest (7:44), reappears, controverts, escapes stoning (8:59), performs the sign of healing the blind man, and escapes stoning and arrest even though his adversaries literally have stones in their hands during this last episode (10:31–39)."[39] In the dizzying rush of daily actions and last-minute escapes, John gives us an account of Jesus's hunted, pressured life—there is a hellhound on his trail.

There appears to be widespread agreement among all of the Gospels about this one factor: Jesus's cryptic, labyrinthine movements are responses to constant crisis and conflict. "In Galilean towns and synagogues, he confronts violent demonic forces and antagonistic authorities. In Gentile territory, he meets a legion of demons and a crowd of angry residents. In the hostile atmosphere of Jerusalem, he faces overwhelming political opposition."[40] Wherever Jesus turns, opposition finds him. As I have mentioned, Mark's prose conveys this pall of menace: the writing is enigmatic and only semitransparent; it is filled with gaps and silences and appears to be rushed, as if the author follows his own counsel in chapter 13, "flee to the mountains." (Many scholars presume that Mark was a product of diasporic Christianity, possibly a community of exiles fleeing the Roman-Judean war or other forms of persecution.)[41] The author of Mark's gospel seems to do his best to organize Jesus's scurrying movements into a coherent pattern, but the result is hardly rational—the pattern is, instead, discontinuous and agitated, a pattern of abrupt transitions and surprising interruptions. Yet this is part of its genius. Mark's disjointed design is a parable in itself of the apocalyptic disarray of his age, or, speaking existentially, of the shocks and blows that human flesh is heir to. In traversing the land mines of his time and place, Jesus comes across as a rolling stone that winds its way through the terrain, rushing and absconding to avoid arrest. Gary Wills attempts to capture this restless movement with a musical metaphor: "If I think of a music to be heard in the background of his restless mission, it is the scurrying *agitato* that opens Khachaturian's violin concerto. He went into cities as into alien territory. He was a man of the margins, never quite fitting in, always 'out of context'."[42]

Though I prefer the analogy of the blues or hip-hop for Jesus's passage in the world—the desperate flights and departures of Robert Johnson; the apocalyptic urgency of Chuck D; the staccato barks of DMX; the looming threat of death and dying in Tupac; the frenetic, plaintive raps of Bone Thugs-n-Harmony; the spiritually minded lyrics of KRS-One, Kendrick Lamar, and Chance the Rapper; and the roguish and defiant words of all of the above—the point is that Jesus had to move with deft, nimble care, had to keep on the move, to slip, slide, and dodge threats of violence and persecution (Mark 7:24). These narratives present the reader with an image of the soul under great duress, in times of great crisis and tribulation, a soul that is an alien and a sojourner on earth (1 Pet. 2:11; Lev. 25:23). Jesus's erratic and surreptitious movements are reminders that the soul of man and woman in these texts is nomadic and restless, even when rooted in the Promised Land.

Consider also the Gospel of Matthew, in which the author describes the Messiah's infant life in harassed terms (with obvious echoes of the plight of the patriarchs in Egypt and, of course, the Exodus of the Israelites from Egypt). Fresh from the womb, Jesus already has a death sentence hanging over him and must flee Herod's murderous intent (like Moses fleeing from the Pharaoh in Exod. 2:15). Almost immediately in Matthew's depiction, a link is established between Jesus and a long history of expulsions and exoduses in Jewish history. Before he is able to walk, he will know the trial of long walks and desperate exoduses. In the "flight to Egypt" episode, Matthew gives us a startling account of a Messiah figure unlike any king or aristocrat in the annals of history, a Messiah who shares the experience of displacement with countless refugees and exiles throughout time.

Matthew's fascinating account of Christ's passion thus begins as soon as Jesus enters the world. While still dressed in swaddling clothes, Jesus is already baptized into a tragic destiny. I can't help but think of the birth of Tupac Shakur when contemplating his own emergence into the world: his mother, Afeni Shakur, was pregnant with him while she was in prison (she was charged with conspiracy to blow up a police station with the Black Panthers, but was later acquitted). Tupac attached great significance to this fact, as if it had already been written in the stars that he would be a voice for those who felt trapped and caged in, tossed up to a life of marginalization and imprisonment. Tupac recalls the circumstances of his mother's pregnancy as a metaphor of innumerable lives that have their beginnings behind bars, locked up in penitentiaries and projects, and preordained to face the unrelenting legacy of racism in America.[43] Keeping in mind Foucault's unnerving definition of racism—"the social distribution of death"—we might say that Tupac's music is a raging objection to the inequitable distribution of death in the world.[44] The statistics on black children and adults in America are worth considering here (with Latinos fast approaching the same levels): in our own day and age, close to half of black men between the ages of eighteen and twenty-five are in jail, on probation, or on parole; blacks are five times more likely to die of homicide than white Americans; half of black children grow up in poverty; and one-third of all African Americans live in poverty.[45]

If nothing else, Tupac's music is testimony to these grim facts. His raps are attempts to add up and assess statistics of this sort, to give an accounting for the lives subtracted by these troubling numbers. I discuss hip-hop in greater depth in chapters 6 and 7, but consider some snapshots here. This first is from Tupac's song "Trapped":

> They got me trapped
> Can barely walk the city streets
> Without a cop harassing me, searching me
> Then asking for my identity
> Hands up, throw me up against the wall
> Didn't do a thing at all. . . .
> Sweated me, hunted me
> Trapped in my own community.
> Why did ya lie to me?
> I couldn't find a trace of equality.[46]

A similar note is struck in Wu-Tang's classic, "C.R.E.A.M.":

> A man with a dream, with a plan to make CREAM
> Which failed; I went to jail at the age of 15.
> A young buck sellin' drugs and such who never had much
> Trying to get a clutch at what I could not touch.
> The court played me short, now I face incarceration,
> Pacin', going up state's my destination,
> Handcuffed in back of a bus, 40 of us
> Life as a shorty shouldn't be so rough.[47]

Whether in Tupac or Wu-Tang, rap lyrics flow out of memories of bondage, from slavery and Jim Crow to the industrial prison complex of the late twentieth century. As Tupac saw it, being black in America carried the stigma of being hunted and dogged, of children born into fetters and fears, like having to fear the police before you can walk, or avoiding bullet shots on your way home from school. Tupac saw the world through the barred windows of the ghetto, where girls had babies that they could not feed; where boys got locked up before they could read; and where death came in a bum rush, with little warning. In articulating these fears and forebodings, Tupac showed how pervasive the feelings of exile and exclusion were among poor blacks in America. Cast in the role of fugitives and convicts, black folks' progress in the United States seemed stalled to Tupac, as if the situation had remained the same since the blues era of Skip James: "The people are driftin' from door to door, can't find no heaven no matter where they go."[48] Similarly, Tupac's vocals and lyrics—rants and rages, prayers and chants, guttural croons and aching sighs—are measurements of the remoteness of heaven and the hiddenness of God on the one hand, and evidence of God's abiding presence in the souls of all drifters like him on the other. Though he was prone to wild misapprehensions, sins, and transgressions (like Jesus's disciples), Tupac shared through these narratives the anguish of an outsider and the hopefulness of a seeker of wisdom: "trapped, black, scarred and barred / searching for truth."[49] At least in his most sublime moments, he grasped the good news that the biblical texts offer and transformed his music into an effort to order and calm his soul in the face of dangerous storms and tempests.

Ethical Magnanimity and the Music of the Soul

Though I insist throughout this book that hip-hop can provide a unique ghetto perspective on the scriptures, there are numerous ways in which hip-hop disappoints. It frequently has brilliant explanatory and diagnostic power, but fails when it comes to a prognosis for a better, deeper, more soulful life, especially in the matter of ethics. And there is no doubt that this is a significant failure, because soulfulness in the Christian tradition is profoundly shaped by ethical codes and creeds. The Jesus of the biblical texts enjoins upon his followers the values of service and sacrifice in order to "gain one's soul" (Luke 21:19). Perfunctory observances of the law—tithing, sacrificial offerings, and so forth—will not suffice if one neglects "the weightier matters of the law: justice and mercy and faith" (Matt. 23:23). The tales in the Gospels seek to move and sustain us with their truth, persuade us with their simple beauty, and shake us out of our moral complacency. They make stories come alive before our eyes, arresting and holding the reader or listener in a state of thrall and helping us imagine a fuller life. If readers are not swayed in these ways, the soul of the Bible will escape their grasp. And worse yet, without moral depth—the leavening presence of love above all—the soul will waste away and become a lifeless, spectral figure, dried out and insubstantial, spiritually moribund.

By schooling us on ethical matters, Jesus transforms the precepts and stories of the Torah into dangerous memories that threaten the inertia, indifference, and injustice of his age. Like the prophets of old, his vision is both recapitulative and prospective—it looks back to Moses, Elijah, and the story of Exodus, while looking to the future, to the dawning of the kingdom to come. Past, present, and future intersect constantly: when Mark begins his tales with Jesus's baptism in the wilderness at the Jordan River, for example, we know that the text is evoking older stories, such as the crossing of the Jordan by the Israelites under Joshua, the miracles performed by Elijah and Elisha at the Jordan, or the return of the Babylonian captives to Israel (Josh. 3:15–17; 2 Kings 2:8–14). The author is drawing here from a deep well of memory and painting the figure of Jesus as a new Moses, a prophet who liberates those whom Egypt or Rome had ground into its soil.

Again, Jesus was bringing about nothing less than a revolution in morality. That revolution welcomes sinners and whores into the banquet before the pious and respectable (Matt. 21:31); it humbles the proud and mighty and exalts the poor and lowly; and it confounds the wise and learned, defending the street knowledge of the marginalized.[50] Mary's beautiful canto puts it this way:

> My psukhe magnifies the Lord,
> And my spirit rejoices in God my Savior,
> For he has looked with favor on the lowliness of his
>   slave/servant. . . .
> He has brought down the powerful from their thrones,
> And lifted up the lowly;
> He has filled the hungry with good things,
> And sent the rich away empty. (Luke 1:46–53)

It is so appropriate for Luke to record Mary's words as a soulful rhapsody because the bars are bursting with joy, and prose seems unworthy of them. In so many words, Luke tells us that the good news of Christ is best felt at a gut-bucket level, with blue and yellow notes alike, sometimes mournful like the winter, and sometimes yellow like the spring. With the Messiah blooming within her, in fact, Mary, this lowly *doules* (Greek for slave or servant), strikes a jubilant note about the favor shown her and for all the downtrodden of Israel. An ode of joy suddenly interrupts the laments and dirges that echo throughout Israelite history. One can imagine that Mary's canto sounded smooth and honeyed yet rough and rugged, maybe something like the "queen of gospel," Mahalia Jackson's, deep, transcendent voice. However it sounded, there are shared sensibilities among these feminine voices, similar memories of slavery and similar syncopations of freedom. When Mahalia Jackson spoke of the impulses in her music, she could have been speaking of Mary's canticle: "I sing God's music," she once explained, "because it makes me feel free."[51]

Much like Mahalia Jackson's music, the New Testament is a collection of songs of freedom, and it must have soothed the troubled nerves of its first audiences as much as spirituals and jazz, reggae and hip-hop have relieved black agony in North America. As the artwork of children of slaves, black music bears a striking resemblance to the world and characters of the Bible. When they first heard these stories, American slaves must have experienced something like a shock of recognition, as if the stories of exile, diaspora, and crucifixion in ancient Israel were coded ciphers of their own trials and afflictions. In no time, these stories were adopted and transfigured for a new purpose, as they became the beating heart of African American music and culture.

And even when black music adopted a secular tone, this biblical legacy continued to reverberate in its tonalities, worries, and hopes. Consider the Isaac Hayes and David Porter classic, "Soul Man": the song reinterprets the story of Passover and Israelite bondage in the context of civil rights struggles (specifically in the context of riots in Watts and Detroit). For Isaac Hayes, the song profiles a "soul man" who has been able "to rise above one's present conditions" in the manner of the ancient Israelites during their journey from bondage to freedom.[52] In countless cases, black musicians have conjured and reimagined biblical themes of hardship and promise. By tapping into the biblical world, these artists have quarried the Bible for its explosive potential, the buried gas and energy under its surface. They have sought out the more dangerous substratum of these texts, one that might blast conventional American interpretations.

By circling back to black music here, my point is simply that this legacy has frequently been more faithful to the radical Jesus of biblical narratives than the more typical and sentimental portrait painted by many Christian churches. Consider how fierce Jesus becomes when confronting the rich and powerful of his time; sounding like a Jamaican "rude boy" in the era of Ska, or a "soul man" in the age of Stax records, or like Tupac's black Jesus, the character who appears in the New

Testament often assumes a threatening tone when faced with mountains of inequality and injustice. Threats, curses, and imprecations come
to his tongue like a mad rapper; he uses abrasive terms to shock and
awaken his followers to the craven failures that he witnesses in the
world around him. Whether in cursing fig trees or overturning money
tables in the temple, Jesus uses hyperbole and aggression when the
world seems deaf and blind to the commandments of the Torah. On the
subject of wealth, for example, he is a relentless antagonist and gadfly.
One story describes a rich man who asks Jesus about inheriting eternal
life: What must he do, he asks, to become worthy of it? He has kept the
Jewish Law and commandments, but Jesus calls for more. "Sell all that
you have and give to the poor." This extraordinary demand leaves the
man downcast, for he knows that he cannot possibly follow the advice.
And then comes Jesus's searing remark: "It is easier for a camel to pass
through the eye of a needle than for one who is rich to enter the kingdom of God (Mark 10:21–25; Matt. 19:16–24).

In contrast to this man, or the "rich fool" in Luke's gospel, Jesus
envisions the achievement of soul through the dispossession of one's
power and wealth, through the loss of self and the abasement of ego.
Jesus assumes that the soul of man and woman is capable of growth and
expansion, but the process requires painful sacrifice, and this is a lesson
that many, including his innermost circle, have a hard time understanding. They expect to have an easier time of it; suffering is not exactly part
of their plan. For Jesus, though, there are always birth pangs in the
soul's expansion, there is always the need for deconstruction and tearing down before the temple of the soul can be rebuilt, before the soul
can get churched. The intelligence and ego must, to invoke Keats yet
again, be schooled by the pains of the world in order for the soul to
become what it was meant to be.

Tragic Wisdom and Christ Crucified

As suggested in chapter 1, Jesus's famous adage, "For what does it
profit a man to gain the whole world and lose his soul?," belongs to a
rich prophetic history in Israel (Mark 8:36). The question has a concentrated force to it that is bigger and more potent than its lean body; it
accosts the listener or reader and calls his values and priorities into
question (to restate Rudolph Bultmann's well-known definition of the
Christian *kerygma*).[53] Instead of synchronizing the relationship of the
soul with the values of the world, this message introduces a note of

dissonance between the matter of soul and the normative standards of society. Like a high-pitched frequency that shatters glass and breaks windows, Jesus's voice in these texts shatters commonplace portraits of power, glory, and material success. In the eyes of the Gospel writers, these are the values of Judas, not Jesus.

While the Christian message clearly samples prophetic voices in this way, Jewish wisdom literature was also a formative influence. Matthew, in particular, includes numerous allusions to the wisdom tradition, so that his protagonist comes across as a sage and seer in addition to everything else. The presence of the book of Sirach is one example: "Come to her with all of your soul, and keep her ways with all of your might. . . . For you will find the rest she gives, and she will be changed into joy for you. . . . Then her fetters will become for you a strong defense, and her collar a glorious robe. Her yoke is a golden ornament and her bonds a purple cord" (Sir. 6:24ff.). Matthew's Jesus speaks in similar terms: "Come to me, all you who labor and are burdened, and I will give you rest. Take my yoke upon you and learn from me, for I am meek and humble of heart, and you will find rest for your *psychais*" (Matt. 11:28–29). In both cases, the message assumes total dedication and devotion: to put on the yoke of Wisdom is to walk in the way of righteousness and the path of justice (Prov. 8:20), it is to consume the bread and wine that she offers (Prov. 9:5), and it is to take Wisdom as your bride (Ws. 8:2). For Matthew, needless to say, Wisdom is exemplified by the figure of Jesus, the embodiment and incarnation of *Sophia*, the bread and wine for all the appetites of the soul.

Perhaps we can get a better sense of the scandalous nature of this vision—Wisdom embodied in an outlaw—if we contrast it with a Stoic portrait. If the purpose of a Stoic sage is to align his individual logos or reason with the Logos in the universe, the disciple of Christian wisdom must seek to align his or her soul with the Logos incarnate and crucified in Jesus of Nazareth. This aim is less an act of pure reason than an act of love and divine illumination; it assumes a turning of one's soul in the manner of a nuptial bond. In wedding our minds and souls to this humble king, we are given eyes for what is invisible, despised, and insignificant in the ways of the world, a mystic ability to peer into the other side, or better underside, of things. The tiered norms that govern the possession of wisdom are suddenly disrupted, and wisdom is offered to the lowly and ignoble of the world, "for the foolishness of God is wiser than human wisdom" (1 Cor. 1:25). In prying wisdom away from cultural and economic elites and redistributing it, Christianity insists that those on the outskirts of society—the lowly and the despised of the world in St. Paul's words—can evince a clear-eyed and imaginative form of understanding (1 Cor. 1:28).

Unlike the wisdom of the Stoics (in which slavery is read allegorically, as a state of mind), Matthew's Jesus draws from a wisdom tradition that is informed by the memory of actual slavery and that "executes justice for the orphan and the widow, and loves the alien, giving them food and clothing" (Deut. 10:18). Jesus is the embodiment of Wisdom crying out in the streets, in the squares, at the busiest corners, at the crossroads, and at the entrance of the city gates, sounding a loud warning to sleeping souls (Prov. 1:20, 8:2–3). In the guise of Wisdom, Jesus directs our attention past courtly and priestly affairs to "all the oppressions that take place under the sun: the tears of the victims with none to comfort them" (Eccles. 4:1). His voice is a public and inclusive proclamation, and it seeks to inspire mindfulness about the plight of the poor and needy, along the lines of this beautiful passage from the book of Job: "The poor of the earth hide themselves together. Indeed, as wild asses in the desert, they go out to their work, searching for food. . . . They spend the night naked, without clothing, and have no coverings in the cold. They are wet with the showers of the mountains, and huddle around the rock for want of shelter" (Job 24:4–8).

In the Gospels, the search for wisdom is synonymous with this cognizance and solicitude, with moral imperatives that draw our attention to the poor's taxing search for food, their desperate need for clothing, and their shivering quests for shelter. The purpose of wisdom is to prod, urge, disturb, and draw us out of ourselves, urgently alerting us to privations previously overlooked. In this same spirit, Bartolomé de Las Casas (1484–1566) picked up the book of Sirach and came across a passage that would unnerve and jolt him: "The bread of charity is life itself for the poor; whoever withholds it is a murderer" (34:25). With this text agitating his mind and soul, Las Casas sought to fundamentally reorder and recalibrate his soul to the voice of Wisdom in Sirach and elsewhere in the Bible, especially, as one might guess, in the prophets: "Wash yourselves clean! Put away your misdeeds from before my eyes; cease doing evil; learn to do good. Make justice your aim: redress the wronged, hear the orphan's plea, defend the widow" (Isa. 1:16–17).

In the case of Las Casas or the biblical books, Wisdom is clearly more than just knowledge or belief; it is an entire way of life, achieved through *pathos* (suffering), *passio* (passion, endurance), and *compassio* (to suffer with others). It is a wisdom born of suffering, a tragic clarity, a painful enlightenment. Aeschylus spoke of it as a divine law: "He who learns, must suffer." (Several scholars, incidentally, argue that Mark was familiar with Greek tragedy.)[54] And Mark spoke of it as the way of the cross, the way of humility, service, and suffering (Mark 8:31–10:32).[52]

Whether or not Mark knew Greek tragedy, many of the collisions in his Gospel—between Jesus and the authorities, Jesus and the "strong man," Jesus and his hard-headed disciples, and Jesus and the Father—have a tragic nimbus to them. By repudiating the image of Jesus as a miracle-working hero or triumphant military leader, Mark gives us a Messiah who is vulnerable, distressed, and above all, an innocent victim of an awful fate. And he allows his hero to plead for an alternative destiny: "Abba, Father, take this cup away from me" (Mark 14:36). More than any other gospel, Mark's narrative is shrouded with this sorrowful spirit and by the sorrowful events of the author's age: the death of his beloved teacher, the destruction of his beloved Jerusalem, and the impending destruction of an age in its death throes. Mark paints his canvas with a black, Goya-like brush, depicting a world that is haunted by dark shadows with restless edges, rapid movements, trembling angles, and swaying borders like the shadows of a tree in a storm.

The pregnant silence in Mark's passion narrative is also related to these explosive, solemn moments of anguish in which the reader picks up the tremors of Jesus's faith. Mark knows how to concentrate and condense agony into a few words and then, when words are inadequate, he becomes reticent, elliptical, and silent. There are ominous silences throughout his gospel—none louder than the silence of the Father on the cross—but Mark turns these silences into tragic beauty, a haunting melody with a brooding but hopeful strain.

Mark's silences are even more pronounced when we read them in light of the other Gospels: the latter, in fact, seem uncomfortable with his silence and frequently offer elucidations to fill in the blanks of Mark's narrative. When it comes to the death of Jesus, for example, Matthew adds a note that is absent in Mark, namely, that the passion represents "atonement for sin" and fulfillment of the scriptures (Matt. 26:28–54). John, too, follows suit, seeing Jesus's death in sacrificial terms, as the death of the paschal lamb of God (while mitigating Jesus's agony). Unlike the writers of these Gospels, Mark holds his tongue and leaves the reason for Jesus's death unexplained. In the abstemiousness and starkness of his account, Mark reveals his sympathy with a fundamental motif of biblical literature: that there are characters, events, and forces of the world that defy and confound human understanding.[55] When sketching the story of Jesus using this principle, all justifications for the death of the Son of God—and the death of countless innocents throughout history—are quieted and emptied to make room, in place of rationalizations, for amazement and awe.[56] In lieu of a theological solution to the terrors of evil, Mark gives us a narrative response, a representation of a Messiah who entered the human drama with a prodigal love for our misshapen and disfigured humanity and surrendered his life in the process, pouring it out like water, bones disjointed, his heart like wax, melting away (Ps. 22:15).[57] Mark, in short, gives us the full humanity of Jesus; he gives us, as Melville noted, a man of sorrows: "The truest of all men was the Man of Sorrows, and the truest of all books is Solomon's, and Ecclesiastes is the fine hammered steel of woe."[58]

While Nietzsche considered Christianity and tragedy incompatible, oil and water, Melville recognized the "fine hammered steel of woe" in the biblical tradition, and he used it to contest superficial versions of Christianity, ones that "dodge hospitals, jails, and walk fast crossing graveyards."[59] It is Melville who would have understood the tragic genius of African American portraits of Christianity; it is Melville who is the spiritual ancestor to the existential and somatic anguish of black Christianity, as described by Cornel West:

> The trauma of the slave voyage from Africa to the New World and the Euro-American attempt systematically to strip Africans of their languages, cultures and religions produced a black experience of the absurd. . . . With the slow but sure 'death of the African gods,' many blacks creatively appropriated the Christian gospel . . . and thereby transformed a prevailing absurd situation into a persistent and present tragic one, a kind of 'Good Friday' state of existence in which one is seemingly forever on the cross, perennially crucified, continuously abused and incessantly devalued, yet sustained and empowered by a hope against hope for a potential and possible triumphant state of affairs.[60]

I suppose that one can, to return to Nietzsche, call this "hope against hope" and the related dreams of mercy, justice, and faith a form of illusion, vengeance, and resentment, but in the Bible, and for the slave morality of a Dr. Martin Luther King Jr., Christianity represented the promise made to shepherds and slaves, day laborers, and refugees that they would be cherished and loved. The empty tomb in Mark's gospel is the hint of this promise and covenant and represents a counterweight of joy and surprise to the tragic gravity of the narrative; it represents the vivifying breath of hope, "the thing with feathers that perches in the soul and sings the tune without the words, and never stops at all."[61]

It should be obvious by now that I stand firmly with a figure like Dr. King, or Cesar Chavez, or Mahalia Jackson, or Tupac, against Nietzsche. That is not to deny, however, Nietzsche's psychological genius in exorcising the whole legion of demons of Christian history. He was, of course, right about the self-delusions, deceitful masks, and virulent will to domination in the Christian soul (Augustine argued as much). He was also right about the dark underworld of the soul that frustrates any attempt to make the psyche transparent and clear. He was right about many things when it comes to the maladies of the soul, especially when these maladies are painted over with a superficial layer of innocence and virtue, when ugliness is meretriciously covered up with cheap makeup. Something of this sort happened, for him, in the Christian revolution, when the lust for power and revenge was dressed up as compassion and humility, when resentment and envy were masked by the guise of equality, and when weakness and indigence were exalted over aristocratic and noble instincts; when everything, in short, that is truly beautiful and elevating about life was cursed and renounced.

For my purposes, at least, we need Nietzsche, the psychologist and master of suspicion, to keep us honest and remind us of our capacity for self-deception. When assessing any struggle for justice or equality, it is always important to consider the unspoken motives and base impulses that always reside in the souls of oppressed people as much as anyone else, as Richard Wright came to believe after reading Nietzsche.[62] Without this sort of vigilance, the soul can easily slide and sink into a morass of hatred, bitterness, envy, and resentment.

In the end, Nietzsche was both right and outrageously wrong. If he had understood what it was like to be a slave in the modern West, or a Jew in modern Germany, or understood the "enormity of the breach instituted by the transatlantic crossing of black captives and the consequent processes of enslavement, violent domination, dishonor, natal alienation, and chattel status," he might have been less absolute and less metaphysical in denouncing the Jewish-Christian soul and its "slave morality."[63] Perhaps if he had had a more expansive musical ear beyond the range of classical music, one that picked up the lower frequencies and plebeian blues of a Billie Holiday or Mahalia Jackson or Lauryn Hill, he would have discovered new dimensions and still unexhausted possibilities of the human soul.[64] Perhaps, with these bouncing rhythms and lyrical acrobatics in his ear, his faith in Dionysus would have been shaken somewhat, maybe enough to cause a trembling or quake in his pagan worldview that would have, at the very least, opened a crack and crevice for the place of the "god on the cross" in his soul. And maybe, if he had been born after the age of hip-hop, he would have learned the crucial difference between "selling out" and being "souled out." In the end, the Christian tradition (along with hip-hop) includes a lot of sell-outs, but it is finally about being souled out, about keeping your deen true, about a wisdom that is more precious than silver and gold and can be found among the brokest and illest in the world, as this track from Lauryn Hill suggests:

> I'm about to change the focus from the richest to the brokest.
> I wrote this opus, to reverse the hypnosis. . . .
> Make a slum lord be the tenant,
> give his money to kids to spend it.
> And then amend it, every law that ever prevented
> Our survival since arrival, documented in the Bible, like Moses and
>   Aaron,
> Things gonna change, its apparent,
> And all the transparent gonna be seen through.
> Let God redeem you, keep your deen true. . . .
> Watch out what you cling to, observe how a queen do.
> And I remain calm reading the 73rd Psalm,
> 'Cause with all this going on, I got the world in my palm.[65]

PART TWO

Profane Accents of Soul

4

In Search of *Duende*

Lorca on Spanish Soul

Duende has something to do with *soul*, with an art that
deepens with so much black feeling, so much humanity, that
it needs to break loose into fresh form—an art that would
transfigure suffering, that would surpass itself.

—Edward Hirsh[1]

In the very essence of poetry there is something indecent.
That's why poetry is rightly said to be dictated by a daimonion, though it's an exaggeration to maintain that he must
be an angel. It's hard to guess where that pride of poets come
from, when so often they're put to shame by the disclosure of
their frailty.

—Czeslaw Milosz[2]

I believe that being from Granada gives me a fellow feeling for
those who are persecuted: for the gypsy, the Negro, the Jew,
and the *morisco,* whom all *granadinos* carry inside them.

—Federico García Lorca[3]

Federico García Lorca (1898–1936) was one of the earliest victims of the
Spanish Civil War, killed in 1936 by the fascists in the vicinity of Víznar,
a town to the northeast of his beloved Granada. It is likely that Lorca
was shot near a famous spring known by the ancient Arabs as Aina-
damar, the "Fountain of Tears." Since Lorca had so cherished the rich
and varied history of Spain, especially the history of its subjugated cultures, there is symbolic significance in his body languishing close to this

natural spring, as if the Andalusian earth, with its layered sediments of Jewish, Moorish, and Catholic cultures, would anoint his body for burial. As strange as it sounds, he was accused of being a Russian spy, someone who had "done more damage with his pen than others with their guns."[4] Though the accusation that he was a spy is absurd, the second part of the criticism is more accurate: it chances upon a fundamental truth of all great art, the way that it can crawl under the skin and cause great disturbances and inflammations in the body politic. Lorca's conception of soul—what he called *duende*—bears this out: As the muse of Lorca's imagination, *duende* transported his poetry and music to great heights and simultaneously agitated and menaced the powers of his age. To his fascist critics, *duende* was the stuff of heresy, a kind of disease and deviation from the canonical values of society that if not checked could lead to full-blown plague. Critics of this sort sought to sanitize or sterilize Lorca's pen of all such rebellious instincts. His murder was no doubt an attempt to control Lorca's unruly, disruptive genius.

As Edward Hirsch suggests, there is something in this *duende* that is related to the notion of "soul" in black American traditions. Shaped and created in a similar likeness to "soul," *duende* is a Spanish translation of the creative grace that transfigures suffering into some of the finest achievements in music, poetry, religion, and the arts. In this respect, we might also translate *duende* by what Muddy Waters called his *mojo:* the magic spell or dark charm that confers distinction and excellence on an artist, allowing him or her to bewitch and enchant a crowd of listeners. As in Lorca's poetry and plays, the *mojo* that appears in the art of the blues inspired remarkable soundscapes, ethereal and earthy, but also provoked a throng of Puritan-like detractors. With its origins in voodoo (the term refers to a small flannel bag worn as an amulet), mojo—just like its understudy in the blues—was accused of being the work of the devil. If mojo was behind the hollers, grunts, and grinds of the blues, then it was dangerous indeed, for this was a music that seemed to many church folk in America to be perilously close to the carnal delights of hell. The blues, after all, arose out of the American underworld of Jim Crow in Mississippi, where death and poverty haunted the countryside like unappeased ghosts. In embellishing on this theme with the theatrical flair of a Lorca, one of the masters of the blues, Son House, evoked gruesome details of death and dying in his piece "Death Letter": a macabre recital of a funeral scene, with the body prepared for burial, pall in the air, coffin lowered, the earth swallowing the corpse.[5] This staging of death and dying became Son House's way of grappling with and fending off the threat of death; music was his amulet against the dark side.

We find something eerily similar in the work of Lorca: He was fascinated with dramatizations of death and lived in a culture in which the deaths of Christ and the saints were widely exhibited and paraded as part of the cultural life. Lorca's Spain was a tragic society, as Miguel de Unamuno famously argued, but not world-weary, not listless or despairing. The wild pageantry of death in the culture seemed to inspire an art of life, in which affirmations and revelries trumped negations and gloom. Lorca's art was cut from this cloth. Though he flirted with death in his poetry, plays, and music, his art was steeped in a life-enriching plenitude, bursting at the seams, "stuffed with the stuff that is coarse, and stuffed with the stuff that is fine."[6]

But some of his countrymen could not tolerate so much exuberance. Lorca's mojo-inspired poetry, plays, and essays became dangerous because they allied themselves with a past or future of Spain that was more tolerant and diverse than the dogmatic present; they allied themselves with the persecuted of the earth, with those whom Spain nullified and relegated to the netherworld. Because Lorca's art harvested styles of beauty that came from these locations and that transgressed the boundaries of the sacred and profane, it is not at all surprising that he antagonized the fascist protectors of morality and sanctity. His work celebrated a standard of art that measures the value of an artist without presumptions of education or class privilege, a meritocracy of soul. As unpredictable and riotous as the Pentecostal spirit that was poured out on servants and handmaidens, the shattering revelation of *duende*'s presence enabled Lorca to dream new dreams, to see visions, and to prophesy with a tongue of fire—all hazardous passions.

LORCA'S *DUENDE*: SACRED AND PROFANE SOUL

The reader will note that I have placed the consideration of *duende* in this second part of the book, concerning the profane sense of soul, especially as it is related to a sense of style and aesthetics in Spanish music, dance, and the spoken word. While the idea of *duende* in Lorca is associated with these cultural accents, it doesn't follow that the concept is entirely secular or remote from religious sentiments. Consistent with its African American cousin across the Atlantic, *duende* is charged with deep undercurrents of spiritual voltage and can appear in various forms: in the beatific ecstasy of a mystic or saint, the crazed delights of dance

and song, the bursting hydrant of religious rhetoric, or the enchant-
ments of love. This is to say that *duende* appears where the flourishing
of human creativity is most intense, whether in the holiness of a religious ceremony or in shady and carnal experiences. As if Ariel and Cal-
iban suddenly produced a wild offspring with genes from each parent,
the *duende* can be ethereal and chthonic, transcendent and sensual,
inspiring and terrifying. Because of this inherent complexity, *duende* is
a storm of emotions that blows and swirls in different directions, cross-
pollinating a variety of ideas and experiences, including the spiritual
and elemental, the sacred and profane, that are at the heart of this study.

When considering the raw intuitions and music-inspired delirium in
the experience of *duende*, the figure of Dionysus naturally invites comparison, because *duende* seems to come to the recipient in wild abandon, bodily rapture, and spiritual inebriation. But though the analogy is
illuminating in some ways (especially if we follow Nietzsche's portrait
of Dionysus as a god of music and ecstasy), it can also blind us to the
ethical contours of the term in Lorca. If we examine *duende* in the light
of his colorful spiritual world, pagan and Christian, he begins to resemble more and more a product of Lorca's baroque world. In other words,
duende surely has traits that are Dionysian and pagan, but with Christian elements intertwined, especially in the strands that speak so eloquently on behalf of the poor and the dead or in the filaments that
conflate the experience of death—a condition for the experience of
duende—with the way of the cross. In his own version of despoiling the
Egyptians, Lorca steals this pagan concept and makes it resemble a
Catholic concept, now branded with the image of Christ crucified. Similar to the way African American traditions baptized African traditions
of spirit possession and dance with Christian narratives and images,
Lorca reworked *duende* to bring Dionysus to the altar of Christianity
(something that would have appalled Nietzsche, of course).

DUENDE'S ORIGINS

Duende's etymological origins date back to the term for "master of the
house," *duen de casa*. If the *duende* is master of the house, then the
human person is essentially a stranger in his own territory, never master
of his domain. Though this truth is fiercely resisted by the ego, like a man
resisting eviction, when the self learns how to live with the presence of
otherness and mystery within, when it learns how to surrender to grace,
it can become a conduit of the *duende*. Seen in this manner, the *duende*

incarnates a truth about many of the highest achievements in art and life: they occur when we are possessed or summoned by something outside of us, something that enters us from beyond the domain of our ego or will, like the splendor of beauty, the terror of death, the gift of love, and the arresting force of music. In Lorca's Spain, *duende* came to suggest such moments of spiritual fullness, but in popular lore it was a disruptive spirit or ghostly trickster that could stir up trouble or produce mayhem in one's household. As a personification of unruly and anarchic forces, the *duende* is an undesirable visitor, taking control of our habitat, disinheriting and unhousing us, and banishing us to a life of exile. It can make a beggar out of a king, a wanderer out of a sovereign, or a prisoner out of a prophet. To an artist, *duende* has sublime, if devastating, consequences: "He makes Goya work with his fists and on his knees with horrible bitumins," writes Lorca. "He strips Mossén Cinto Verdaguer in the cold of the Pyrenees, or takes Jorge Manrique to watch for death in the wasteland of Ocaña" (DS, 45). In making wastelands out of mountains, the *duende* has the destructive force of a volcanic blast or the emptying power of a desert whirlwind; it humbles, denudes, and overwhelms.

To speak of the shape-shifting *duende* in purely destructive or ravaging terms does not, however, do the concept justice; as much as it tutors us in the pains of life, *duende* can also enchant and charm, make the soul come undone in order to give it a fuller existence. By the time *duende* appears in Lorca's work, it suggests something enthralling and hypnotic, an experience of vital intensity and preternatural clairvoyance. It transforms itself into a muse-like figure that inspires the greatest artists, especially musicians, dancers, and poets. In this guise, *duende* is the rarefied air that breathes oxygen into the embers of a great artist; it is the spiritual vitality that exalts the ordinary self to unimaginable heights; it is Dionysian mania, frenzied ecstasy, and feverish rapture. Without it, an artist may master techniques and refine skills, but she won't have soul. And without soul, an artist can bring at best a modest breath of fresh air, never a cyclone of ravishing beauty. Lorca's description of the Andalusian singer Pastora Pavón, "La Niña de los Peines," is a case in point:

> As though crazy, torn like a medieval mourner, La Niña de los Peines got to her feet, tossed off a big glass of firewater and began to sing with a scorched throat, without voice, without breath or color, but with *duende*. She was able to kill all the scaffolding of the song and leave way for a furious, enslaving *duende*, friend of sand winds, who made the listeners rip their clothes with the same rhythm as do the blacks of the Antilles when in the lucumí rite, they huddle in heaps before the statue of Santa Bárbara. (DS, 45–46)

In relating the *duende* of flamenco to Santa Bárbara in the lucumí and santería traditions, Lorca points to a secret kinship between these rites across the Atlantic, as if the *duende* will turn up wherever the primitive beauty of music channels the travails and raptures of life (chapter 7 explores these themes in Afro-Cuban music). In the guise of this crazed singer, possessed by Santa Bárbara—or by her companion, the *orisha* Shango—the *duende* explodes on the scene and razes the scaffoldings and systems of music, creating new sounds and beliefs by violating the rulebooks of religious, musical, or aesthetic orthodoxies. Keeping in mind the Enlightenment's drive to create systematic, universal, transcendental rules for aesthetic judgment and value—as propounded in Immanuel Kant's *Observations on the Feeling of the Beautiful and Sublime* or his *Critique of the Power of Judgment*—Lorca's *duende* looks like a principle of anarchy, something resembling the unenlightened, savage beauty of colonized, non-European rhythms and folklore. Like a trickster who disrupts and offends a social gathering dedicated to principles of civility, politeness, manners, and highbrow taste (values that coexisted with modern slavery), the *duende* defies the rules established by the modern canon of aesthetics.[7] As an "eccentric" and "ex-orbitant" creature (outside the center and orbit of modern Europe), the *duende* of Lorca's Spain is the shadowy Other of Enlightened aesthetics, a product of the collective experiences of groups confined to the margins of modern taste and thought: gypsies, Moors, Jews, Hispanics, blacks, and the poor. For Lorca, the *duende* is a "friend of sand winds" because it forms bonds with dispossessed and wayfaring groups across the world, blown into the wind by modern forces of change.

The scorched, torn voice of the flamenco singer thus symbolizes a conception of sublimity that swerves wildly from a European science of aesthetics (as envisioned by Kant, G. W. F. Hegel, David Hume, Alexander Baumgarten, Edmund Burke, and others). To those dedicated to the privileging of European culture and taste, the sound of the *duende* passing through the gypsy throat could only be like the babel and bedlam of barbaric exclamations, devoid of reason, decorum, and propriety. With its abrasive, grindstone timbre, gypsy song is a coarse mouthpiece of forgotten, screaming memories: "The gypsy siguiriya begins," Lorca writes, "with a terrible scream. . . . It is the scream of dead generations, a poignant elegy for lost centuries, the pathetic evocation of love under other moons and other winds. . . . No Andalusian can help but shudder on hearing that scream" (DS, 25). In its fidelity to the souls of the dead, "deep song" hearkens back to the howling fury of a medieval mourner, a shouting prophet, or a rapturous psalmist. This music employs a rich sonic palette that mixes colors and shades of pigment to create a montage of Spain's disinherited legacies. It has the ability to communicate with the dead and to recall their troubles, complaints, and grumblings. Deep song has the affection and tenderness of Jesus for Lazarus, the power to raise the dead. It is life giving.

To some, Lorca's own overflowing vitality and range of artistry (as a playwright, a musician, a poet, and an essayist) were *duende* incarnate. Salvador Dalí, for example, described Lorca in this way: "The poetic phenomenon in its entirety and 'in the raw' presented itself before me suddenly in flesh and bone, confused, blood-red, viscous and sublime. . . . And when I felt the incendiary and communicative form of the poetry of the great Federico rise in wild, disheveled flames, I tried to beat them down with the olive branch of my premature anti-Faustian old age" (CP, xxii). Fearful of such excessive, orgiastic emotion, Dalí appears here as a disciple of Apollo instead of Dionysus, and he advocates the composed wisdom of old age, not the brashness of youth. He testifies to the incendiary, raw power of *duende* in Lorca, but warns against a wild conflagration of passion. Dalí was a fire hydrant dousing Lorca's blaze, a ship's line tying Lorca's soul to the shore. He feared for his friend's safety, feared that Lorca might lose his moorings and end up adrift. Dalí advocates the caution of old age: stick to the coastline.

There is wisdom in Dalí's discretion, and Lorca learned from it, orchestrating his emotions and poetry with necessary flashes of discipline and reason. Reason and logic form a guiding principle of Lorca's art, a raft to keep one afloat in the sea of the unknown. But it will only keep one floating in place; if the purpose of poetry is to explore the uncataloged variety of life under the sun, then the fainthearted student, restrained by what is logical or prudent, is not one's best guide. Instead, look to those who cast aside all caution and lead others through transcendent depths and profundities, the deep sea divers of life. The poetic imagination is this sort of guide for Lorca, one that can extend the frontiers of knowledge to new horizons. "By means of poetry," he writes, "a man more rapidly approaches the cutting edge that the philosopher or mathematician turns away from in silence" (DS, 112; CP, lx). Going to places where philosophy or science cannot go, *duende* uses poetry as a psychic medium to explore the uncharted world of the human soul.

But even more than poetry, especially in its written form, *duende* has a special bond with the phenomenon of sound and the oral arts. This shouldn't be surprising if we consider the nature of sound. In contrast to sight, which situates an observer outside of what is seen and leads to the capacity for abstract thought and objectivity, sound has a way of invading and pouring into the listener. Music or the spoken word immerses and submerges a listener in what is heard, so that it is deeply felt and experienced, never purely theoretical. Considering that the biblical texts would have historically been read, chanted, and sung aloud, in contrast to private readings in the modern world, the biblical Word would have immersed the listener in this way. (The Hebrew word *dabar,* in contrast to the Logos of the Stoics, can mean both event and word.) When most artfully performed and recited—employing the same skillful range of timbres, pitches, and time signatures as a contemporary rapper or singer—the truth of what was recounted was tied to the art and beauty of the delivery, a combination that would have engrossed the listener and called for the soul's submission. Bearing a resemblance to Martin Heidegger's understanding of truth in the pre-Socratics (aletheia), *dabar* is a disclosure, happening, or occurrence that insinuates itself into the lifeblood of the listener, entering the ears, racing through the veins, exciting the skin, and seducing the heart—all effects of the incantatory power of the spoken and sung Word.[8] Both in the Bible and the ancient Greek tradition, there are numerous indications of these bewitching effects of language, such as when Odysseus hears the Sirens singing to him and his heart, Homer says, is throbbing in his chest, filling him with a longing that is maddening. (He has to be tied up to the mainmast in order to resist the desire to steer the ship toward the delightful sound.) Music and the spoken word can be entrancing and wrenching experiences, and Lorca thought of them as special vehicles of *duende.*

THE *DUENDE* AND THE DAIMON

When raising the specter of the Greeks, we also have to consider the possible connection between the *duende* and the ancient daimon. (Lorca specifically mentions the daimons of Socrates, St. Teresa of Ávila, and Nietzsche—odd bedfellows, to be sure [DS, 43–50].) The similarities are uncanny. According to E. R. Dodds, the daimon is a mysterious spirit that attends a particular individual and that influences, if not determines, the destiny of that person.[9] In this role, the daimon is associated with an individual's natural endowments and divine aptitude. It is an elevating spiritual force and guide, which propels a person's quest for excellence, courage, or beauty.[10]

However, when the concept of the daimon reaches the philosophers, such as Socrates and Plato, it undergoes changes that make it more suitable to the rational standards of a philosopher. Plato seeks to subdue the irrational sway of the daimon the way Dalí would later seek to temper Lorca's poetic pyrotechnics, trying to prevent uncontrollable combustions and fevers. That said, it is also true that Plato clearly acknowledges the blind spots in the faculty of reason—as in the matter of dreams, prophecies, love, and the gods—and this allows him to concede a place for the daimon. The daimon consequently comes to represent for Plato the authority and soundness of irrational intuition, "whether it is expressed in dreams, in the inner voice of the 'daimonion,' or in the utterance of the Pythia."[11] In these cases, Plato admits the revelatory intrusion of the supernatural into human life. He also acknowledges the epiphanies that happen beyond the control of the rational self, the divinatory moments in and out of time, the unveiling of truths that leaves us breathless and astonished, at a loss for words. In short, he clearly acknowledges the divine-daimonic gift of *mania:* a madness or *enthusiasmos* that is a possession of the human psyche by the divine *pneuma.*[12]

Plato describes eros, among all the types of divine madness, as the most formidable and vexing. Under the spell of eros, the daimon can appear in convulsive paroxysms and sweeping surges, as the lover is covered in sweat, his heart in tumult, his tears lashing his eyes, and his stomach in knots. The lover feels sick, can neither eat nor drink. Eros has arrived with the electric frenzy of lightning, causing the heart to skip a beat and the mind to become unhinged. At least in the *Phaedrus* or *Symposium,* Plato gives free rein to the rushing, careening power of eros and does not try to confine it to the authority of reason. In fact, he allows eros to soar, if we recall the myth: once welded to the common clay of the body, the wings of the soul fall into disrepair and find themselves in desperate need of water, like a plant in the desert summer. When eros is present, however, the wings begin to germinate and sprout, eventually spreading out and bearing the soul into the heavens (*Phaedrus* 255D). It is love and beauty, then, not reason or truth, that raise the soul to transcendent heights and return us to our divine origins—in our end is our beginning. For Plato, the daimon is thus an intermediary between gods and mortals, a link in the cosmic chain between heaven and earth. Though the daimon wears different guises—the masks of Apollo, Dionysus, the Muses, and above all Eros—Plato insists that it is a lofty spiritual guide and the source of our kinship with the divine.[13]

While Lorca's view of *duende* is darker than Plato's view of the daimon, as if Francisco Goya had a hand in Lorca's portrait, it still maintains ties with Plato's figure as divine mediator. When speaking of Teresa of Ávila's widely celebrated mystical experience, for example—the contorted mouth, rolling eyes, exhausted body, piercing wounds, and sexual agony—Lorca says that the *duende* tried to kill her "for having stolen his deepest secret, the subtle bridge that unites the five senses with the raw wound, that living cloud, that stormy ocean of love freed from time" (DS, 50). In her carnal experience of God, Teresa is swept off her feet by divine love and is wounded in the process. Through this experience of both love and death, Teresa has stolen the secrets of the grave, says Lorca, and she returns to speak of this newfound truth, the omnipresence of the "stormy ocean of love" in the universe. Like the prophet Tiresias, blinded for revealing the secrets of the divine, she is scathed in this encounter with God, but blessed with clairvoyance at the same time. She sees and senses God with her whole being, each faculty of her body and soul bequeathed with supersensory awareness.

Lorca regarded Spain as being in the mold of Teresa, a channel of excruciating grace, if only because of the intensity of its religious devotions and its familiarity with suffering. Spain had been ravished by the *duende*, whether in the dark nights of mysticism, the contorted body of a dancer, the undulating and tremulous voice of a flamenco singer, the poise of a bullfighter, or the fevered festivals and ceremonies of baroque culture. When the vital spirit of the *duende* rushes upon such artists, the *duende* serves an aesthetical and mystical end and is a medium of "communication with God through the five senses" (DS, 46).

DUENDE AND TRAGEDY

Just when we think that Lorca's *duende* is an unambiguous messenger of God, maybe an angel, he introduces a less desirable, more frightening dimension to this night prowler. In order not to confuse the *duende* with an angel, Lorca adds descriptions that we recognize from tragedy or when we are in the throes of affliction. To make sense of these severe and dreadful experiences, Lorca seems to want something more coarse and earthy than a starry-eyed, sentimental, cloud-dwelling angel. He requires something with authority among dispossessed groups, an indecent figure, in Czeslaw Milosz's sense. Without equating the *duende* with the devil—it does not have the same empty, vile, evil character—Lorca does let it appear as a symbol of a dark fate, or dreadful power, a *mysterium tremendum et fascinans*. In the worst moments of suffering, the *duende* appears as an awe-inspiring, even violent creature, and it pursues us with the unflagging determination of death, perhaps something like the hellhound that dogged Robert Johnson:

I got to keep movin', I got to keep movin'
Blues fallin' down like hail, blues fallin' down like hail.

And the days keep on worryin' me
There's a hellhound on my trail.[14]

Whatever else it is, Lorca's *duende* figure shares this pedigree; it can be
a personification of tragic curses and implacable suffering, like that
faced by Robert Johnson, the house of Atreus, or gypsies and slaves in
the modern world. Neither angel nor demon, the *duende* is something
more uncanny, perhaps a hybrid of the two, combining the elevating
potential of the former with the gritty, rebellious spirit of the latter.[15] If
there is an obvious ambivalence and logical inconsistency here, a split
personality in the *duende*, that is so largely because it reflects the complexity of human experience, the tragedies and ecstasies alike. Or perhaps it even shows the complexity of God: we cannot forget that God is
not only tender and loving in the Bible, but also awesome and terrifying. God wounds Jacob; batters Job; and causes Israel to suffer captivity, exile, and enslavement throughout its history. Martin Luther
referred to this aspect of God as the *deus absconditus*, the hidden God,
and it caused him much grief.[16] Ultimately, Lorca's portrait of the
shadow side of *duende* is related to a similar effort to make sense of the
absurd in human experience; it is related to the encounter with suffering, especially the kind of suffering, to quote David Tracy, "caused less
by personal sin than some mysterious necessity: fate, fortune, choice,
providence."[17] As Lorca sees it, the greatest artists bear the battle marks
of these forms of agony, as if they were in a deadly contest with the
duende, wrestling with God, or in the throes of delivery, panting and
shrieking, trying to give birth to a form of art that has tragic grace.
Lorca often turns to the term *amargo* (acrid, bitter) as another Spanish
illustration of these difficult truths, as a way of naming the bitterness
and pain in all human experience. "This figure," he writes, "is an obsession in my poetic work" (DS, 118).

Sprinkled with the pungent and bitter taste of *amargo*, Lorca's *duende*
is a bittersweet concept, love mixed with death, beauty with the cross,
the sacred with the profane. When an artist successfully mixes these different experiences, she tames the *duende*'s fury and blunts its terror.
Whether in the furious glottal attacks and vibratos of a flamenco singer
or in the gentle flow of the ballad-inspired guitar, Lorca emphasized the
Orpheus-like power of music to subdue and entrance the forces of chaos.
In one poem he designed the cadence of the lyrics to correspond with the

strumming of a guitar as it synchronizes its pace with the relentless movement of death, striking a chord that is grim but not bleak:

> La muerte
> entre y sale
> de la taberna.
>
> Pasan caballos negros
> y gente siniestra
> por los hondos caminos
> de la guitarra.
>
> La muerte
> entre y sale
> de la taberna. (CP, 144)

> Death
> goes in and out
> of the tavern.
>
> Black horses and sinister people
> pass along the sunken roads
> of the guitar.
>
> Death
> goes in and out
> of the tavern. (CP, 145)

With words that mirror the musical tempo and tonal restraint of a ballad, this poem aims for a direct exposition of death's menacing gait. The sonorities follow the lament of the guitar and stay in step with the unyielding footfalls of death as it strolls in and out of taverns or churches, pestering its prey. Lorca's poetry demands vigilance on this matter, as if the poet is a bullfighter in the ring and a momentary distraction could lead to a gory end; one's concentration, whether in poetry or life, must remain steady in this deadly contest with the majestic bull, summoning, evading, and spurning its powerful advances. Lorca's life was lived, it seems, in close proximity to these dangers, to the dagger-like horns of the bull. Death haunted and harassed him and wanted to plunder his native Spain. "Everywhere else, death is an end. Death comes, and they draw the curtains. Not in Spain. In Spain they open them. . . . A dead man in Spain is more alive as a dead man than any place else in the world" (DS, 47).

Lorca's poetry flings the curtains open when it comes to Spain's *ars moriendi*. He wants to share Spain's ornate art of dying with the broader world: death adorned and paraded around during festivals or funerals, death flirted with in the combat with a bull, and death remembered and defeated in the Catholic mass. Lorca didn't think an artist would ever possess the power of *duende* without engaging with and braving death. "The *duende* does not come at all unless he sees that death is possible. The *duende* must know beforehand that he can serenade death's house and rock those branches we all wear, branches that do not have, will never have, any consolation" (DS, 50). Stripped of simplistic consolations and sentimental clichés, the tortured voices of "deep song" quiver and tremble with the weight of these themes. We can hear similar burdens in the voices of the blues, whether in Charlie Patton's "Prayer of Death" or in Ma Rainey's down-home moaning blues:

> Black cat on my door-step, black cat on my window sill,
> Black cat on my door-step, black cat on my window sill,
> If some black cat don't cross me, some other black cat will.
> *Black Cat Hoot Owl Blues* (1928)[18]

Like Ma Rainey's plaintive voice in this song, Lorca's poetry is written for lives that are vexed by a black destiny. It is for those who are dueling with a cross daimon that drags ruin into the house, like so many dead birds (or diseased bugs, as when Son House speaks of the boll weevil as putting everybody on the "killing floor").[19] Lorca's poetry is for those who are fighting the bull of heaven as Gilgamesh and Enkidu did, or for those in a life and death struggle with none other than God himself, like Jacob, Jeremiah, and Job.

Whatever else it does, Lorca's poetry gives voice to every torment suffered under the sun and refuses any contention that such pain is necessary or excusable. He can strike an irreverent tone: "At the bottom of all these poems lurks a terrible question that has no answer," Lorca writes. "Our people cross their arms in prayer, look to the stars, and wait uselessly for a sign of salvation" (DS, 31). Purged of solutions to the problem of evil, Lorca's poetry is the stammering and sighing voice. It mirrors the sound of the flamenco or blues guitar, hollering and shouting for mercy, wailing away in wordless beseeching, praying in a language of pure emotion and gesture.[20]

If there were a hint of an answer to suffering in Lorca's art, it is evident in the folklore of the *duende* or the theology of the cross, both species of tragic beauty. He preferred the myth *of duende* to any logical justification for the presence of evil (theodicy), for the same reason that he embraced the crucified God: because both represented a poetics that did not pontificate about suffering, but instead expressed solidarity with the depths of human anguish, a willingness to enter the sordid mess of the world. In approximating this pattern, Lorca's poetry sought to incarnate itself in the dirt and mire of earthly existence, to achieve transcendence only through intimacy with the chthonic roots of life. "These black sounds," Lorca writes, "are the mystery, the roots fastened in the mire that we all know and all ignore, the mire that gives us the very substance of art" (DS, 43). Unlike Greek muses, or Catholic angels, these black sounds of the *duende* are not confined to Olympian heights or church walls, but emanate from the mud and funk of human experience. They do not come from the head of Zeus like Athena, but rather from the seedy corners and ghettos of the human soul.

THE *DUENDE* OF FLAMENCO AND DEEP SONG

Flamenco is a product of those seedy corners. Most historical studies of flamenco or deep song (they are virtually the same thing) have shown that they emerged from desperate slum conditions, in which poverty, hunger, crime, prostitution, and violent death polluted the air like the smog of a big city, making it difficult and taxing for people to breathe. As if the musicians were inhaling this oppressive air and then converting it into melodic gasps, cries, and shrieks, the music made something beautiful out of inharmonious atmospheres. Timothy Mitchell remarks about the origins of flamenco:

> More significant than the places of flamenco, however, were its spaces: slum neighborhoods, ghettoes, bordellos, taverns, penitentiaries, hospitals, hideouts, inns, tobacco shops, smuggling routes. . . . And most important of all, were the people who occupied these spaces for centuries: not exactly the proletariat or the working class, to be sure, but a newly urbanized subproletariat composed of gitanos, moriscos, pícaros, slaves or ex-slaves, men or women banished from their communities by the Inquisition, forced laborers, and any offspring of interbreeding among these groups. In sum: the human debris of a de facto caste society.[21]

Since flamenco came of age among despised and banished groups, as Mitchell suggests, it picked up the ghetto inflections and urban argot of these communities and was accused, like the gaucho music of the pampas or the blues or jazz or hip-hop, of being dissolute and licentious, an indecent eruption of human instincts. It was associated with the ordeals and passions of homeless *gitanos*, exiled *moriscos*, and the uncouth poor. Flamenco dwelled obsessively on "poverty, hunger, prisons, jails, hospitals, prostitution, alcohol consumption, taverns, insanity, violent death, the caprices of cruel fate, and the futility of effort."[22] Not surprisingly, the cultural heroes of this music were dissidents and rebels, those who defied bourgeois, conventional values: *pícaros* and thieves, thugs and pimps, gangsters and mulattoes. In fact, the word "flamenco" comes from nouns that suggest defiance and isolation: "knife," "thug," "braggart," and "Andalusian gypsy."[23] Fittingly for its rough world, "flamenco" conveyed an attitude of rude defiance or insolence.

But in its most eloquent form, of course, flamenco became an enthralling art of sound and dance, a musical genre. Since many of the groups mentioned above found themselves excluded from various sectors of society, including higher education, music presented itself as the most democratic medium available to them, an art that permitted the contributions of the lower classes. Instead of expressing their anarchic energies in written form, through flamenco members of these groups put their bravado on display in sound and dance, transforming inelegant and brute passions into something dramatic and soul-wrenching, something robed in flamboyance.[24] Every movement, every bodily feature communicated their rebellious values: the dancer's writhing body, her wild, Medusa-like hair, her furious clapping hands and stomping feet, her entranced and haughty eyes and pomegranate lips. To Rainer Maria Rilke, the flamenco dancer would raise her hands "like startled serpents," and this, too, was a gesture of the dancer's brash spirituality, as if she now had the Moses-like power to subdue the sinister creatures of the earth.[25]

Flamenco eventually became synonymous with the style and soul of Spain as a whole, and I want to take note of its origins among the alienated communities of Spain, beauty at its most raw. One can hear the whole speckled, motley history of Spain in its various timbres and tonalities: the Moorish call to prayer, African beats and rhythms, gypsy cries and laments, and the Catholic liturgy. There is no doubt that its sounds were forged at the crossroads of many cultures, from both west and east, and always with a promiscuous affection for beauty wherever it might be found, in the clouds or in the mud of the earth. As a poet, Lorca sought to follow the same design: "The artist must laugh and cry with his people. He must set aside his bunch of white lilies and sink to the waist in the mud to help those who are looking for lilies" (DS, 128).[26]

THE SACRED DIMENSIONS OF *DUENDE*

As much as deep song can be earthy and profane, it also throbs with religious intensity, one moment echoing the profane speech of a criminal, then sounding like a benediction. In flamenco, the sacred begets the profane, then in a sudden reversal, the profane is interrupted by the sacred, as if they were part of a duet that sometimes harmonizes and sometimes engages in battle. For Carlos Fuentes, the circuitous path between the two is evident in the spellbound flamenco dancer, "sexual turbulence clad in saintly longings . . . sensuality repressed by faith but sublimated in mystical dreams."[27] Whether at these intersections of sexuality and mysticism or in the prayers of convicts and exiles, deep song is a house of many different rooms and niches. It is well known, for example, that religious *saetas* are part of this household and influenced the evolution of deep song. (*Saetas* are plaintive songs sung by prisoners to images of Christ or the Virgin Mary during Holy Week processions.) Accompanied by the guitar, the *saetas* are rueful outpourings of emotion by inmates. They express the psychological and spiritual aspects of incarceration: loss of freedom, corrupt authorities, abuse, poverty, and through it all, the longing for God in a troubled world.[28] These *saetas* are part of a larger corpus of flamenco prison songs.[29] Following is an example:

> Look at me Mother, and pardon
> that I sing to you in this style;
> it is flamenco and comes out deep
> and one's soul rides on a sigh.[30]

The song apologizes for its rough and rude language (a guilt present in most blues songs), but it trusts that the Mother of God will understand the sincerity of the emotion and the humility of plain speech. As a distillation of vernacular wisdom, the song concentrates its anguish in simple and straightforward lines, sparse and direct. If the *duende* appears in these guises, it is a companion of terse speech, of nouns without adjectives and verbs without adverbs. The emotion is big and extravagant, but its expression is tight and compressed.

One famous flamenco singer of recent years, Fosforito ("little match"), describes this musical extravagance in these terms: "Deep song can make you cry or explode in ecstasy; it shakes you and it hurts you, though with pleasurable pain; it boils over and floods your insides and brings you closer to God."[31] This "little match" will set your house on fire and cause the roof to come tumbling down. He will inflame your eyes and ignite your passions, char your brow like Moses, and make you moan like Teresa of Ávila.

Though removed culturally and religiously from these specific ecstasies, even the iconoclastic Nietzsche defended revelations of this sort, ones that enable the soul to find a "widely extended rhythm": "If one has the slightest residue of superstition left in one's system, one hardly finds it possible to repudiate the idea that one is a mere incarnation, the mere mouthpiece, the mere instrument of supremely powerful forces. The term revelation, in the sense that suddenly, with indescribable certainty and refinement, something becomes visible, audible, something that moves one profoundly and overwhelms one, is but a plain description of the facts. . . . Such an expanse, such a need for a widely extended rhythm, is almost the token of the power of inspiration."[32] It is surprising for the deconstructive Nietzsche to defend these "residues of superstition," but he is unapologetic here about the experience of revelation: a power that makes one shake and shudder, that brings about an intensification of reality and an expansion of one's being. In these pregnant moments of time, the artist or savant is a mere midwife of beauty or love, an instrument whereby revelation assumes visible or audible form.[33]

Lorca fashioned all of his poetry with these intoxicating rhythms in mind, believing with Nietzsche that the greatest artists are mouthpieces for spiritual inspirations and prophecies. In contrast to Nietzsche, though, Lorca's hymns were both pagan and Christian, in honor of Dionysus and the crucified Christ. He wanted his poetry to be more expansive than Nietzsche's philosophy, to include both paganism and Christianity in a baroque-like parade or delicious paella of ideas: "I feel full of poetry, strong poetry, simple, fantastic, religious, bad, deep, wicked, mystical. Everything, everything, I want to be all things" (SL, 9). Or: "Poetry exists in all things, in the ugly, in the beautiful, in the repugnant. . . . One must be religious and secular, uniting the mysticism of a severe Gothic cathedral with the wonder of pagan Greece" (IL, 3; G, 69).[34] With this kind of bursting, inclusive mysticism, Lorca dug deep into the underground reservoir of folk ballads in Spain, searching for the hot springs that would release the pent-up energy of the earth. He was looking for the subterranean rivers and eddies that would unite, in a swirling current, mysticism and music, the sacred and indecent in the history of Spain. His *Gypsy Ballads* (1924) and *Poem of the Deep Song* (1931) were outlets of these whirlpools of emotion. These works became his interpretations "of the soul of the people," in which he tried to capture in poetry the tormented, torn, whiskey-scorched voices as the singers he so admired (DS, 41).

Gypsy Ballads

According to Lorca, the themes of *Gypsy Ballads* vary from crime and poverty to violence and spirituality, but one constant protagonist is anguish, *pena*: "The book, therefore, is a *retablo* expressing Andalusia, with gypsies, horses, archangels, planets, its Jewish breeze, its Roman breeze, rivers, crimes, the everyday touch of the smuggler and the celestial touch of the naked children of Cordoba who tease Saint Raphael. . . . And there is just one protagonist, *Pena,* great and dark as a summer's sky, which filters into the marrow of the bones and the sap of the trees" (DS, 105; G, 135). His referring to these ballads as a *retablo* is significant, because a *retablo* is a devotional work of folk art that expresses gratitude or supplication; when painted and carved in the style of a *retablo,* his poems became sacraments that bestow grace on a variety of God's creatures, from criminals to the naked children of Cordoba. The poems transubstantiate the ordinary and familiar elements of Andalusia into something extraordinary and holy. Instead of striking the studied pose of a scholar or art connoisseur, Lorca demanded that his poems be considered with the liturgical and contemplative devotion of a believer, someone who approaches these poems with his entire heart and soul, someone who suspends his disbelief.

In particular, his ballads are prayerful meditations on the *retablos* found in many Andalusian churches, devoted to the three archangels, St. Michael, St. Gabriel, and St. Raphael. In Lorca's reading, the archangels—along with St. Joseph and the Virgin Mary—share in the plight of the gypsies and adopt their customs and dress. Gabriel is the "great-grandson of the Giralda"; St. Joseph appears "badly wounded, and lays a shroud upon a girl"; the Virgin is a "dark wonder of a woman," dressed in gypsy attire, though she has lost her castanets; and at a shrine of Christ, "the angels and seraphim sing: holy, holy, holy." Saturated with a baroque imagination, Lorca's ballads are crowded with angels and saints, who are fully alive and involved with the drama of gypsy existence. Only a poet would dream of these idiosyncratic images: angels and saints garbed in gypsy clothes and implicated in gypsy lives, moving and gyrating among poor street children, criminals, gypsies, Jews, and other disaffected groups. When Lorca imagines gypsies as broken and bruised, the angels, saints, and Jesus are seen as sharing in the passion of their struggle, like pieces of Christ in the Eucharist broken for each of them to consume.

As Lorca suggests, however, the main protagonist is the enigmatic and mournful Pena, a character with shades of Christ crucified, the grief-stricken widow in *Lamentations,* the sorrowful Madonna, with her beautiful sad eyes, and mother Rachel in Jeremiah, weeping for the desolation and ruin of Jerusalem. With Pena added to the drama, the ballads assume a dirge-like quality, as though they are now smeared with ashes and robed in sackcloth. For Lorca, Pena is a personification of the distress that the flamenco guitar simulates, the distress that is impossible to explain in words. It names the mysterious "ache in the flesh of the soul," the "cautery that burns the heart, throat and lips of those who speak it" (SV, xi; DS, 40). With or without words, Pena is a cry of anguish and a cry of protest, a refusal to remain silent in the face of injustice, like the cry of the horse in Picasso's *Guernica*.

In the hue and cry of his ballads, therefore, Lorca's words combine lament and dissent, as they cry out on behalf of the victims of Spanish history. He does what he can to keep the memory of the dead alive, as in the following poem, "The Feud," about a hunted and murdered gypsy:

Ángeles negros traían
pañuelos y agua de nieve.
ángeles con grande alas
de navajas de Albacete.
Juan Antonio el de Montilla
rueda muerto la pendiente,
su cuerpo lleno de lirios
y una Granada en las sienes.
Ahora monta cruz de fuego
carretera de la muerte.

El juez, con guardia civil,
por los Olivares viene.
Sangre resbalada gime
muda canción de serpiente. (CP, 552)

Black angels were bringing
handkerchiefs and snow water;
angels with big wings
of Albacete knives.
Juan Antonio de Montilla
rolls dead down the slope,
his body full of irises,
a pomegranate in his temples.
Now he rides a cross of fire
down the road of death.

Through the olive groves
come judge and Civil Guard.
The sliding blood is moaning
the mute song of a snake. (CP, 553)

The blood of the gypsy, Juan Antonio de Montilla, is oozing away *(res-balando)* as death comes to him in a violent rage at the hands of the dreaded Civil Guard and their "souls of leather." Once he has been killed, his body decomposes until it becomes one with the irises of the earth, and his blood, pomegranate red, is moaning and lamenting, but no one can hear the "mute song"—save perhaps the black angel, who brings a hand-kerchief to bind his wounds and water to his dying mouth. It has to be a black angel, for who else would show such kinship with this outlaw gypsy? Then again, if there is another advocate for him and his kin, it is the *duende*-inspired poet, as he turns the tale of this persecuted people into a lyrical lament. Together, Montilla and the *duende* refuse to forget the plight of the gypsies:

> Oh ciudad de los gitanos!
> En las esquinas banderas.
> La luna y la calabaza
> con las guindas en conserva.
> Oh ciudad de los gitanos!
> Quién te vio y no te recuerda?
> Ciudad de dolor y almizcle,
> con las torres de canela. (CP, 591–92)

> Oh city of gypsies!
> Corners hung with banners.
> The moon and pumpkins,
> and cherries in preserve.
> Oh city of gypsies!
> Who could see and not remember you?
> City of musk and sorrow,
> city of cinnamon towers. (CP, 591–93)

Though Lorca refers to the "city of gypsies," there is tragic irony in the line, for his elegy is about the dispossession of the gypsies, their absence of place and belonging. This poem echoes Psalm 137:5–6, a lament of the exiles in Babylon: "If I forget thee, Oh Jerusalem, . . . let my tongue cleave to the roof of my mouth." In lieu of the rivers of Babylon, the ballads substitute the Guadalquivir, but the sense of anguish is similar. While the Civil Guard sacks and burns their towns, the gypsies fly away in agitated patterns, like bees expelled from their hives, like the Israelites after the destruction of Jerusalem. "Por la calles de penumbra huyen las gitanas viejas" (CP, 594). "The old gypsy women flee through shadowed streets" (CP, 595). Disoriented and dismayed by these events, they don't know where to go next:

> Cien jinetes enlutados,
> dónde irán,
> por el cielo yacente
> del naranjal?

Ni a Córdoba ni a Sevilla
llegarán.
Ni a Granada la que suspire
por el mar.
Esos caballos soñolientos
los llevarán
al laberinto de las cruces
donde tiembla el cantar.
Con siete ayes calvados,
donde irán
los cien jinetes adaluces
del naranjal? (CP, 126)

One hundred horsemen in mourning,
where will they go,
under the recumbent sky
of the orange grove?
They will never get to Córdoba,
or Granada that sighs
for the sea.
Those sleepy horses
will carry them
to the labyrinth of crosses
where the song trembles.
Pierced by seven *ays*
where will they go,
the one hundred Andalusian horsemen
of the orange grove? (CP, 127)

This is a song of crucified, displaced peoples. We can hear the trembling sighs and piercing cries (ay!) of these horsemen in mourning, with no one to receive them. Lorca's poem is a psalm of desolation, and he engraves these events and memories on his forehead the way a Jew in prayer attaches the tefillin to his arm and head: "Let them seek you on my brow," the poet sings about gypsy lives. As an antidote to forgetfulness, Lorca's poetry is torah on behalf of the disinherited and dispossessed of history. He cries out on their behalf, screaming until the mirrors shatter, as he once said about the flamenco vocalist Silverio Franconetti: "Su grito fue terrible. Los viejos dicen que se erizaban los cabellos y se abría el azogue de los espejos" (CP, 136–38); "His cry was terrible. Old people used to say it stood your hair on end and opened the mercury in mirrors" (CP, 137–39). And when the howling voice begins to falter, the guitar hollers, sighs, and complains in its place. "Empieza el llanto de la guitarra. / Es imposible callarla. / Llora por cosas lejanas" (CP, 100); "The weeping of the guitar begins. / Impossible to silence it. / It weeps for distant things" (CP, 101). With a flood of tears welling in one's eyes, the guitar weeps for truths that escape the purview of vision, as if blindness in these artists (as in so many blues artists) has made possible a different, deeper mode of seeing. "Deep song sings like a nightingale without eyes. It sings blind, for both its words and its ancient tunes are best set in the night, the blue night of our countryside" (DS, 32).

LORCA IN NEW YORK: 1929–1930

Though Lorca's poetry always utilized the cadences of music, it is certainly true that his style underwent significant development in his later years; the cadences changed their tune. By the 1920s and 1930s, the years of *Poet in New York,* Lorca's style was moving away from his ballad-inspired verse and picking up inflections from modernism and the avant-garde, a shift that parallels, in my view, the transition from the blues to jazz in America. Unlike the skintight lyricism of the blues, jazz introduces far more complex and ornamental sounds: intricate syncopations, melodic elaborations, and elliptical phrasings.[35] In contrast to the more direct and taut prosody of the blues, jazz can appear downright byzantine and baroque, a sphinx-like arrangement of sound that is pleasurable for its inscrutability. Even more than his early work, Lorca's *Poet in New York* echoes these modernizing trends heard in jazz. His later poetry recorded the new spirit of experimentation and improvisation—the "labyrinthine subdivisions of the beat," in Ted Gioia's apt description—that became synonymous with American jazz.[36]

Lorca arrived in New York in June 1929, and the chic of those times—the jazz idiom, surrealism, and apocalypticism—entered his bloodstream. By copping bits and pieces of these trends and adding them to the pathos of his earlier poetry, Lorca created poetry that was filled with secret meanings, Dadaist mystique, and existential dread. He arrived right before the onset of Great Depression (a few months before the stock market crash in fact), and soon the roaring parties of the 1920s came to a crashing halt. As the Depression arrived, it seemed to quickly end the intoxicated jubilation of the Jazz Age. New York was suddenly hemorrhaging money, confidence, and optimism, and Lorca was there, by sheer coincidence, when the market crashed. Going forward, his poetry would register many of these changes, and accentuate, in particular, the impact of these crises on the most vulnerable and abused residents of America.

New York seemed to Lorca a wasteland of the modern world, "a heap of broken images, where the suns beats, and the dead tree gives no shelter, the cricket no relief, and the dry stone no sound of water."[37] As if he had drunk from the same cup as T. S. Eliot, Lorca's poetry became more fragmented and enigmatic as he adopted an apocalyptic style and transformed his words into comets streaking across the sky, warning of further calamity. As strange and eerie as these apocalyptic images were, Lorca embraced them because they seemed to him, ironically, to be the most lucid images of the deranged reality of modern life. His poetry became more disjointed and surrealistic to keep up with his wrenching perceptions of a world gone to pieces. To read Lorca's *Poet in New York* is a disorienting experience, especially for those familiar with his earlier work on deep song and gypsy ballads. Following him through New York City is like following Dante into purgatory and hell, only worse, since Lorca had no Virgil or Beatrice to be his guide. Lorca's journey through New York was unguided and unmoored, a portrait of a castaway on an island, or worse, of an entire shipwrecked civilization. Lorca's discovery of America was a scathing indictment of an urban inferno.

His impressions of New York were thus synonymous with imprecations. In New York, Lorca was somewhat like the prophet Jonah, denouncing and thundering against the Assyrians, but in this case it is Lorca who will swallow the whale, the whole of New York, and spit it out like a rotten apple (to borrow a metaphor from Nas).[38] Indeed, everything around him in New York had the majestic power of a great white whale—the grandeur of the skyscrapers, the mammoth ambitions of Wall Street, the titanic achievements in science and technology—but it was a whale without soul, a city hostile to mystery and spirituality, drained of song. It was a city where the captains of industry counted their money as the groans of the poor sounded in the night. It was a city that transformed prosperity and success into a sign of virtue and consequently turned poverty into a sign of vice:

Cuando el chino lloraba en el tejado
sin encontrar el desnudo de su mujer,
y el director del banco observaba el manómetro
que mide el cruel silencio de la moneda,
el mascarón llegaba a Wall Street.

No es extraño para la danza
este columbario que pone los ojos amarillos.
De la esfinge a la caja de caudales hayt un hilo tenso
que atraviesa el corazón de todos los niños pobres. . . .

No es extraño este sitio para la danza, yo lo digo.
El mascarón bailará entre columnas de sangre y de números,

entre huracanes de oro y gemidos de obreros parados
que aullarán, noche oscura, por tu tiempo sin luces. (CP, 662–64)

While the Chinaman wept on the roof,
not finding the nude of his wife,
and the bank director examined the manometer
that measures the cruel silence of money,
the mask [of death] arrived on Wall Street.

It isn't a strange place for the dance,
these cemetery niches that turn the eyes yellow.
Between the sphinx and the bank vault, there is a taut thread
that pierces the heart of all poor children. . . .

This isn't a strange place for the dance, I tell you.
The mask will dance among columns of blood and numbers,
among hurricanes of gold and groans of the unemployed,
who will howl, in the dead of night, for your dark time. (CP, 663–65)

Lorca named this section of the poem "dance of death," but the title is misleading, because it describes a world that no longer can dance with death. Death has been emptied of transcendence, flattened out and trivialized. It has lost the enchantment and aura of mystery; it is crass and inelegant and turns the eyes yellow like a sickly jaundiced man, like one sapped of blood. Lost in this modern city is the baroque drama on death: the rituals and festivals, the colorful extravagance and musical ostentation, the kisses and arguments with which Spanish and Latin American cultures confronted death. If death still dances in New York, he dances alone, because no one knows how to follow his steps, no one has the grace to respond to his rhythms.

This kind of civilization was terrifying to Lorca. He curses it the way Jesus cursed the fig tree, or the way John of Patmos once cursed Babylon/Rome: "The kings of the earth . . . will stand at a distance, for horror of her torment, and say, 'Alas, alas for the great city, the might city of Babylon! In a single hour your doom has struck!' The merchants of the earth also will weep and mourn for her because no one any longer buys their cargoes of gold and silver, jewels and pearls, cloths of purple and scarlet" (Rev. 18:9–15). Beneath the bright colors and resplendent wealth of Rome, this ancient prophet of doom sees a false and cheap civilization. Though the city is clothed with jewels, pearls, and brilliant attire (purple and scarlet were royal colors of Roman magistrates), the seer envisions a future when Rome will be undressed and undone. Lorca's prophecy is similar. He cries out against New York for its idolatrous appetites, its temples of greed, its orgies of violence, its banquets of gluttony. Disgusted by so much waste, he calls attention to the putrefying odors of the streets, if only to underscore the gross injustices of the age:

Ay, Harlem! Ay, Harlem! Ay, Harlem!
No hay anguistia comparable a tus rojos oprimidos,
a tu sangre estremecida dentro del eclipse oscuro,
a tu violencia granate, sordomuda en la penumbra,
a tu gran rey prisionero, con un traje de conserje. (CP, 652)

Ay, Harlem! Ay, Harlem! Ay, Harlem!
There is no anguish like that of your oppressed reds,
or your blood shuddering with rage inside the dark eclipse,
or your garnet violence, deaf in the penumbra,
or your grand king, a prisoner in the uniform of a doorman. (CP, 653)

Nauseated and lost, Lorca describes an experience of urban disorientation that recalls in my mind the stressed psychology of urban dwellers in American life, with their "blood shuddering with rage." As though he is wandering through Nas's Queensbridge or Jay-Z's Bedford-Stuyvesant, Lorca describes a dark, etiolated world that does not let in enough light, making it difficult to breath, grow, and flower. The streets he walks are littered with trash, stained with urine, threatened by the police, and inhabited by "shadowy people who stumble on the curbs" (CP, 671). While Americans pay homage to the sanctuaries and shrines of the golden calf, Lorca's anger burns in the manner of Moses, throwing his tablets at the people and making powder out of their gods. He refuses their devotion and instead turns his attention to the "hurricanes of gold and groans of the unemployed," or the cruelty of greed that "pierces the heart of all poor children." Years later, Grandmaster Flash and Melle Mel voiced the same sentiment in "New York New York":

A castle in the sky, one mile high
Built to shelter the rich and greedy
Row of eyes, disguised as windows
Looking down on the poor and needy.

Staring at a skyscraper reaching into heaven
When over in the ghetto I'm livin' in hell.[39]

Lorca saw New York with the same eyes as this song from Grandmaster Flash and the Furious Five: a vision of skyscrapers and monuments of mammon reaching into the heavens, built to protect the rich and to grind the poor into the dust of the earth. He gives us an account of urban ruin through hymn, psalm, and rhapsody, an account of life lived close to the edge. We can hear his cries and protests through the violent windstorms of the city: "Every day I protested. I protested to see little black children guillotined by hard collars, suits, and violent boots as they emptied the spittoons of cold men who talk like ducks" (DS, 96). Indignation and acrimony are always right under the surface of this poem, bubbling up and burning the surface of the verses. Lorca collects the rage of blacks in America and then matches it with a poetic rhythm and beat á la Grandmaster Flash or Public Enemy. When his words are disregarded, screams burn through his throat:

> Mientras tanto, mientras tanto, ay!, mientras tanto,
> los negros que sacan las escupideras,
> los muchachos que tiemblan bajo el terror pálido de los directores,
> las mujeres ahogadas en aceites minerales,
> la muchedumbre de martillo, de violin or de nube,
> ha de gritar aunque le estrellen los sesos en el muro,
> ha de gritar frente a las cúpulas,
> ha de gritar loca de fuego,
> ha de gritar loca de nieve,
> ha de gritar con la cabeza llena de excremento,
> ha de gritar como todas las noches juntas,
> ha de gritar con voz tan desgarrada
> hasta que las ciudades tiemblan como niñas
> y rompan las prisiones del aceite y la música.
> Porque queremos el pan nuestro de cada día,
> flor de aliso y perenne ternura desgranada,
> porque queremos que se cumpla la voluntad de la Tierra
> que da sus frutos para todos. (CP, 728)

> Meanwhile, yes, meanwhile
> the blacks who empty the spittoons,
> the boys who tremble beneath the pallid terror of executives,
> the women who drown in mineral oil,
> the multitudes with their hammers, violins, or clouds—
> they'll scream even is they bash their brains against the wall,
> scream in front of the domes,
> scream driven crazy by fire,
> scream driven crazy by snow,
> scream with their heads full of excrement,
> scream as if all the nights converged,
> scream with such a heartrending voice
> until the cities tremble like little girls
> and knock down the prisons of oil and music.
> Because we demand our daily bread,
> alder in bloom and perennially harvested tenderness,
> because we demand that Earth's will be done,
> that its fruit be offered to everyone. (CP, 729)

With the repetitions in this verse and elsewhere (common in his ballad-inspired poetry), Lorca composes his words with the descanting voice of ritual or ceremony. The repetitions (scream, scream, scream) are stacked together like a mountain of emotion, and they indicate to us the gradual escalation of intensity. The pitch begins with gentle tones and whispered asides, then swells into a fierce, shouting falsetto as the reader ascends the verses. The repetitions rock and roll in our minds; they plead and persist like uninterrupted waves crashing on the cliffs, slowly but relentlessly sculpting the rocks of our nature. He is trying to awaken vigilance: "Wake up. Be still. Listen. Sit up in your bed" (CP, 703). He will scream until the cities tremble and their citizens are roused from their slumber. He will scream until the nations respond to the anguish of the poor, until the fruit of the earth is shared with everyone.

Though it's sometimes difficult to see, the poem is not entirely blind to the vestiges of light that remain buried under these mountains of injustice. In fact, the poem does what it can to gather these fragments to shore up the city against its ruin, the way Noah gathered the creatures of the land to save them from the coming deluge. With so much wickedness on the face of the earth, we must look for another Noah or Moses to protect us from the tsunami-like weight of the sea that threatens the island of New York. And this is where the poem becomes more captivating. Lorca looks for a new Moses to clear a redemptive trail through America, a prophet who will hold out a light for the territory and build a better world—and his hope is fixed on black American culture to bring forth this Moses-like luminary.[40]

In the heart of such darkness, Lorca suddenly introduces a mysterious prophet to the poem, someone who certainly will continue to denounce, bewail, and censure, but now with an added dimension of love and hope and faith. This black prophet will bring a radiant, uncontrollable light to America, even in the midst of graves:

> Será preciso viajar por los ojos de los idiotas,
> campos libres donde silban mansas cobras deslumbradas,
> paisajes llenos de sepulcros que producen fresquísimas manzanas,
> para que venga la luz desmedida
> que temen los ricos detrás de sus lupas,
> el olor de un solo cuerpo con la doble vertiente de lis y rata
> y para que se quemen estas gentes que pueden orinar alrededor de
> un gemido on en los cristales donde se comprenden las olas nunca
>   repetidas. (CP, 670)

> We will have to journey through the eyes of the unlearned,
> open country where the tame cobras hiss in a daze,

landscapes full of graves that yield the freshest apples,
so that the uncontrollable light will arrive
to frighten the rich behind their magnifying glasses—
the odor of a single corpse from the double source of lily and rat—
and so that fire will consume those crowds still able to piss around a
moan or on the crystals in which each inimitable wave is understood.
    (CP, 671)

Lorca would have us journey through New York with the unlearned and
lowly as our guides, so that we can see the world through the eyes of the
poor. As docents of the ghetto, they will help us see a world obscured and
whitewashed by triumphal celebrations of capitalism. In joining his vision
to these farsighted eyes, Lorca offers a radically different image of New
York than the view of Wall Street millionaires or Main Street consumers.
Now looking through the windows of these burning, prophetic eyes,
Lorca holds out hope for a fire that will do more than fume and rage; he
envisions a purgatorial or Pentecostal fire that will purify and renew. He
echoes the sentiment of Eliot in *The Four Quartets*:

> The dove descending breaks the air
> With flame of incandescent terror
> Of which the tongues declare
> The one discharge from sin and error.
> The only hope, or else despair
> Lies in the choice of pyre or pyre—
> To be redeemed from fire by fire.[41]

To choose the right fire—the one free from sin and error—is to partake
in the refining redemption of the Holy Ghost. Lorca dreams of something similar, but only in his vision will a black child play a providential
role in this passion play. I repeat: Lorca prophesies the emergence of a
black prophet to release the doves of peace and justice:

> Quiero que el aire fuerte de la noche más honda
> quite flores y letras del arco donde duermes
> y un niño negro anuncie a los blancos del oro
> la llegada del reino de la espiga. (CP, 736)

> I want the powerful air from the deepest night
> to blow away flowers and inscriptions from the arch where you sleep,
> and a black child to inform the gold-craving whites
> that the kingdom of grain has arrived. (CP, 737)

This black voice—a child's voice—will sing with a melody that has the
desperate loneliness of the blues, the anger of hip-hop, and the loving

hopefulness of gospel. This prophet will come from the barrios of the wronged and wounded and will announce the kingdom of bountiful grain, where everyone will be fed by the bread of life. (The grain in the poem, as Richard Predmore suggests, symbolizes the Eucharist.)[42] This voice will announce an era of eschatological abundance and justice.

In the end, Lorca's poem is a tribute to the wisdom found in humble and marginal places, a proclamation of the Word dwelling in the mangers and thatched huts of the modern city: "Love is in the flesh shredded by thirst, in the tiny thatched hut struggling against the flood" (CP, 729). Black music was a gift of this sort for Lorca, and it gave him hope that diamonds could be forged out of the pressurized circumstances of modern life: diamonds out of coal. In his reading, the blues, gospel, and jazz were mined out of the underground of human experience and immersed in the same musty, earthy smell as deep song and flamenco. In their best forms, these rhythms and melodies were something like Karl Marx's definition of religion: the sigh of the oppressed creature, the heart of a heartless world, the soul of soulless conditions. Or better, commensurate with a mystical purpose lost on Marx, these genres of music were fallen sparks of light trapped in the broken shards of modernity, and Lorca, now as Kabbalist, sought to release them for the purpose of *tikkun olam,* the mending of the world. In redeeming these broken shards, Lorca's poetry brings together, in a baroque musical ensemble, black American rhythms with Spanish melodies. *Poet in New York* pulses with unions of this kind, in which cultural variations are joined in a common redemptive purpose, making the writhing serpents of sorrow and misfortune dance to the beguiling sound of words and music.

Though Lorca's expedition to New York began with a Dantean descent into the abyss, it ended with an ascent and dance on the farther shore of the Spanish New World, as he made his way to Cuba. He arrived in "perfumed" Havana and was transported to a transcendent realm, in which he described Afro-Cubans dancing a *son* (discussed in greater detail in chapter 7). "Against three great horizontal lines—the line of the canefields, that of the terraces, and that of the palm trees—a thousand blacks, their cheeks dyed oranged, as though running a fever of 152 degrees, dance this 'son'" (DS, 101):

> Cuando llegue la luna llena iré a Santiago de Cuba.
> Iré a Santiago
> en un coche de agua negra.
> Iré a Santiago.
> Cantarán los techos de palmera . . .

Iré a Santiago.
Oh bovino frescor de cañavera!
Oh, Cuba! Oh, curva de suspiro y barro!
Iré a Santiago. (CP, 742–44)

As soon as the full moon rises, I'm going to Santiago, Cuba.
I'm going to Santiago
in a coach of black water.
I'm going to Santiago.
The thatched roofs will sing. . . .
I'm going to Santiago.
Oh, the bovine coolness of sugar cane!
Oh, Cuba! Oh, curve of sigh and clay!
I'm going to Santiago. (CP, 743–45)

His own cheeks flushed with feverish enthusiasm, Lorca celebrated the music of Cuba's folk culture, this *son* that combined the Spanish guitar with African rhythms and percussion. Regarding the fusion of Spanish and African traditions in the New World, Lorca gushed like a newly liberated underground spring that has been dammed up for way too long. The miasma and pall that had hung over New York suddenly gave way to the burning delight of the sun over Hispaniola, and he basked in it like a child with his face full of wondrous expectancy, stretching himself on the sand and tossing himself into the waves on Cuban seashores. In a very real way, he had come home, and in lieu of the gypsies, Jews, and Moors of Spain, Lorca was welcomed by the exuberant *duende* of American blacks in New York and Cuba.

Lorca's poetry testifies to the light that shines in the darkness, the light that the darkness cannot overcome. In spite of the black shadows in the *Poet in New York*, the light remains obstinately present, even dazzling, and this fact remains as miraculous as the Hanukkah candles that flickered and flamed in the face of the destruction of the temple. Like his distant Jewish ancestors, Lorca did what he could to keep the flame burning and cried out against the powers of his age that would snuff it out. The result of these efforts is the kind of soul that squeezes transcendence out of suffering and that moves with grace and poise even as death is charging at one like a snorting minotaur.

The Souls of Black Folk

Ralph Ellison's Tragicomic Portrait

Instead of the sublime and beautiful, the near, the low, the
common was explored and poetized. . . . The literature of the
poor, the feelings of the child, the philosophy of the street,
the meaning of household life, are the topics of the time.

—Ralph Waldo Emerson[1]

If you can't manage to put tinges of Spanish in your tunes,
you will never be able to get the right seasoning for jazz.

—Jelly Roll Morton

With the ghostly presence of *duende* as our guide, I hope that we can
begin to notice some of the synergies between Spanish soul and black
American traditions, especially as we explore in this chapter Ralph Ellison's depiction of soul. In turning to Ellison, a contemporary of Lorca,
we place ourselves in the thick of musical and cultural currents of soul.
Like many black writers of the twentieth century, Ellison brought musical cadences and flows into the mighty river of American literature,
injecting some of its stagnant waters with a fresh tributary of style. By
adding his lyrical voice to American literature, he used his pen the way
black musicians used their instruments, making it sing on behalf of a
black American experience that was invisible in many parts of America.
He not only honored conceptions of soul in black music, folklore, literature, and religion in this way, but also simultaneously exposed the
blindness and tone deafness of many Americans.

Ellison's project, which brought shades of black and blue to the pale
cast of soul in America, resembles Lorca's use of the *duende* as a force
of revitalization for tired and spent conceptions of soul. Music—gypsy

ballads and deep song for Lorca and spirituals, blues, and jazz for Ellison—gave them their formula for a richer view of art and literature, one with sparkle and fresh vitality, one that renovated rusted and worn-out words. Both of them came to literature from an early, formative affair with music—Ellison played the trumpet and studied music at Tuskegee, while Lorca was a trained pianist—and both wrote as if the flows and meters of music were always playing in their ears, lending harmony and synchronicity to the stridency of their lives. More than all other art forms, music, dance, and the spoken word were revelatory for the two men, breaking open the secret chambers of a culture's soul (DS, 47).

Besides sculpting their language with a lyrical sensibility, affection for music kept the musings of Lorca and Ellison close to the ground and close to the poetry and folklore of common people. Although the reclamation of vernacular and folk traditions had been a widespread trend among European and American writers since the nineteenth century, Lorca and Ellison avoided some of the most glaring deficiencies of this fashion. Unlike romantic caricatures of non-European cultures—examples of exotic and noble savagery, rich in flair and passion but lacking in intellectual sophistication—Lorca and Ellison displayed a more intimate, thick knowledge of their traditions; they were participants, not just voyeurs.[2] While they, too, ascribed a certain primitive inspiration to black and Spanish traditions, they avoided stripping them of their intellectual complexity and spiritual depths.

With their omnivorous cultural appetites, Lorca and Ellison also knew that the artist in search of genius must be willing to look in a variety of places, inside and beyond one's heritage and inside and beyond one's comfort zone. In contrast to the genteel scholar, who stays confined to chaste sectors of society, the disciple of *duende*, says Lorca, must be willing to venture into funky and shady arenas of life—taverns and road-houses, prisons and boat docks, alleyways and streets—all in search of the visceral and unprocessed manifestations of the human spirit (DS, 43). Ralph Waldo Emerson had some of this spirit; rumor has it that he walked backstreets to hear gutter slang, urban humor, teamster argot, Irish curses, and so forth.[3] Learning from these voices, Emerson added a sharp edge to his style, a gritty and slick note to his refined eloquence, and Lorca and Ellison later followed this lead. They, too, insisted that there are forms of learning best nurtured in the company of exploited workers, rugged sailors, and disreputable groups. In this schooling of the intelligence in the interest of soul, to repeat a line by John Keats, sailors and slaves, gypsies and Jews, Arabs and black folk could become the high priests of the soul's apprenticeship.

For many dissenting, avant-garde artists of the twentieth century, this intuition had transfiguring if not revolutionary consequences, allowing for the introduction of accents and experiences previously spurned in many circles of art. Black and Hispanic artists contributed to this cause, featuring the brightest prodigies and sensations of their traditional cultures and oral traditions. (In Latin America literature, this trend is reflected in José Hernández's *Martín Fierro* [1872] and later trends like *costumbrismo,* the regional novel, and of course "magical realism.") Though the vernacular drift of literature in Latin America lagged behind the North American scene—the baroque in Latin America had an aesthetic stronghold on the culture and tended to disdain the speech and customs of the masses— groundbreaking trends and crazes could be found in many of the musical genres in Latin America, especially in fashions born from African and Spanish American relations (discussed in chapter 7). When an elitist condescension prevailed in official and educated circles toward the vulgar masses (as in Leopoldo Lugones's *El payador* [1916]), music answered back with liberal notes, qualities, and intonations. "The vitality of the tango in the period when Lugones delivered his lectures," writes Angel Rama, "its intimate connections with the city's plebeian culture, its insouciant tendency to straddle the division between colloquial orality and clumsy writing, its distance from urban high culture, and more than anything else, its uncontainable popularity, made it impossible to incorporate immediately into the rigid parameters of the lettered city."[4] In its evolution in the lower-class districts (the *orillas flacas,* the "shallow outskirts") of Buenos Aires and Montevideo—packed with immigrants and blacks—the distinctive music and dance of the tango captured the explosive possibilities that existed in black and Hispanic collaborations. Prohibited from other means of communication, peasants and slaves throughout the Americas would use music as a vehicle of self-definition and self-assertion in the face of numerous threats to their existence.

As the twentieth century progressed, various artists on the *orillas* of Europe and America began to consider and utilize the shared struggles and shared aesthetics—especially in music, dance, and folklore—of black and Hispanic traditions. Alejo Carpentier, Jelly Roll Morton, Richard Wright, Langston Hughes, and Miles Davis, to name a few, examined many of the contiguous patterns in black and Hispanic cultures or spoke of the tinges of Spain in black music. Lorca and Ellison echoed many of these tendencies.

It seems to me that black and Hispanic crops of music and spirituality were received with so much enthusiasm in the twentieth century for an obvious reason: there was a palpable hunger for soul food among many citizens of the modern world. In a world that was famished for and lacking in spiritual resources, these kinds of musical and aesthetic revelries provided nourishment, a cornucopia of emotional and sacred sustenance. In the case of Ellison, he looked to his own traditions for this kind of food, while at the same time recognizing a similar diet, rich in music and dance, in Hispanic culture. And Lorca did the same with black American traditions; as we have seen, when he visited New York and Cuba, he was immediately seduced by black rhythms and creativity, and this made him feel at home in an otherwise foreign world. Lorca came to recognize the magnetism of *duende* at work in Afro-American and Afro-Latin cultures, as if the *duende* of deep song had accompanied the diaspora of African slaves to the New World, like the *Shekinah* following Israel into exile. In fact, Lorca revised his famous essay on deep song after listening to jazz and blues in Harlem in 1929.[5] And for his part, Ellison spoke of a "shock of recognition" after attending performances of flamenco in Madrid and Paris in 1954 (CE, 23). He subsequently wrote a fantastic piece, "Flamenco," for the *Saturday Review* in December 11, 1954, discussed below.

Though this chapter focuses on Ellison's view of soul, it's also part of a larger jam session on the notes shared by and collaborative efforts between Spanish and black American styles. With our ears tuned to the lower frequencies, as Ellison puts it, we might be surprised by the haunting, compelling sounds that determined and defined conceptions of soul in these cultures.

ELLISON'S AMERICAN SOUL

Since I ended chapter 4 with Lorca in New York, I pick up here in the heart of the city that became Ralph Ellison's home and later the birthplace of hip-hop. As discussed previously, New York was in a state of extreme distress when Lorca landed there. As he wandered the streets of New York, evidence of the broken times littered the streets, and he stumbled upon many of the lives gripped by the crisis of the age, especially black men and women who were struggling not only with economic depression, but also with the discrimination of their contemporaries. Outside the luminaries of African American culture, all Lorca noticed were the anemic spirituality and oppressive conditions of New

York, which made his poetry sound like some of the later scathing indictments of American life in hip-hop (e.g., by Public Enemy, NWA, Immortal Technique, and Nas).

By contrast, Ellison's outlook on New York was much more nuanced. Instead of expressing an unconditional negative judgment, Ellison stressed the ambiguities of America, the blue-gray shades instead of black and white. As an outspoken critic of black nationalism and all cultural equivalents, Ellison defended the "sacred principles" of American democracy in spite of its glaring shortcomings, hypocrisies, betrayals, and moral failures (GTT, 17, 26). He could be hard on American deficiencies, but he was equally "repelled by works of art that would strip human experience—including American experience—of its wonder and stubborn complexity," and this certainly included unqualified condemnations (GTT, 13). America was a complicated work of art for Ellison, with an extravagant variety of colors and beguiling polyphony of sounds; to denounce it without reservation was to miss these fantastic shades and gradations, as if one were color-blind and could only know a world of pale extremes.

On the matter of the soul, Ellison sought to complicate the idea in a similar way, making it resemble a polychromatic and multihued creature, with a capacity for chameleon-like alterations, adaptations, and improvisations. If he was intolerant of many forms of cultural nationalism, it was because of their tribal hostility toward the endless variety of human identity, toward otherness without and within. With their aggressive and brash pieties, cultural nationalists were quick to categorize, name, and stereotype, and in the process they desecrated and diminished the mysteries of the soul. Cultural nationalism simply smelled wrong for Ellison, "an odor rank of enclosed rooms of the mind."[6] With their dogmatic assertions of racial purity and homogeneity, the nationalists closed the curtains and locked the doors to the intricacies and differences that constitute human identity, creating a stale odor in a room that never opened itself to other voices, sights, and smells.

In contrast to this "puritan" version, Ellison's American soul is representative of the patterns of *mestizaje* throughout the Americas. Pregnant with odd fragments from cultures and religions far and wide, this sort of soul is a multicolored mosaic of mysterious gods, angels, demons, and God knows what else. Or if not a mosaic, Ellison's soul is something like Jorge Luis Borges's library of Babel, stacked with books that encompass the whole universe in its infinite variations and endless permutations. It contains a whole cosmos, as Whitman famously said:

> I am of old and young, of the foolish as much as the wise . . .
> Of every hue and trade and rank of every caste and religion,
> Not merely of the New World but of Africa Europe or Asia, a wandering savage. . . .
> I resist anything better than my own diversity.[7]

Like Whitman's wandering savage or the perpetual wandering of the protagonist in *Invisible Man* (who is kept running throughout the novel), Ellison was always restless in his search for the right note that would capture the diverse hues, ranks, and castes of American life. Fearing being confined and caged in, he advanced a "social mobility of intellect and taste" that would explore American identity like the original pioneers of the New World, all strangers in a strange land, having to re-create their identities out of the meager circumstances of their surroundings (GTT, 9). Based on his own experience of life on the frontier (in Oklahoma), Ellison settled on images of human nature that were provisional and inconclusive, images that epitomized the trailblazing spirit of American explorers.

In his musical and literary work, Ellison always tried to capture these rambling patterns—similar to the way the howling and whistling of the blues later tried to capture the sound of trains departing for the West and setting out toward the great, orgiastic future. Standing at railroad crossings, "where the Southern cross the Dog," Ellison conjured frontier energy, change, movement, action, and unlimited possibility like a blues musician. For Ellison, as for Houston Baker, the blues musician was skilled at reproducing and reinventing the raw energy of the locomotive and consequently the energy of America: "Afro-Americans responded to the railroad as a meaningful symbol offering both economic progress and the possibility of aesthetic expression. This possibility came from the locomotive's drive and thrust, its promise of unrestrained mobility and unlimited freedom. The blues musician at the crossing became an expert at reproducing or translating these locomotive energies."[8]

Learning from these thrusts and vibrations, Ellison celebrated the unlimited potential of America, what it could become instead of what it was. Even more than the blues, jazz has been the standard example of this potential, and Ellison saw it as America's signature sound. He detected in jazz music American impulses: the rapid-fire improvising, extemporizing, and riffing on classic customs and conventions; the introduction of hot, unrestrained imaginings to frozen ways; the dream of freedom; and homage to the new. Jazz embodied everything ingenious about America in the way it shook off the tired, dead hand of the past and replaced it with the manual dexterity of a great pianist or trumpeter who is quickened by the winds of change. Instead of demonstrating servile fidelity to premeditated scores and compositions, jazz would bring spontaneous and mercurial inspirations to music and make possible sudden breakthroughs in aesthetics and spirituality. In this creative process, the once mummified hand of tradition was reanimated and brought back to life, so that new, previously unheard possibilities of sound were fashioned, and the "sound of surprise" (that characteristic sound of jazz) blazed its way into the inner sanctum of the soul.[9] For Ellison, America always remained an experiment in the state of becoming, a burst of polyphonic and polyrhythmic vibes; a fantastic symphony of various scales and harmonic structures; and an elegance adopted from black, Indian, European, Spanish, French, and countless other traditions (GTT, 317). It had so much potential and gave so much reason for hope.

SOUL: THE TRAGICOMIC VISION

Although there is an extraordinary, Gatsby-like capacity for hope exhibited in Ellison's work, *optimism* is certainly the wrong word for it. In fact, Ellison's version of "soul" is propped up by the flying buttresses of both tragedy and comedy. It swings wildly between the two, like the swinging rhythms of jazz in Stanley Crouch's eloquent description: "What I refer to is the expression of sorrow or melancholy in a melodic line that is contrasted by a jaunty or exuberant rhythm, that combination of grace and intensity we know as swing. In jazz, sorrow rhythmically transforms itself into joy, which is perhaps the point of the music: joy earned or arrived at through performance, through creation."[10] In identifying these oscillations of sorrow and exuberance in jazz, Crouch taps into what Ellison named "soul." Crouch essentially parses and explains Ellison's grammar of soul, noting the way a high-spirited rhythm can transform a melancholic line into a stirring and uplifting performance. Here and elsewhere, Crouch takes cues from Ellison on when and how to add tragic and comic elements in the right proportions. An excessive focus on one element could ruin the rhythm. If tragic lessons are erased from memory, we end up with banal and artificial sounds, like elevator music, a ditty for advertising, or the most trifling forms of pop music; at the same time, without the comic sense we will be left with cheerless and drab sounds, music that turns the living soul into stone and causes it to sink and drown in gloom. For the soul to grow to its fullest temple-like potential, Ellison required elements of each: the comic sense would be a leavening grace to lighten the gravity of suffering, allowing the American soul to rise to its fullest potential. With both ingredients in the right balance, soul is attained, a kind of multigrain bread of life.

Ellison's definition of soul is key to my study: "It is its ability to articulate this tragic-comic attitude toward life that explains much of the mysterious power and attractiveness of that quality of Negro American style known as 'soul.' An expression of American diversity within unity, of blackness with whiteness, soul announces the presence of a creative struggle against the realities of existence" (GTT, 100). As we can see here, Ellison's concept of soul is born from the conjunction of tragedy and comedy; it skates and slides between the two like the careening legs of James Brown, carrying us from the Apollo Theater to the church, from barrelhouses to the bedroom. In the process—one of the many lessons of the resilient history of black music in America—it displays, even flaunts, an existential toughness and ability to survive no matter the troubles it sees. It's no wonder that Ellison speaks of an "apprenticeship" when educating us on soul: "Here it is more meaningful to speak, not of courses of study, of grades and degrees, but of apprenticeship, ordeals, initiation ceremonies, of rebirth" (SA, 208).

As an apprenticeship and initiation by fire, soul cannot be achieved in a scholastic manner; it requires the kind of verve, daring, courage, resilience, and shrewdness shown by the main character in Ellison's *Invisible Man*. Though the protagonist is a scholarship recipient, his real education occurs outside the walls of the university, in the course of the numerous "battles royal" and contests of nerve that mark his life. He ends up living in an underground room—he speaks of being "clubbed into the cellar," in point of fact—and must find his voice and perspective in this confined basement (SA, 57; IM, 572). The narrative begs for allegorical elaboration. Whether one is driven into the underground like this young man or ingested by a whale like Jonah, Ellison implies that being black in America automatically puts one in the darkest dungeons of life, so that the gestation of soul will have to occur in Sheol-like spaces, in the face of death. Thus, there is a sepulchral or mausoleum-like quality to the cellar that Ellison's invisible protagonist must enter and endure before he can be reborn, as if he were a seed that must fall and sink into the earth before germinating and blooming. (Early Christian baptisteries were shaped like mausoleums with this exact logic in mind.)[11]

Besides possessing this phoenix-like ability to raise black lives from the ashes, Ellison's concept of soul also casts a dark shadow over the American psyche. By speaking from the American underground, Ellison adds a blues-like color and prophetic edge to his concept of soul; it is a force of dissent against vain and jingoistic versions of American greatness. Ellison's "soul" is not unlike biblical understandings—vital spirit, life force, or essential self—but he clearly adds the particular shibboleths of black history and culture to the religious account. Consistent with many romantic portraits, as discussed in chapter 1, "soul" is accordingly a vital spirit and life force but now applied to African American traditions, a symbol of the "spirit of a race," to quote José Vasconcelos (1882–1959).[12]

Seen as the tragicomic attitude of African American culture (blending high and low culture, as well as the sorrowful and hopeful, in black history), the constitution and complexion of soul in Ellison juxtapose a variety of incongruent fragments. At times, his emphasis falls on the comic ingenuity and spiritual resilience of black culture, its indefatigable spirit of resistance; at other times, he invokes the tragic sense as homage to the defining impact of woes and griefs on the black experience in America. Faced with American refusals to recognize past and present wrongdoings, Ellison invokes tragic features as a way of placing the unperturbed conscience of America on trial, dragging it in front of a jury and marking it in bloody red. In lieu of scarlet letters, though, Ellison etches the American soul with burning crosses, dark shadows, and foul crimes, all with the aim of blackening the simple daylight of American narratives (GTT, 246). He had learned enough from his Calvinist forebearers to know that sin was aggressive and implacable, that the wolf, the snake, and the hog were not wanting in the American soul.[13] And he had also learned what many Puritan divines were reluctant to acknowledge: that even the Christian story could be conscripted in campaigns of prejudice and violence and be employed in the service of wolfish ends; that our country had the potential, to quote Harriet Beecher Stowe, of being ruined by pious white people.[14]

However, Ellison thought that once these sins and tragedies have been confronted, America can become worthy of its highest ideals, that America can give birth to a democratic code that graces and dignifies the most abased souls. This dream was built from the same theological stuff as Melville's vision:

If, then, to meanest mariners, and renegades and castaways, I shall hereafter ascribe high qualities, though dark; weave round them tragic graces; if even the most mournful, perchance the most abased, among them all, shall at times life himself to the exalted mounts; if I shall touch that workman's arm with some ethereal light; if I shall spread a rainbow over his disastrous set of sun; then against all mortal critics bear me out in it, thou just Spirit of Equality, which hast spread one royal mantle of humanity over all my kind! Bear me out in it, thou great democratic God![15]

In ascribing high qualities and exalted graces to the meanest lives, Ellison followed Melville's precedent, but with an obvious concern for black castaways and renegades in American life. He, too, used words and lyrics to spread a rainbow over all of God's creatures, especially those who have only known the deluge, only the "disastrous set of the sun." He aimed for a wholly American style of writing, mingling the high and low and dignified and colloquial speech. Just as the American Renaissance adopted popular idioms, especially the religious rhetoric of the revivals, Ellison sought to add black experiences and black vernaculars to the table of American literature, elbow to elbow with the boisterous multitudes, the roughs and rowdies of this New World (SA, 165).[16] He wanted to play the game "dozens" with American literature and bring "cursing vocabularies," "exalted praying," "shouting and playing the blues," and even "the limping walks affected by Negro hustlers" to a broader, more widespread audience (SA, 158). He wanted to celebrate the "rich babel of idiomatic expression" and wordplay of young black kids, which "would make the experimental poets, the modern poets, green with envy" (SA, 103; GTT, 67).

Though Ellison was referring to a wide variety of black language arts—from the blues and various proverbs to preaching and street idioms—we might take his statements as an eloquent prophecy of what was to come in rap music (GTT, 66; SA, 149). He was speaking of the linguistic ingenuity—"shit, grit, and mother wit"—that matured and incubated in the heat of "dismembering pressures" (IM, 176). He was also talking about the moments of creativity and transcendence that can be won on the battle lines when the enemy seems close to victory. In short, he was referring to the grace to be discovered in the grinding teeth of tragedy:

> Any people who could endure all of that brutalization and keep together, who could undergo such dismemberment and resuscitate itself, and endure until it could take the initiative in achieving its own freedom is obviously more than the sum of its brutalization. Seen in this perspective, theirs has been one of the great human experiences and one of the great triumphs of the human spirit in modern times. . . . So, let's not forget that the great tragedies not only treat of negative matters, of violence, brutalities, defeats, but they treat them within a context of man's will to act, to challenge reality and to snatch triumph from the teeth of destruction. (GTT, 287–88)

As I have been discussing, "soul" in Ellison's writing is the bravura or elegance or panache that emerges from these triumphs over suffering; for him, black music was one of the finest examples of this capacity. By parlaying threadbare opportunities into cultural achievements of the highest order, black musicians would become quintessential exemplars of the soul's ability to resuscitate itself after experiences of degradation and death.

THE BLUES AND *DUENDE*

For Lorca and Ellison, in short, music was the purest language of the soul. Better than other forms of understanding, music enables us to express complex ideas and emotions when speech alone is inadequate. The soul, *duende,* and of course God, are all examples of such complex, ineffable notions: with each we are faced with mysterious realities that cannot be fully explained. Lorca's definition of the *duende,* "a mysterious power which everyone senses and no philosopher can explain," fits this blueprint, as do Ellison's stabs at explaining the meaning of the soul (DS, 43). As a language of "turgid, inadequate words," the blues probes the soul in this way, expounding on it with certain tones, rhythms, moods, slurs, and harmonic structures, trusting in intuitions more than rational arguments (IM, 443). For both Lorca and Ellison, language must be carried to its furthest limits, until it is necessary to surrender speech to the vocal qualities of a musical instrument or to the kind of horn-like lines and wordless syllables evident in, say, Armstrong's scat singing or Southern rap's melodic shouts, bellows, and croons.

But since we are speaking of gifted writers, Ellison and Lorca naturally believed that something can be said about each of the three concepts before the sentences and syntax begin to crack and crumble. In this regard, it is obvious that they embraced some form of interpretation and explanation—albeit poetic, lyrical, provisional, and experimental. Ellison's definition of the blues is a case in point: "The blues is an impulse to keep the painful details and episodes of a brutal experience alive in one's aching consciousness, to finger its jagged grain, and to transcend it, not by the consolations of philosophy but by squeezing from it a near-tragic, near-comic lyricism. As a form, the blues is an autobiographical chronicle of personal catastrophe expressed lyrically" (SA, 78–79). In this version of the blues, the memory of suffering is not only kept alive against the destructive forces of amnesia (the enemy of wisdom, in Plato), but it is also carefully, almost lovingly, recalled and evoked. The music of the blues recalls suffering the way Mexicans, according to Octavio Paz, recall death: "The Mexican is familiar with death. He jokes about it, caresses it, sleeps with it, celebrates it. It is one of his favorite toys and his most stead-fast love."[17] The way Mexicans mourn or joke about death, blues music caresses and succors the memory of loss or catastrophe. The jagged grain of the blues—the long history of slavery and its malevolent aftermath—is fingered by a blues artist like the beads on a rosary. As a secular prayer of sorts, the blues is surely seeking transcendence, but only—as in Lorca's *duende*—through the corporeal experiences of people on earth. What Peter Guralnick says about soul music holds true for its ancestor in the blues: "We should always remember that soul music could stink as bad as the nastiest blues, could offer redemption, like the church, only after acknowledging the basest of human needs."[18]

There is a rich festival of meanings in the blues, whether as prayer or complaint or groan or dirty grind, which explains its extraordinary impact on so many musical genres in America. (Without the blues, there would be no jazz, rock 'n' roll, R & B, funk, soul, or hip-hop.) The blues is a great river that breaks off into numerous streams and eddies of emotion, into mellow pools of tenderness or steamy vortexes of passion. Sometimes in jest, sometimes in elegy, the blues transcends the brute experience of suffering not by philosophical abstraction, but by a tragic-comic lyricism, according to Ellison. The blues, when sad, can affect a sorrowful, down-hearted strain like the funeral processions in New Orleans in which the horns toll and the drums grieve. When the mood is comical and festive, the blues can sound like the music of the garden of earthly delights: sensual, ecstatic, Dionysian, irreverent, mocking, and funny.

The range of these emotions can be explained in light of the onomato-poeia that clearly influenced the blues. The blues might mimic a wide spectrum of sounds and feelings: the guttural, frantic sound of maternal lamentation; the rumbling, tumbling, clattering, whistling sound of a train; the soul-testing cries and wails of unrequited, frustrated love; the warbling loneliness of a bird without her mate; or even the bumping and grinding of human sensuality. The earth has music for those who listen, George Santayana once wrote, and the blues artist, it seems, excelled at listening, parodying, and re-creating the sounds of the earth.

By re-creating the harmonies and dissonances of life in the American South, the blues would swing and groove to its logic, outside the parameters of mathematical reasoning and its unbending geometric lines. In lieu of theoretical solutions to tragic predicaments, deep song and the blues provide an outlet for troubles that would otherwise sink the soul if they couldn't be released to the winds. In releasing these emotions, in throwing them overboard, the blues stave off the ruin of the entire ship, as in the story of Jonah or Iphigenia in Aeschylus's *Agamemnon*. Catastrophe can only be averted, the story goes, if something is sacrificed, and in the blues, it is the pent-up torment and inner demons that must be exorcized.

Because music, theology, and tragedy each grapple with enigmas and conundrums that overwhelm the modest resources of the human mind, each one of them honors the apophatic insight that there are things in our world that are unspeakable, like the deepest, blackest suffering, like the spark of the soul, and like God's name. If inscrutability is a key signature of these genres, the greatest foe is the Oedipus-like presumption that intelligence can solve the riddles of life, as Oedipus boasted in the case of the Sphinx. In his handling of this myth, Sophocles warns his age—the age of the Greek enlightenment—of the hubris in depriving life of its shadows and mysteries, and in denying the gods and prophets proper reverence: "Zeus and Apollo know," the chorus sings, "they know, the great masters, of all the dark and depth of human life" (*Oedipus Rex* 561–62).

In their own way, blues artists also know this truth, these great masters, and like the Greek tragedians, they also resort to myth and music when the soul wishes to plumb the dark and depth of human life. When handling suffering, for instance, the blues artist turns explicitly to myth to make sense of it all—hence the fables of hellhounds and blue devils in the music (obviously akin to the *duende* in Lorca). Indeed, it is worth remarking here that the blues as such (distinct from the music) are often personified as menacing, foreboding creatures. Albert Murray begins his conversation in *Stomping the Blues* with references to baleful spirits, haunting demons, ancestral curses, and so forth. In this construction, the blues are personifications of the anguish that dogs human experience and degrades human dignity; they are synonymous with destructive, depressive forces, with figures that resemble T. S. Eliot's eternal footman, holding his coat with a snicker, a man with the look of death.[19] Consider the following examples of these personifications:

Blind Lemon Jefferson: "Black snake, mmmmm, black snake crawling in my room."[20]

Robert Johnson: "Got to keep moving, got to keep moving, / blues falling down like hail / and the days keep 'minding me, there's a hellhound on my trail."[21]

Son House: "Oh in my room I bowed down to pray / Oh I was in my room I bowed down to pray / Say the blues come 'long and they drove my spirit away."[22]

Little Brother: "The first time I met the blues, mama, they came walking through the wood / They stopped at my house first, mama, and done me all the harm they could / Now the blues got at me, Lord, and run me from tree to tree. / You should have heard me begging, 'Mister Blues, don't murder me!'"[23]

Whether in the form of snakes, hellhounds, or dark spirits, the blues can poison your blood, assault your dignity, drive you out of your home, and send you wandering with a troubled, worried mind. It can beat and batter you like a crooked cop; it can run you from tree to tree; or it can make you feel invisible and run-down like the protagonist of *Invisible Man* or like Louis Armstrong when he crooned, "What did I do to be so black and blue."

Even though blues music is hardly equivalent to social protest or sociological analysis (Ellison and Murray are both emphatic on this point), we would have to turn a deaf ear to not notice the indications of racism, persecution, and tyranny in many blues songs. When Little Brother cries out, "Mister Blues, don't murder me," we know not only that the blues in question is the devil in hot pursuit, but that he wears a badge of prejudice and persecution, perhaps is an officer of the law, a prison guard, a militia member, or part of a mob. We know that the soil and culture of the blues were tilled by a long history of subjugation and exclusion. Though these factors are rarely on the surface of the blues, we can hear grievances and grumbles on the edges of the notes, in whispered sighs, wailing chords, and verbal signifying. The music may sing of small, everyday details of individual lives, Ted Gioia contends, but there is a larger catastrophe in the background.[24]

That said, we would do blues music wrong if we ignored the bursts of life that ring throughout the music. With a guitar lick and a ragged, throaty voice, the music prevents misfortune from having the last word; it takes the grief out of the lyrics, as Toni Morrison puts it: "Misery colored by the greens and blues in my mother's voice took all of the grief out of the words and left me with a conviction that pain was not only endurable, it was sweet."[25] Like the greens and blues in this mother's voice (a character in *The Bluest Eye*), the blues is a taste of the bittersweet flavors of human life, and it has healing properties. It can extract poisonous venom from the blood of its victim like the bronze snake of Moses—

gaze and listen, and you just may be healed. Something like this happened to King Saul; we are told that in the years before David became king, he once visited a deeply troubled Saul and soothed him with his music. (Recall that David was a masterful musician, elegist, and psalmist.) "And so, when the evil spirit of God was upon Saul, David would take up the lyre and play and Saul would find relief, and it would be well with him and the evil spirit would turn away from him" (1 Sam. 16:23). We might imagine that David played a psalm to drive away the evil spirit that had settled on Saul. If a psalm is, as Robert Alter says, "an act of chanting or singing, rhythmically and regularly, to implore, to admonish, to reflect, and above all, to celebrate," then we can imagine that David intoned or chanted one that was a wild mixture of these themes, a psalm that was prayer and threnody, lullaby and praise.[26] Whatever it was, we know that when David composed these elegiac, blues-like psalms, he was already conjuring the spirit of the blues.

However preoccupied with loss, disappointment, and deprivation, then, blues music is played to cleanse, not pollute, the atmosphere of the overcast blue of the air. The music is more than the color of a sullen, haggard mood like the broken blue guitarist in Picasso's painting; agony is only one of the garments in its multicolored wardrobe. Like the Mexican festival Día de los Muertos, the blues creates aesthetic, festive pleasure out of existential dread or physical degradation; the blues gathers and channels the kind of "subversive joy," to quote Cornel West, that has been a feature of black American artistic life: "This full-fledged acceptance of the body deems human existence a source of joy and gaiety. . . . Rhythmic singing, swaying, dancing, preaching, talking and walking—all features of black life—are weapons of struggle and survival."[27]

Soul is evident in these rhythmic movements of the body and tongue: the bobbing and dipping of the head, the clapping of hands, the pounding of feet, the swinging of arms, and the twirling and twisting of the tongue in speech and song. Through these strutting displays, a "full-fledged acceptance of the body" is inseparable from the boisterous life of the soul. No accusation of the soul's enmity with the body will stick here. Albert Murray adds a similar gloss on the philosophy of the blues:

> Sometimes the Blues Set in a dance program used to be referred to as the one that put the dancers, and in fact the whole event, into the alley, back out in the alley, out in the back alley, or way down in the alley. . . . Which meant that it was not only from the drawing room (and the over-extensions and over-refinements thereof) but was of its very essence the sound-equivalent of the unvarnished or unpainted back-alley actualities of every day flesh-and-blood

experience. . . . Which by the same token is also why the Blues Set is sometimes said to be the one that gets things back down from the cloudlike realms
of abstraction and fantasy to the blue-steel and rawhide textures of the elemental facts of the everyday struggle for existence.[28]

Read this way, the blues brings a realistic strain to the most glamorous
portraits of America and thus grounds us in a world far removed from
cloudlike realms of fantasy. With its rawhide textures; its unvarnished,
unschooled beauty; and its aching guitar sounds and voices that grunt,
slur, and wail, there can be no mistaking the blues for the ethereal,
refined music of the "drawing room." The blues finds its voice in the
alleyways of history, in the coarse company of transients, drifters, and
workers. With society's throwaways, in all their sweaty commonness
and flesh-and-blood actuality, the blues shouts out its high-spirited and
barbaric yawp.

Growing from the seeds of tragedy and comedy, and the desires of the
flesh and spirit, the blues eventually thrived in a variety of contexts: in
prisons and plantations, on chain gangs and in churches, in taverns and
dance halls, and in barrelhouses and juke joints.[29] Ted Gioia makes the
point that the blues has been proficient in knowing when and how to
modulate its sound to win over its audience; when it migrated from the
countryside of the Delta and entered urban spaces in Memphis and Chicago, for example, the blues became more festive. "The languorous melancholy of the Delta," he writes, "is replaced by a sunnier disposition;
the darker corners of the music are cast in sudden illumination; songs
aim to move the audience's feet even more than their feelings, and a
holiday spirit prevails, an escape from drudgery and despair."[30] Murray
also insists on this more convivial and exuberant flavor of the blues. "On
occasion, the Bacchanalian music of Saturday Night Function becomes
forthrightly orgiastic, as everybody not only knows but expects. . . .
Accordingly, in addition to its concern with forthright confrontation and
expurgation, the Saturday Night Function also consists of rituals of resilience and perseverance through improvisation in the face of capricious
disjuncture."[31] As rituals of resilience and expurgation, these celebrations stared down the threats of physical and spiritual death and used
juicy, invigorating abandon to rout the evil spirits within and without.[32]
The blues, in Murray's reading, may be nocturnal but not macabre,
black but not despairing, tragic but not without the redeeming thrill of
comedy, dance, and Bacchanalian rapture.

In celebrating these same purgative dimensions of the blues, Ellison
naturally saw the music as an inspirational source of his literature, the

way it bottled black genius and black mojo for therapeutic purposes, the way it healed the wounds of gnawing futility or debasing sorrow, and the way it deposed the destructive demons of life and replaced them with sublime spirits. In his novels and essays, he was summoning blues music to help him write poetry out of the experience of being invisible (IM, 8). He was summoning it to help him give voice to black lives so frequently unsung and unvalued by mainstream America. "Ask your wife to take you around to the gin mills and the barbershops and the juke joints and the churches, Brother. Yes, and the beauty parlors on Saturdays when they're frying hair. A whole unrecorded history is spoken there, Brother" (IM, 471).

THE SOUL OF THE BLACK PREACHER

If there are unrecorded histories to be found in juke joints, barbershops, and gin mills, Ellison surely felt the same about the sacred liturgies of black Christianity. Ellison's novel *Juneteenth* takes up this motif, specifically the liturgy of the Word in the black church. This sprawling novel, likened to a jam session by Adam Bradley, treats the relationship between a former jazz musician turned preacher, Reverend Alonzo Hickman, and an orphaned white boy named Bliss.[33] Though the racial identity of Bliss is unclear (his physical features are unrevealing), he has been raised in the black church by Reverend Hickman. As the boy grows up, he eventually turns his back on the black community and becomes first a filmmaking charlatan and con man, then a racist senator named Adam Sunraider ("the most vehement enemy of their people in either house of Congress") (JT, xvi). The significance of this character for understanding America is plain: all Americans are partially black, like Bliss, "a marvelous child of Ishmaelian origin and a pariah's caste," but a host of moral evasions and historical subterfuges have erased this recognition from memory like a Lethean drink of forgetfulness or some kind of bleaching agent.[34] Black cultural traditions have seeped into the subsoil of American life, but for many they remain too embarrassing, so they are repressed and pushed down into the caverns of the subconscious. The result is a pale and pallid shadow of the true American soul, the American soul puritanized and whitewashed. The story of this orphaned child is thus also the story of America.

Though American life, seen through the figure of Bliss, tends to be evasive and outright mendacious about the matter of black blood in American veins ("ignorance is bliss"), Reverend Hickman plays the role of prophet and seer, with the uncanny ability to read the entrails of the

American soul. But Reverend Hickman is a prophet in the biblical sense as well, a messenger of the divine and master of the spoken Word. In the person and speech of a prophet, says Abraham Joshua Heschel, God rages and gives voice "to the silent agony, a voice to the plundered poor."[35] This characterization fits Reverend Hickman like a glove: God storms furiously in his preaching and confers the gift of tongues on the preacher, enabling him to speak on behalf of the poor and unseen in America. Though words come to him from some otherworldly source, the reverend knows how to skillfully manipulate them; he knows when to slow his roll, as if he is mimicking the billowy drowse of the sea, and then, suddenly, to speed up to the tempo of a race horse. He knows when to echo the quiet, muted elegance of Al Green, the windy equilibrium of Dizzie Gillespie, or the holy madness of James Brown. Each measure and pace is adroitly marshaled for the right purpose.

An example is the crucial sermon in the novel on the subject of Juneteenth (June 19, 1865, the day emancipation reached Texas). Reverend Hickman's sermon uses Ezekiel's story of the dry bones, but seen through the eyes of the black Israelites of America. When Ellison comes to this moment in the novel, the flow and rhythm of his prose swells and speeds up as if he is prefiguring the fast-paced flows of Busta Rhymes, Twista, or Krayzie Bone. He gathers the blistering breath of an inspired preacher or rapper, and he spits, scats, and whoops with the best of them. With his booming voice (he's known as "God's trombone"), the reverend stretches language until he moves speech "beyond words back to the undifferentiated cry" (JT, 117). The reverend is weaving and bending his tongue at this point like a master horn player suddenly dragged into the whirlwind of the *duende*, leaping into a higher register. The congregation is caught up, too, and they all experience a mystical unity, as if the Holy Ghost has them speaking in the same tongue, perfectly comprehensible to each other: a language of pure, fiery emotion. Reverend Hickman is preaching in a language of music so sweeping that they become enraptured by the sound bursting from the preacher's mouth:

> We had mourned and rejoiced and rejoiced and moaned and he had [another preacher in this revival] released the pure agony and raised it to the skies. So I had to give them transcendence. Wasn't anything left to do but to shift to a higher gear. I had to go beyond the singing and the shouting and reach into the territory of the pure unblemished Word. I had to climb up there where fire is so hot it's ice, and ice so cold it burns like fire. Where the Word was so loud that it was silent, and so silent that it rang like a timeless gong. I had to reach the Word within the Word that was both song and scream and whisper. (JT, 139)

In words that reach him from a transcendent source, the reverend finds the still point of the turning world, where the sway of logic fails and where contradictions—hot/cold, music/silence, stillness/dancing—are metaphorical markers for otherworldly truths. This is Reverend Hickman's rain dance for a community that has suffered a drought. He dances and chants and grunts with rollicking delight in language, until the language spills over into transcendence, overflowing, torrential, with words that are excessive but without ostentation, are common without vulgarity, the perfect consort dancing together.[36] This preaching Moses climbs high up Mount Sinai and brings his people the Word engraved by fire, the Word that is song, scream, whisper, and cry all at once—and of course, praise.

In fact, on this celebratory occasion of Juneteenth—when the emancipation of American slaves is related to the Christian dream of resurrection—praise is the most fitting description (JT, 116). The time of mourning has given way to a time of exultation, as the people, once "scattered in the ground for a long dry season," are now freed from death (JT, 125). In Ezekiel's story, in the valley of dry bones, the Israelites lie buried beneath the fallow, scorched earth, dead to any future. In this sterile condition, with the Israelites gnashing their teeth on the dry clay of the earth, a miraculous, moistening wind begins to stir until they began to hear a whispering voice, which is the Word of God calling them to life. God breathes his spirit into the dry bones and puts flesh and sinews on wasted skeletons. Now, Reverend Hickman shouts, we can walk, run, and, yes, strut once again: "'That's the way. Now walk on back. Life your knees! Swing your arms! Make your coattails fly! Walk! And him strutting me three times around the pulpit across the platform and back. . . . And if they ask you in the city why we praise the Lord with bass drums and brass trombones tell them we were rebirthed dancing, we were rebirthed crying, affirmation of the Word, quickening our transcended flesh'" (JT, 127).

Ellison must have recalled from childhood the style and form of black sermons, because he summons them so well, with words that radiate with swagger, eloquence, and emotion. Through the voice of Hickman, he modifies Ezekiel's allegory the way the slave spirituals once modified the stiff hymns of Protestantism into more supple inflections, syncopations, and call and response patterns.[37] The preacher gives his congregation the rush of the *ruah* (spirit, breath, wind, soul) that once quickened the dead flesh of the Israelites. This "trombone of God" becomes an instrument of a heavenly muse, and everyone within earshot is a frenzied witness. The spirit has come to make the congregation shake and quiver like leaves in a violent storm, like Dorothy's house in the heart of the tornado in Kansas. The *duende* has arrived with house-wrecking power to produce "wild exaltation, the rending of veils, grown woman thrown into trances, screaming, tearing their clothing. All that great inarticulate moaning and struggling" (JT, 112).

With so much joy, laughter, and transcendence in this concert of language, one might wonder if this is another vision of Christian triumphalism, the kind of theology that skims over tragedy. It is closer to the truth, however, to say that the reverend's preaching (like Ellison's brooding over soul) is constantly navigating the terrain where the tragic joins the comic, celebrating the resurrection, while clinging to the battered and bruised body of Christ:

> On a cross on a hill. His arms spread out like my mammy told me it was the custom to stretch a runaway slave when they gave him the water cure. When they forced water into his mouth until water filled up his bowels and he lay swollen and drowning on the dry land. Drinking water, breathing water, water overflowing his earthbound lungs like a fish drowning of air on the parched dry land. . . . There He is, with the spikes in His tender flesh. Nailed to the cross. . . . His face twitching and changing like a field of grain struck by a high wind—hanging puzzled. Bemused and confused. Mystified and teary-eyed. (JT, 151–52)

Those who prefer the dark side of Ellison's soul get it here. Consistent with black riffs on evangelicalism, he removes the sentimentality of some forms of Christianity so that the tragic essence of the tale of Christ stands out clearly.[38] Now Ellison gives us a psalm of abandonment and anguish; this is the crucified Christ who is hanged in solidarity with a tortured slave, Christ spread out on a tree to become, as Billie Holiday sang in her careworn, smoky voice, "strange fruit hanging from a tree." Here Ellison gives us an image of the crucifixion as the unending agony that spans the centuries and reaches into America's slave era and beyond. "Jesus will be in agony until the end of the world," Pascal writes, "there must be no sleeping until that time."[39] If Ellison's preacher has a voice like a trombone or a clashing cymbal, it echoes Pascal's sentiment and seeks to disturb the pervasive somnolence of many Americans, to awaken vigilance to the agonies endured by countless victims of crucifixion, bodies twisted and broken like those tortured icons in Latin American churches. In fact, in this sermon the preacher's words are exactly icon-like: he paints a picture for his congregation to help them imagine the spikes piercing Jesus's flesh, the twitching face, the stretched-out body, the inability to breathe.

In theatrical and poetic forms, his homily gives voice to the "silent agony" of Jesus and all innocent sufferers.

In these examples of soul drawn from the black church, the *duende* makes its appearance in the rhapsodizing, oracular voices of preacher and choir. Ellison gives us the glory of the Word here, a view of Christianity that revels in verbal elegance. In Reverend Hickman, the Protestant voice is substituted for the visual splendor of Catholic theater, art, and ritual in Lorca's Spain. Instead of the sumptuous spectacle of Catholicism, he gives us a cathedral of language that brings us to our knees and arouses reverence. He gives us the word as sacrament and pageantry, bursting forth in the melodious rhetoric of a *duende*-possessed preacher, the word as a spark thrown into a tinderbox.

While Ellison aims for the sobriety of realistic prose in this novel and others, there are many moments like this in which the prose becomes "inebriated" on words. Under these Dionysian and modernist inspirations, literary realism undergoes an expansion—Ellison calls it "dilated realism"—to account for everything surprising, excessive, and magical about human experience.[40] Ellison seems to have required this capacious imagination to translate the wonders and terrors of black history into an appropriate literary form. Like many of his generation (surrealists, magical realists, and modernists), for him realism was too much of a straitjacket, prohibiting the full extension of the imagination, preventing the play and pirouettes of the mind. Many writers of that generation looked for alternatives to realism in other cultures and found in Spain a cupbearer for eccentric and intoxicating inspirations. Ellison was no different. He came to see Spanish customs, music, and dance as cousins of black American styles. They became an important ingredient in his cauldron of soul.

ELLISON ON SPAIN

When Ellison visited Madrid in 1954, he recognized something familiar and ravishing in flamenco, as if it were another branch in the Dionysian family tree that shaded his own culture (CE, 23).[41] True to his understanding of soul, Ellison stressed the tragic-comic dimensions of flamenco, the way it flaunts and defies suffering with joyful license, erotic play, and ostentatious beauty. In his reading flamenco, with its crazy mixture of Iberian, gypsy, Byzantine, Arabic, Hebraic, and Moorish/African elements, is a cosmos unto itself, and one can hear the distant corners of the globe in its piercing cries and affected postures. Both primitive and modern, flamenco is foreign to the separations of tragedy and comedy, sacred and profane, emotion and reason, theory and practice that have become widespread in the modern, Western world. It is, Ellison wrote, a "folk art which has retained its integrity and vitality through two centuries during which the West assumed that it had, through enlightenment, science and progress, dispensed with those tragic, metaphysical elements of human life which the art of flamenco celebrates" (CE, 22).

Heedless of modern creeds of progress and scientific knowledge, flamenco flaunts and revels in cultural styles now considered out of step with European developments, as I noted in chapter 4. If syncopation means a disturbance or interruption of the regular flow of rhythm, flamenco is this disturbance, a discordant and jagged note that is at odds with highbrow aesthetical norms. Flamenco gives expression to all the fragments and debris that have been trampled underfoot and forgotten in the new world order.[42] Inherent in the codes and contortions of flamenco is the sound of marginalized and colonized cultures, the sound of insolence and defiance. In this regard, Ellison saw the Spanish/gypsy/Moorish folk cultures as Caliban-like companions of blacks in North America:

> It can be just as noisy and sweaty and drunken as a Birmingham "breakdown;" while one singer "riffs" or the dancers "go to town" the others assist by clapping their hands in the intricate percussive manner called *palmada* and by stamping out the rhythms with their feet. . . . Great space, echoes, rolling slopes, the charging of bulls, and the prancing and galloping of horses flow in this sound much as animal cries, train whistles, and the loneliness of night sound through the blues. The nasal, harsh, anguished tones heard on these sides are not the results of ineptitude or "primitivism"; like the "dirty tone" of the jazz instrumentalist, they are the result of an aesthetic which rejects the beautiful sound sought by classical Western music. (CE, 23–24)

In the earthy harmonies of the blues or flamenco—collected, as Ellison says, from the sounds of charging bulls, galloping horses, nightingales in mourning, train whistles, and so forth—Western conceptions of beauty are destabilized and forever altered. Through these earthquakes of rhythm and swing, things fall apart; the center cannot hold.

Approximating the same fluctuations of tragic and comic notes in the blues or jazz, flamenco writhes and dances with the most excruciating troubles of life while mocking despair and despondency. Flamenco is a graphic illustration of Ellison's vision of soul, simultaneously an art of dying and an art of living. "In its more worldly phases the flamenco voice resembles the blues voice, which mocks the despair stated explicitly in the lyric, and expresses the great human joke directed against the universe, that joke which is the secret of all folklore and myth: that though we be dismembered daily we shall always rise again" (CE, 24–25). In flamenco wails, cries, warbles, and trembling voices the singer sums up the sadness of life, but always with a concurrent clapping of hands, prancing of feet, and squashing of the blues.

When speaking of the *duende*-inspired priestess of gospel, Mahalia Jackson, Ellison could have been speaking of the range of ideas and emotions in flamenco, full as it is of Eastern sounds: "It is an art which depends upon the employment of the full expressive resources of the human voice—from the rough growls employed by blues singers, the intermediate sounds, half-cry, half-recitative, which are common to Eastern music; the shouts and hollers of American Negro folk cries; the rough-edged tones and broad vibratos, the high, shrill and grating tones which rasps one's ears like the agonized flourishes of flamenco; to the gut tones, which remind us of where the jazz trombone found its human source" (SA, 216). In celebrating Mahalia Jackson's ability to achieve rapid variations with the human voice, from rough growls and half-cries to tremulous vibratos and grating tones, Ellison is not only celebrating the power of music to hit upon a variety of human tones and desires; he is also describing his own portrait of an artist, someone who reaches for the full expressive resources of the human voice. His prose searches for the same range of human expression: It mimics the cadences of music in highbrow and lowbrow forms, in symphonic and orchestral arrangements, in shouts and hollers, in gutbucket laments and ecstatic highs. His prose gives us the human drama in dark shadows and luminous flashes, an image of the soul sketched with chiaroscuro brushstrokes.

If Ellison exploits the full range of possibility in the human voice and soul, he also attributes a similar range to American life. With his ability to paint the dark spots of the soul, Ellison's view of America is nothing like the self-righteous portraits of American exceptionalism: light without blackness, triumphalism without catastrophe, innocence without sin and guilt. If the American soul is a shining knight to the maidens of the world, Ellison knows it to be a quixotic knight, full of noble dreams and no less brash flaws and vices, a source of both good and harm in modern history. To continue with this analogy, Ellison's vision of soul has something of the tragic beauty of Cervantes's great novel: it is comprised of both transcendent and earthly impulses, joining together Don Quixote's lofty, ethereal flights of the imagination with Sancho Panza's pragmatic, guttural realism (after all, *panza* means gut or belly in Spanish). Ellison ultimately sought to give us a reason to love America the way Don Quixote loved Dulcinea even after he realized that she was neither young, nor beautiful, nor perfectly virtuous—he loved her in spite of her imperfections, a kind of gallantry stripped of delusions of grandeur.

ELLISON AND HIP-HOP IN NEW YORK

One might say that both Ellison and Lorca explored the strange regions of the soul in this quixotic manner, sailing into unknown parts of the human person the way earlier explorers sailed for Asia. In a sense, everything that was found in the Indies—dark-skinned Calibans, strange gods, savage landscapes, ravishing beauty, impossible creatures, and wondrous phenomena—could be found, as they saw it, closer to home in the soul, in its wild labyrinths and terrifying temples. If they differed on key matters, it was in their dissimilar judgments of the American experiment. Lorca arrived in New York and saw nothing but savage hordes glutted on human blood, offering sacrificial victims to the idols of gold and greed. And he inveighed against the situation the way his fellow countryman, Las Casas, once inveighed against the colonizers for ravaging and sacrificing Indians to the god of avarice. For Lorca, New York resembled Rome in the pages of an apocalyptic text ("whore of Babylon") or Rome after the barbarian invasions: spiritually in ruins and withered, in desperate need of a new Moses to arrive and wring water out of the dry rock of the city.

To Ellison, New York wasn't irredeemable; it merited criticism, just not perdition. In avoiding Lorca's apocalyptic vision of the new Rome on the one extreme, and the mythical, glorious vision on the other, Ellison believed that America combined republican promise with infernal betrayals and sins, perhaps something like Dante's portrait of Rome. In this way, Ellison placed America in purgatory, not in hell or heaven, and this enabled him to cling to hope—malice toward none, charity toward all—for some purgative fire that would incinerate American sins and fuel American ideals. Ellison tried his best, in other words, to shape and mold the American experiment into something more worthy of "that condition of man's being at home in the world which is called love and which we term democracy."[43]

In this Dantean spirit, Ellison's peregrine soul would begin its journey with a plunge downward into the hell and purgatory of America before it would ascend, with the power of love, to the light. Like hip-hop artists of our own day, Ellison took his readers into the street corners and dungeons of America and produced lyrical narratives out of the experiences of estrangement and invisibility before turning a bright light on suffering, imbuing it with the possibility of redemption. Black music is one of these lights for Ellison, and an antidote for the serpent's venom that threatens the blood of the soul. (Saint Ambrose's metaphor for the grip of sin, by the way.) In wildly unique ways, both Ellison and hip-hop echo the same lament heard from Robert Johnson: "I was standing at the crossroads, I tried to flag a ride. / Nobody seemed to know me, everybody passed me by."[44]

Ellison, of course, preferred songs of this sort to the G-Funk that came out of the Bronx. In his later years, Ellison recoiled from the new sounds emanating from boom boxes and rap stations, but if we follow his own contention that serpents have the ability to teach theology and worms can teach small earthly truths, we might reconsider some of Ellison's judgments of rap (GTT, 149). In reminding us to be wise as serpents, Ellison would give legitimacy to the kind of street knowledge that hip-hop has put on wax and broadcast throughout the world, a knowledge that teaches small earthly truths in big beats and brash lyrics. By burrowing, worm-like, into the American psyche and conscience—often through biting criticism of the Big Apple—hip-hop has continued Ellison's efforts to represent lives that have been confined to the underground and obscured in invisibility. Though Ellison operated with far greater decorum and propriety than the ghetto voices of hip-hop do, his lyrical and vernacular rhythms are responses to similar concerns and similar dreams.[45] More than Ellison would have conceded (and certainly more than his conservative disciples concede), much of what appears in his work can be found in the sounds and sentiments of hip-hop: the psychological scars of ghetto life; the pounding, conflicted anger; the wounding despair; the swaggering style and grace; the embittered lyrics and exploding beats; and no less, the resilient and robust joy.[46] When Big Boi, of Outkast fame, named his basement studio in Atlanta the Dungeon, he was sampling the spirit of Ellison and suggesting that he, too, will formulate plots and rhymes out of the stank and clay of the South, out of the underground experience of a young black man in the United States.

Though the generation of Ellison and Lorca was no doubt different from the hip-hop generation, some of the sounds, moods, and colors bleed together and speak eloquently of many of the festering wounds that continue to plague our contemporary situation. As we move on to reflection about hip-hop in the following chapters, the nature of these constantly reopened wounds is the main focus, but I want to keep in mind the configurations of soul in Ellison and Lorca, if only to appreciate some of the ancestral sources of the tortured soul of our own age. At the very least, we might learn that there were kindred melodies and beats playing in the minds of Ellison and Lorca, kindred ideas of soul or *duende*. As we have seen, they adopted the dialects of their respective tribes, but they also purified these tongues and raised them to higher, transcendent levels, where they eventually converged in similar patterns of beauty. Through Lorca singing and intoning deep song, with its laments and joys, its heart pierced with Ay!, and Ellison singing and crooning the blues, with its elegies and praises, its soul crying Amen!, their poetry and thoughts found the right beat in playing the music of the soul.

From Soul to Hip-Hop

The Rise of the Apocalypse

When prophecy fails, apocalypticism takes over.

—Ernst Kasemann

Born just like Christ, in the damn ghetto.

—Poor Righteous Teachers[1]

For many artists of the twentieth century, apocalypticism was the preferred style of the age. For all of its strange and surreal features, apocalypticism put its finger on the pulse of the century, sensing and identifying many of the conundrums, conflicts, and tortured histories of the modern world. In narrating the story of "deconstruction," for example, Jacques Derrida pointed to the end-times fury of the twentieth century, when everything—history, metaphysics, the Western conception of man—seemed to be ebbing into the night. "We had this bread of apocalypse in our mouths naturally, already, just as naturally as that which I nicknamed after the fact, in 1980, the 'apocalyptic tone in philosophy.'"[2] In a century that was reeling from mass graveyards as a result of world wars, totalitarianism, imperialism, and dire poverty in developing countries, many artists turned their scrambled minds to the bloodred sun of the apocalypse. Whether among European avant-garde writers, Latin American "magical realists," or African American artists living behind the iron curtain of Jim Crow racism, things seemed to be falling apart, so it was not surprising that a genre defined by intuitions and revelations of crisis would be seen as visionary.[3] In the blues, as early as the 1930s, Son House sounded the apocalyptic mood and began prognosticating an imminent end to "this old world."[4] In Alan Lomax's estimation, Son House's apocalyptic songs "channel[ed] the rage that fills all our hearts when we are unjustly and cruelly treated and cannot fight back."[5] Later on, other musicians chimed in: John Coltrane played his sax as if he were trying to blow it apart in an eschatological climax; Jimi Hendrix made the eerie whine of his guitar speak for the betrayed hopes of a generation; Bob Dylan used his howling, shrieking harmonica to capture the disappointments and terrors of his times; and of course, hip-hop rose out of the ghetto and embraced apocalyptic diction as the most fitting style for an age of mass incarcerations, drug epidemics, deadly violence, and gnawing nihilism.

Hip-hop, coming of age in a situation marked by turmoil, injustice, and spiritual discontent, is a child of our apocalyptic era. Though the stirrings of its body and spirit came from the music of soul, R & B, funk, blues, and jazz, it went much further than its predecessors into the modern heart of darkness. In hip-hop studies, this swerve from the music of the past is frequently traced to a rupture that occurred sometime between the civil rights era and the generations that immediately followed. Forced to dwell in the rubble of the dreams of the 1960s, the children who came of age in the late twentieth century became increasingly disenchanted with traditional values and claims of progress. From their ghetto-centric vantage point, a view through broken windows and ruined infrastructures, injustice had not disappeared as much as it had disguised itself in new forms. Nelson George and Mark Anthony Neal were among the first critics to call this the "post-soul" generation. "This story begins as another is ending," George wrote. "The first story is full of optimism and exalted ideas about humanity's ability to change through political action and moral argument. The next story, the plot we're living right now, is defined by cynicism, sarcasm and self-involvement raised to art."[6] Not surprisingly, the story of hip-hop in Nelson George's telling is rife with pessimism and the grammar of endings, as if hip-hop came into the world like an orphaned child, born out of the dearly departed aspirations of civil rights.

SOUL AND POST-SOUL

When we compare hip-hop with its immediate musical forerunners in R & B and soul music, the contrast is conspicuous. What strikes one in soul music is the feeling of unlimited possibility—the dream of freedom, in Peter Guralnick's words—that throbs and pulsates in the music.[7] Born in a context of flagrant segregation, soul music picked up the uninhibited ecstasies of gospel music and channeled them in new directions.

The music of the black church became a rich resource for soul artists, as they culled its energies and vibes and used them on behalf of civil rights aspirations. By mixing the electrified body and soul of the church with the profanity and sexuality of the blues, soul musicians produced a combustible formula that fueled the struggle for justice and equality. They produced an explosive art, one that invigorated and boosted the old liberal hope once described by Emerson: the liberation of American culture from the foreclosure of possibility.[8]

In this respect, soul music reveled in a "house wrecking" that not only made the soul come undone, but also threatened the white-picket fences that excluded and barred colored folks from belonging to the American dream. When we consider that a label like Stax Records, born in Memphis, or Muscle Shoals, born in Alabama, helped turn some of the whitest bastions of the post-Confederate south into vital centers of black music, the story of soul music looks rather astonishing and miraculous.[9] The sound waves produced by these labels—along with Motown, Atlantic, Fame, and others—had a remarkable, almost tsunami-like influence; inspired by these raging rivers of soul, racial barriers suddenly started to buckle and break, as different races began to wade and baptize themselves in black music, all to the horror of segregationists and racists. The surging ecstasy of the music led to the breakdown of inhibitions, the smashing of whatever impeded the cross-fertilization of music, culture, and human affections. In essence, something dangerous was afoot in the age of R & B and soul music, as the American soul began to move to savage jungle rhythms that were, in some judgments, equivalent to the rhythms of the devil. In short, an earthy, lowdown, miscegenated kind of soul was getting to white America (to paraphrase a 1967 article in *Rolling Stone*).[10]

What seems especially impressive about this musical achievement is the way it advanced the civil rights struggle through feeling and sound alone, by working the audience over until it was on the verge of rapture, until it felt so good you'd want to scream, in James Brown's sense. Soul music was an education in feeling and sentiment, one that enlarged the scope of American taste and affection for black sounds and experiences. Stax executive Al Bell put it succinctly: "When the white audience discovered us, we didn't get whiter, they got blacker."[11] Through a combination of exhortation and exhilaration, soul music seemed to catch the tenor of civil rights without needing words, distilling music down to its simplest essence and making it speak at a sonic level for the basic rights of oppressed groups in America. Rhythms and words and emotions were let loose to describe the specific burdens of color and to carry the emotion that Solomon Burke sang about: "I wish I knew how it would feel to be free."[12] By exposing the constricted and segregated souls of many Americans to these liberating and edifying emotions, black music instigated a cultural revolution that led to the recalibration of the American soul, tuning it to pick up previously unnoticed vibrations, aesthetics, and experiences. Daring and bold, the spirit of the music played its part in the marches and protests of the age. It was a music of agitation and affection all at once, and many young Americans, hungry for change and intercultural fellowship, turned to this soul food not only for spiritual nourishment, but also as an opportunity to release their dammed-up passions. Nathaniel Hawthorne's comment about nineteenth-century New England culture—that its feelings were less developed than its mind—seems to have remained true in America long into the twentieth century. Whatever else they did, R & B and soul music rocketed into U.S. culture as emergency relief to this underdeveloped condition.

As time marched on into the 1970s and 1980s, however, the pulse of soul music, along with its transcendent impulses borrowed from gospel music, began to weaken and waver in the face of new threats and traumas to the urban body politic. In some ways, the circumstances of American life became worse for those living on the peripheries of America, where the prison industrial complex grew to monstrous proportions, where drugs and violence assaulted family and communal bonds, and where civil rights' advances seemed to be aborted and arrested. The hope that Sam Cooke had expressed, "A Change Is Gonna Come," gave way to the foreboding fear that "ain't nuthin' changing." The civility, racial decorum, and good diction of Sam Cooke and his generation soon gave way to the insolent and foul language of street poetry and hip-hop; a polite "supper-club" brand of soul gave way to a grittier, roughneck soul; utopian visions gave way to dystopian allegories; and prophetic dreams of moral and social justice gave way to the dark and chilling hieroglyphs of apocalypticism. As if the tough circumstances of the age had broken the back of words and split the psyche of young kids, ghetto language assumed a new pattern: fractured, cracked, and staccato.[13]

Instead of the "end of metaphysics" discussed in academic circles of the late twentieth century—a preoccupation with the loss of epistemological assurances and certainties—these black and brown youths were rapping about the end of so many young lives in the hood, about the demise and decay of the inner cities of America: "[A]ny day could be your last in the jungle. Get murdered on the humble, guns'll blast, niggaz tumble."[14] In essence, the music of this black and brown youth culture struck a menacing, dangerous tone and came to represent tales of life in the deepest levels of an apocalyptic inferno, tales straight outta Compton. Jay-Z rapped in this tone when he described the bullet-riddled bodies of Dr. King and Malcolm X as violent parables and premonitions of the decades that would follow. "Everybody want to be the king till shots ring. You laying on the balcony with holes in your dream. Or you Malcolm Xed out, getting distracted by screams."[15] While these lines from "Most Kings" do not renounce the dreams of civil rights, they do lament their failure to prevent so many lives from getting "Xed out." As Jay-Z once said about the boys who appear in Basquiat's paintings—"they didn't grow up to be men, they grew up to be corpses, skeletons and ghosts"—Dr. King's dream met a grim fate in many ghetto communities and never was given the support to fully ripen.[16] And so it has been with civil rights in general: the legacy haunts most rappers like a ghost that demands recognition and appeasement, but it has remained spectral, has been unable to achieve a fleshly, incarnate, material existence. Out of these disappointments and frustrations, hip-hop emerged as a renegade voice that would spook and unnerve mainstream culture, a voice that delighted in the renegade role, but now as a renegade of culture and funk more than of politics (Afrika Bambaataa).[17]

Hip-hop brought about a linguistic insurrection, in which the polite decorum of civil rights was scorned for a new "wild style" that used words like a violent weapon against the forces of ghetto decay and urban blight. Rap artists started slangin' words as a matter of survival, as a way of battling the demonic forces and bleak circumstances that threatened their bodies and souls. Without many resources at hand, black and brown kids used poetry and beats as guerrilla warfare, ambushing the status quo with slick lines and deft jams.

This tectonic shift in American cultural history can be understood by considering the subtle yet revolutionary transition from the prophetic vision of civil rights/black power to the apocalyptic vision of hip-hop. Though there is most certainly continuity between the two—apocalypticism is on the same continuum as the prophetic heritage—apocalypticism emerged in the wake of the failures of prophetic oracles ("when prophecy fails, apocalypticism takes over"). Consequently, apocalypticism has often registered the dark mood of a culture in upheaval and disarray, in which even the prophets seem ineffective. Out of the leftover scraps and fragments of the prophetic message, apocalyptic texts manage to create something authentically new, though wilder and more frenzied than its prophetic forerunner.

Something similar can be said about hip-hop: it is spun and scratched to the jarring beats of apocalypticism, and this has made the vision of the human soul in this tradition appear more conflicted and tormented than ever before. Instead of simulating trains, as in the blues, or envisioning the tense dream of freedom buses, as in soul, hip-hop mirrors and adopts apocalyptic symbols as secret codes for its brand of poetic justice. The graffiti writing on subway trains—scribbled, surreptitious, cryptic, restless, rebellious—is its signature.

APOCALYPTIC THEMES IN HIP-HOP

Like the twisted lines of graffiti or the twisted moves of a break-dancer, the apocalyptic vision has often been a clairvoyant, if contorted, reflection of its age. Consider the book of Revelation: though it seems to reach our age from some foreign cosmos, it is less bewildering if we read it as a wartime text, written during a time of catastrophe, when Christians were suffering under the iron yoke of Roman rule.[18] The author of the book was an exile on the island of Patmos and describes himself as "John, a partner in your tribulation" (Rev. 1:9). Adela Collins argues that Revelation is best understood as a literature of trauma, with the Roman Empire cast as the great adversary of the book.[19] She identifies specific traumas that explain the book's tortured, byzantine representations: the destruction of the city of Jerusalem by the Romans; the emperor Nero's arrest and killing of Christians; the compulsive participation in the imperial divine cult; the death of an important member of the community, Antipas; the banishment and exile of the author; and more generally, the economic stress of the poorest people in the community.[20]

If we hold this litany of traumas before us, the book of Revelation becomes less bizarre. The pages and images of these scrolls gradually divulge some of their secrets when we read them as responses to the early threats and cataclysms faced by a particular Christian community. By deciphering these allegories, the reader is rewarded with a vision of what the author saw: an eerie world that seems to be on the throes of death, dogged and threatened by the minions of Hades (Rev. 6:8). The struggle for survival is intense and desperate in Revelation, as this small, colonized group of people is subjected to an infernal authority, "given authority over a fourth of the earth, to kill with sword, famine, pestilence, and by the wild animals of the earth" (Rev. 6:8). It takes little imagination to crack the code of this line: Rome is surely the culprit here, given authority to rape and pillage whomever it wills. Seen from this anticolonial perspective, Revelation is a harrowing portrait of Roman rule, and it registers the events of its time like a trail of tears.

While the circumstances of hip-hop are obviously different from those that surface in Revelation, hip-hop has often raided apocalyptic motifs as a way of naming and depicting the dangers and distresses of its own world. Even when biblical texts are largely invisible, hip-hop has appropriated many of the tortured images of apocalypticism, including the genre's beleaguered, arcane style. In twisting the texts' speech patterns to approximate racial, class, and social burdens, hip-hop has caught the spirit of apocalyptic writing: harried and harassed, tormented and violent, edgy and stressed, with moments of overwhelming grace tangled with violence. Michael Dyson explains the logic of such convergences: "But a society rife with inequalities—of race, gender, class, social status, sexuality, geography, and age—will produce legends that funnel social critique even as they organize collective memory, articulate social vision, and project communal values."[21]

Tupac Shakur's debut album, *2Pacalypse Now*, and Public Enemy's album *Apocalypse 91* contain classic examples of these legends. "Can't Truss It," for example, which appears on PE's *Apocalypse 91*, tells the story of the slave trade and its enduring influence in black America. The bass is deep, hard, and thumping in the song, with Chuck D's baritone voice—gruff, surly, and truculent—perfectly matching the beat. The rapper's voice is in harmony with the percussive richness of African musical textures, and more significantly, in solidarity with the mutinous attitude of pounding drums. The story, Chuck D implies, calls for this attitude, for a defiance that matches the big, brash sound of the beats. From his perspective, the tale resembles the tribulations of Armageddon:

> Kickin' wicked rhymes like a fortune teller
> 'cause the wickedness by Jack,
> where everybody is divided and sold
> for the liquor and the gold
> smacked in the back, for the other man to mack.
> Now the story I'm kickin' is gory,
> Little Rock where they be dockin' this boat.
> No hope, I'm shackled, plus gang tackled. . . .
>
> Gettin' me bruised on a cruise,
> what I got to lose, lost all contact.
> Got me laying on my back, rolling in my own leftovers,
> when I roll over, I roll over somebody else's. . . .
> Blood in the wood and it's mine,
> I'm chokin' on spit and feeling pain,

like my brain's being chained.
Still gotta give it what I got,
but its hot in the day, cold in the night.
I thrive to survive, pray to God to stay alive. . . .

3 months pass, they brand a label on my ass
to signify, owned,
I'm on the microphone,
saying 1555, how I'm livin',
we been livin' here,
livin' ain't the word I've been given,
haven't got,
classify us in the have-nots, fightin' haves,
'cause it's all about money
when it comes to Armageddon.[22]

Needless to say, the song is suffused with an apocalyptic sensibility and echoes the righteous anger of "John the Revelator" or Malcolm X. This is a tale of history through the eyes of a shackled slave or incarcerated child of the ghetto, a vision that contests triumphal visions of Western history. By choosing to narrate these events in the first person, Chuck D enters the skin of his enslaved characters, participates in their struggle for survival, and embodies their plight in the belly of a slave ship. This gives him the authority of an eyewitness. He speaks with the confidence of Walt Whitman: "I was the man, I suffered, I was there."[23] Or better, he speaks with the authority of Olaudah Equiano's first-person narrative:

> The closeness of the place, and the heat of the climate, added to the number in the ship, which was so crowded that each had scarcely room to turn himself, almost suffocated us. This produced copious perspirations, so that the air soon became unfit for respiration, from a variety of loathsome smells, and brought on a sickness among the slaves, of which many died, thus falling victims to the improvident avarice, as I may call it, of their purchasers. . . . The shrieks of the women, and the groans of the dying, rendered the whole a scene [of] horror, almost inconceivable.[24]

While Equiano's language is more polite and respectable than Chuck D's fire-breathing anathemas and curses, they clearly share the same disgust for and defiance of the racist histories of the Americas.

Chuck D's rap batters the listener like a furious tide and pulls us into his story about the plight of a slave in the Middle Passage: shackled in the underbelly of a ship, rolling over your own and another's vomit and feces, choking on your own spit, losing all contact with your family and culture, and desperately clinging to hope and praying to God to stay alive. Beset on all sides by this wickedness, Chuck D turns rhymes, beats, and flows into weapons of self-defense, into strategies of survival against all odds. He uses words and beats to shock and disturb the easy, untroubled conscience of American innocence and thus casts America as the villain, as Revelation casts Rome (we're back to Lorca's portrait of New York). In fact, with the refrain, "so here's a song to the strong 'bout a shake of a snake, and the smile that went along with dat," we know that we are in the same metaphorical universe as Revelation, only that the latter prefers images of dragons, beasts from land and sea, and demonic horsemen to Public Enemy's iniquitous, deceiving snake. The seething wrath and aggressive insubordination of the artists are similar. Both use poetry to assault the rulers of the earth, who "divide and sell human beings for liquor and gold," all with a smile and shake of the hand. In Revelation 18, there is a remarkable passage that denounces this trafficking of human lives in ways that parallel Chuck D's lyrics: "And the merchants of the earth will weep and mourn for her, since no one buys their cargo anymore, cargo of gold, silver, jewels, pearls, fine linen, purple cloth, silk and scarlet . . . all articles of wine, olive oil, choice flour and wheat, cattle and sheep, horses and chariots, slaves, and human lives" (Rev. 18:11–13). In no uncertain terms, John castigates Rome's predatory involvement in the commerce of human lives, its gross accumulation of material wealth and power irrespective of the human costs. He is sickened by Rome's culture of greed and violence and denounces all attempts at assimilation to Roman norms. In John's uncompromising vision, any involvement with this business amounts to fornication with this harlot and seven-headed beast—in a word, idolatry. Without calling for violence or armed revolution, John's text is hardly less dangerous. It essentially threatens the Roman social order with the only resource that an impoverished, colonized community would have: ideological and civil disobedience.

Writing in the aftermath of the Jewish-Roman war, and in the face of violent persecution, the author concedes the strength of Rome in the present order but envisions a sudden reversal. When he opens one of the sealed scrolls, he sees the coming Armageddon between the "haves" and the "have-nots," to use Chuck D's terms. In dreamlike imagery, the author sees the sun becoming black as sackcloth, the moon turning blood-red, the stars falling to the earth, and the sky rolling up like a scroll (Rev. 6:12–14). And out of this cosmic whirlwind, Christ appears on a white horse to bind Satan and create a new heaven and earth, in which death and pain and mourning will be no more (Rev. 21:4).

For some (notably Nietzsche), this final revolution at the end of times is nothing more than a rabid outburst of vindictiveness. Given the central

image of war and violence in Revelation, this criticism is worth considering here because the question of violence is also a key issue in hip-hop. I
readily concede that in both Revelation and hip-hop there are disturbing
and reprehensible images of violence, such as when God released vultures
of heaven to eat the flesh of kings, captains, and rulers of the earth until
"the birds were gorged with their flesh" (Rev. 19:21). I don't know of
anything in hip-hop that matches this gruesome scenario, but it's true
nonetheless that hip-hop can gorge itself on images of violence and murder. There are countless examples of the music getting stuck, like a
scratched record, on the same tired, played-out refrain about one's prowess with guns and weapons or on a never-ending loop of scurrilous and
hedonistic brags. In these cases, when the lyrics raid the same "gangsta"
sound bites over and over, hip-hop can quickly slip into the dregs of the
industry, where the lyrics aim only at mass consumption and signify
nothing of value, nothing more than sound and fury.

But what the critics of rap do not understand is how much the strategies of rap (and the book of Revelation) revolve around the poetic
power of language and not, as it may seem, physical violence. In the
book of Revelation, Jesus is portrayed with a heavenly army and a
sword, but the sword is described as *coming from his mouth* (Rev. 2:16,
19:15). The sword, in other words, is the Word of God, and it is the
Word that slays and subdues the enemy. (St. Paul also refers to the
"sword of the Spirit" as synonymous with the word of God in Eph.
6:17.)[25] If anything, Revelation outlines a lyrical, theological tactic for
the coming battle, not a violent one. It engages its enemies with the
eccentric, Dada-like products of its mind and mouth, with diction that
is a weapon of protest and nonviolent resistance. Because history is now
in the grip of the beast, Revelation does not believe in active engagement with political power. It advocates neither political involvement
nor violent revolution. Trust in political progress is seen as misplaced in
a world, to quote Tupac, "where only God can save us."[26] The revolution, in short, is coming, but the author of Revelation makes it clear
that it should be fought with the sword of wisdom and faith, not by
violence (Rev. 13:10).

In the culture of hip-hop, where poetry and music are idolized above
politics, this construction generally holds true as well: violent imagery is
used as ammunition for the *lyrical battle*. The rapper's combat is a war
of words, and the spoils of this battle go to the MC with the dopest
flows and rhymes; it is *poetry* that strikes and defeats the enemy. By and
large, metaphors of violence are used in the form of boast and insult, to

signify a rapper's rhetorical mastery over his opponent. For example, the Wu-Tang Clan appeals to the symbol of the sword as the book of Revelation does, where swordplay and martial arts are used as metaphors for the rapper's superior rhymes and flows. The following example is from GZA:

> I swing swords and cut clowns.
> Shit is too swift to bite,
> You record, and write it down.[27]

Here, GZA's swordplay refers to his furious style, which cuts down other clown rappers. His flows are so swift and slick that others want to "bite" (steal) his verses.

De La Soul's lines are another case in point:

> And when we get to racing on the mic, they line up to see
> the lyrical killing, with stained egos on the ceiling.
> My rhymes escalate like black death rates
> over music plates, being played as the rule.
> Kids thinking of stepping to the Soul, you're labeled fools.[28]

Another example is Guru's raps (of Gang Starr):

> I could make your head explode just by my lyrical content
> Get you in my scope and metaphorically snipe ya
> I never liked ya, I gas that ass and then ignite ya
> The flame-thrower, make your peeps afraid to know ya.[29]

There are countless examples of this lyrical warfare, sometimes playful and imaginative and at other times alarming. Tupac Shakur's music is almost always somewhere in between. He certainly could play the role of thug and gangster (this was most disturbing when his acting continued offstage), but he was also one of the most sensitive and thoughtful in the game. And his music is inundated by an apocalyptic temperament, beginning with his debut album, *2Pacalypse Now* (1991), a work that seemed to open the floodgates for the apocalyptic fury of hip-hop in the 1990s.

When we contrast the first decade of rap (say, from the late 1970s to 1985) with the emergence of Tupac, the ambience clearly goes from bad to worse, as the distant drumbeat of doom seems to get louder and closer. Some may have had presentiments of what was to come (e.g., in Boogie Down Production's *Criminal Minded*, Ice-T's *Rhyme Pays*, or Schoolly D's "P.S.K."), but there was little to match the depths of the crisis and conflict in the period of the 1990s.[30] In a sense, we can measure the new tragic haze in rap by its distance from the dreams of the

1960s—the elapsed time seems to proportionately lengthen the shadow of disillusionment and cynicism. "The dreams that defined their horizon," writes Saidiya Hartman, "no longer defined mine. The narrative of liberation had ceased to be a blueprint for the future."[31] Tupac anticipated Hartman in this way, and he used this new, darker paradigm as a source for his brooding genius, as a laboratory for his experimentation with words and beats.

Anyone familiar with Tupac will know that death was one of these sources, a demonic force that bullied and inspired him at once. Not unlike Lorca, death creeped and prowled in the haunted corners of his mind and seemed to concentrate his thoughts like nothing else. It produced a clarity of thought and deep pondering in Tupac that opposed the prevailing sentiments of American popular culture. "This country," W.E.B. Du Bois wrote, "has had its appetite for facts on the Negro problem spoiled by sweets."[32] Tupac's music is a bitter and harsh antidote to this tendency, a collection of grave facts in a culture that prefers fancies and illusions. If one insists on describing this truth-telling as a species of pessimism, it is best seen as a "pessimism of strength," life-enhancing and alive, not a pessimism of resignation, gloom, or decline.[33]

In 2Pacalypse, Tupac presented vexing songs in this tragic vein, as in "Brenda's Got a Baby," a piece about a pregnant twelve-year-old black girl in the hood. Brenda never knew her mom, and her father was a junkie:

> Now Brenda's gotta make her own way,
> can't go to her family, they won't let her stay.
> No money, no babysitter, she couldn't keep a job.
> She tried to sell crack, but ended up getting robbed.
> So, what's next? There ain't nothing left to sell,
> so she sees sex as a way of leaving hell.[34]

Barely old enough for middle school, Brenda finds herself thrown into a pit of destitution, bereft of family or communal support and surrounded by wolves ready to eat her alive. She is left terrifyingly alone, and her child, we assume, will have to face the same heartless circumstances.

When discussing these troubles in this book, it is important to note that Tupac uses a journalistic style, giving his writing a simple, realistic edge. Like many of his raps, this song is metaphorically sparse and sticks to a plain and undressed style of writing. Instead of the inventive metaphors or symbols of, say, Rakim, Big Daddy Kane, Sage Francis, Aesop Rock, or Lil Wayne, Tupac's raps are stripped of rhetorical excess, using the bare diction of ordinary folk instead of more extravagant styles of speech. His stories are presented in the raw, delivered with a visceral and primal directness, as though the specific grammar of suffering requires a more austere style (as Virginia Woolf claimed). By pursuing this stark design, Tupac draws the attention of his listeners to the actions and experiences of his protagonist and doesn't allow poetic license to obstruct our concentration on the story and sound.[35] And by shunning artifice (as unnatural, fake, and elitist), Tupac emphasizes his own familiarity with common struggles; the credibility of the song is enhanced by the unspoken assumption that the rapper has faced similar humiliating ordeals to those the many Brendas must endure in the hood, that he has been in her shoes, has known her worries, fears, and toils. In flashing his camera-like eye back and forth between Brenda's plight and the circumstances of the ghetto, Tupac illuminates the cold and besotted world of this young American and infuses his account with sympathy for such fallen lives. The listener learns to care for her and others in these situations.

If his judgment in favor of the Brendas of the world rouses Tupac's sensitive side, this same judgment suddenly becomes hard and brutal when he addresses the injustices of the America he has known. He is well aware that he and his fellow rappers are frequently accused of barbaric and ruffian ways, and his music hits back with indictments of corruption and savagery among the governing bodies of society, hidden by masks of civility, law, order, religion, or patriotism. Like Las Casas, Montaigne, Melville, or Ice Cube, he essentially flips the accusations of barbarism back onto the self-righteous leaders of the world, snapping and busting on them for their assumptions of innocence and purity. This is Melville: "We may have civilized bodies and yet barbarous souls. We are blind to the real sights of this world; deaf to its voice; dead to its death."[36] And Ice Cube would later sample this sentiment, but in a ghetto context, as he dresses up to attend yet another funeral: "So that's why Ice Cube's dressed up, because the city is so fuckin' messed up. And everybody is so phony. Take a little time, to think about your dead homies."[37] In a society "blind to the real sights of this world" and phony for its "deadness" to the reality of death, the fury of Melville, Ice Cube, or Tupac is a sensible reaction to these maddening derelictions and delinquencies of duty. By narrating the story of ghetto women and men, Tupac cuts through the surface flesh of the civilized body of the United States and uncovers the deeper dysfunctions that prevail at its core. If the label "thug" or "gangster" was a consequence of these exposés, exploding from his tongue with curses and invectives stolen from the pages of NWA and others, we know that Tupac embraced it with pride.

In Tupac's "Trapped," he addresses a theme—the incarceration of young black men—that continues in this vein and that highlights the incongruence of American celebrations of freedom against widespread realities of black detention and imprisonment. In this song and what is to come in future compositions, he stacks together a litany of elocutions— hollers, shouts, grunts, cries, laments, elegies, protests, and prayers—that grapple with the social and psychological damage wrought by the prison industrial complex:

> You know they got me trapped in this prison of seclusion,
> happiness, living on the streets is a delusion. . . .
> Too many brothers daily heading for the big pen,
> niggas coming out worse-off than when they went in. . . .
> Trapped in a corner,
> dark, and I couldn't see the light.[38]

Throughout his rap, Tupac gives his listeners a barrage of such images of confinement. As if "freedom" rings hollow and empty to him and his fellow sufferers, Tupac constantly returns to the feeling of being "coffined" in the hood. If we keep in mind Michelle Alexander's reminder that the United States incarcerates a greater percentage of blacks than South Africa did at the height of apartheid (in terms of sheer percentage), that in the nation's capital three out of four African Americans will spend some time in jail, or that in states targeted by the drug war as many as 80 percent of young African American men have had criminal records that will plague them for the rest of their lives, we might lend a more sympathetic ear to Tupac's insistence that there is a very thin, porous line between the ghetto and the prison.[39] To be born black in certain parts of America almost guarantees one an encounter with the judicial system, if not the undertaker.

In "Words of Wisdom," another song from 2*Pacalypse*, we get the same feeling of internment and aggravation, but now it comes with Tupac's blazing, fiery attitude, as if he's going to blast through the suffocating walls of the new Jim Crow in an apocalyptic cataclysm. In perfect guerrilla fashion, using words as his slings and arrows, he envisions an alternate reality and a radical inversion of the hierarchies of American life:[40]

> This is for the masses, the lower classes,
> the ones you left out.
> Jobs were given, better livin'
> but we were left out. . . .
>
> America, I shine as a reminder of what you've done
> to my people for four hundred plus years.
> You should be scared, you should be running,

you should be trying to silence me.
Just as you rose, you will fall by my hands,
America, you reap what you sow,
2Pacalypse, America's nightmare.[41]

In this prophecy of doom, it is evident that Tupac is echoing the apocalyptic judgments of Public Enemy as well as his mother's community, the Black Panthers. With this tradition behind him, he adds flourishes of "black power" to hip-hop's repertoire, but he does it in a style that is unmistakably his own, that has its own swagger and bluster. To the riled-up, whooping preacher, Tupac adds the foul voice of the pimp and pusher; and he also adds, as I have been saying, the dark prophecies and demons of the apocalyptic imagination.

THE DEMONS OF HIP-HOP: FAUSTIAN BARGAINS

If it's true, as Andrew Delbanco has maintained, that one can track the approach of modernity by the decline of the devil into invisibility and obsolescence, then hip-hop represents a radical contestation of modernity.[42] The reason for this is obvious: the devil may be in retreat among intellectual and cultural elites, but in the hoods of the world, the devil is alive and well, and if anything, he has grown more imposing and hulking from the bounty of twentieth-century calamities on which he has fed. Seen from this ghetto-centric perspective, the devil and his minions are all too real, hovering like vultures over the carcasses of the dead and dying, scattering disease and despair.

Whatever else it is, hip-hop is a testament—a last will and testament—to the flames of the underworld. Even when it does little to put out the fire, it has value for simply alerting us to the dangers and problems faced by millions of people around the globe. Susan Sontag's thoughtful words apply, I think, to this virtue of hip-hop: "To designate a hell is not, of course, to tell us anything about how to extract people from that hell, how to moderate hell's flames. Still, it seems a good in itself to acknowledge, to have enlarged, one's sense of how much suffering caused by human wickedness there is in the world we share with others."[43] Whether or not hip-hop tells us how to extricate people from hell (a rare thing), it enlarges our view of the world and illuminates the searing landscapes of many parts of the modern scene. Hip-hop's preoccupation with tragic misfortunes and trials, or with the terrorizing agents of urban settings, is the music's way of grappling with the intangible malignity of the world and its particular concentration in the ghetto. References to devils and demons in the music are plentiful, if only because the traumas and disturbances in ghetto environments are plentiful. Whether metaphorical or literal, these evil figures appear in hip-hop as expressions of the primal, existential battle with the horned brutishness of suffering.

It is true that in some works of hip-hop, the devil may represent America or the white man or the corporate-controlled music industry (especially in hip-hop inspired by the Nation of Islam and the Five Percent Nation). In these instances, closely matching the portrait of Rome in the book of Revelation, Satan is embodied in the guise of white supremacy, with a white hood and similar symbols, at work in the maleficent actions against Indians, blacks, Mexicans, Chinese, and others. All of the rage and furor of hip-hop, in this tradition, is concentrated on an external enemy. One might say that this construction of evil approximates the manic behavior of Melville's Ahab as he identifies Moby Dick, the white whale, as the cause of all his maimed misery.[44] With his torn body and gashed soul bleeding into each other, Ahab's mind becomes possessed by the single purpose of exacting his vengeance on the whale: "He piled upon the whale's white hump the sum of all the general rage and hate felt by his whole race from Adam down; and then, as if his chest had been a mortar, he burst his hot heart's shell upon it."[45] By embracing a Manichean portrait of evil (a simplistic dualism of good and evil), Ahab traces his tragic lot in life to this particular Leviathan of the ocean, as the source of all demonism in the universe. In his stark vision, evil is an external enemy that is to be confronted with the harpoons of his raging anger and vindictiveness.

I have already conceded that there are some traces of this vindictiveness in Revelation and hip-hop alike, but I protest the judgment that this is the leading strain in either of them. In each case, this vindictiveness is drawing from a deep well of rage and rebellion in response to experiences of persecution, violent murder, and exile, so if the writer of Revelation or rappers throw themselves, Ahab-like, on the Roman Empire or American history like an exploding shell, it is because of legitimate grievances that have mounted into a barricade of distrust.

Nevertheless, this is most certainly not the principal approach to evil in hip-hop. It is more accurate to say that evil is a many-headed Cerberus or Hydra in hip-hop and reaches deep into every human soul. In other words, the enemy is difficult for most hip-hop artists to identify and exceeds any specific representation in person, place, or thing. The devil's work is everywhere, Andrew Delbanco argues, but no one knows where to find him.[46] And so it is in hip-hop: the devil is omnipresent in the distressed conditions of the city, but he is as evasive as a phantom, slipping away just when we think we have him. Like some kind of dark matter, he cannot be directly seen, but his existence is inferred by his destructive effects: the rubble of the ghetto, the dung heaps of the "third world," discrimination, misfortune, and for Tupac, the poisonous experience of hopelessness. Tupac envisions demons as an enemy within, infiltrating his mind and soul, whispering in his ear:

> There was no mercy on the streets, I couldn't rest.
> I'm barely standing, 'bout to go to pieces, screaming peace.
> And though my soul was deleted, I couldn't see it.
> I had my mind full of demons trying to break free.
> They planted seeds and they hatched, sparking the flame
> Inside my brain like a match, such a dirty game. . . .
>
> Lord knows I tried, been a witness to homicides
> And drive-bys taking lives, little kids die.
> Wonder why as I walk by.
> Brokenhearted as I glance at the chalk line, gettin' high. . . .
> Can't take no more,
> I'm falling to the floor,
> Begging for the Lord to let me into heaven's door,
> Shed so many tears.[47]

This song depicts Tupac at his most vulnerable and mournful, with the smooth flow and slow pacing of the beat corresponding with his meditative, broken-hearted mood. His "thug-life" persona is not absent in the song, only submerged into deeper sublime waters, where he feels like he is sinking and flailing for survival. His soul is "deleted" by the demons in his mind, who are hatching seeds of misery and despair and crippling his search for happiness. Instead of endless possibility (the American dream), he envisions himself leaving the projects in a hearse. Death stalks him.

Some critics see songs like this as evidence of depression in Tupac, but even if that were true, the criticism is shortsighted. In presuming to diagnosis Tupac's individual psyche, this approach entirely ignores his art's keen diagnosis of the social and psychological ills that plague the ghetto: the incessant sirens, the engorged murder rates, the imprisonment of the young, the pervasive poverty, the haunting fear and paranoia, and the brutality and prejudice of the police. Tupac's music is contending with personal and social misery alike, so when demons appear in his poetry, they register more than personal threats: His Satan figure lets loose his horsemen on the impoverished corners of the world, running roughshod over the poor and weak; his Satan distributes crack as a way of devastating families and cities ("crack done took a part of my family tree"); his Satan is a cold-blooded killer.[48]

In Jay-Z's raps we find a similar pendulum swinging between social and psychological threats, though Jay-Z has a sharper eye cast on the latter. The devil in Jay-Z's songs, as Ebony Utley explains in her book *Rap and Religion,* is clearly an internal as much as an external adversary.[49] It may manifest itself in institutional and corporate racism, social and political injustice, and mass incarcerations, but Jay-Z's particular signature highlights the pernicious effects on the mind and soul of a vulnerable individual. In Jay-Z's own words: "Hip-hop had described poverty in the ghetto and painted pictures of violence and thug life, but I was interested in something a little different: the interior space of a young kid's head, his psychology."[50] Thus, Jay-Z shifts the spotlight in hip-hop from social landscapes to the dark caverns and potholes of a young person's psyche. In his music, the apocalyptic chaos of ghetto life can be studied by a more intimate approach than we would find in sociological accounts, by diving deep into the turbulent sea of a ghetto dweller's soul, by examining the ripples and riptides in the soul caused by violent disturbances and social revulsions, and by analyzing the scenes and battles that take place in the inner lives of ghetto dwellers. For Jay-Z, in other words, signs of the apocalypse are written all over the soul, and he makes an effort—like a psychoanalyst of the hood—to decipher the strange world contained within.

In his rap "D'Evils," Jay-Z tells the story of a battle in which evil has clearly been victorious. The main character is held in the inexorable grip of the "D'Evils":

> It gets dangerous, money and power is changing us
> And now we're lethal, infected with D'Evils. . . .
> My soul is possessed by D'Evils in the form of diamonds and Lexuses.
> Liquors invaded my kidneys, got me ready to lick off
> Mama forgive me.
> I can't be held accountable, D'Evils beating me down, boo.
> Got me running with guys, making G's, telling lies that sound true
> Come test me, I never cower
> For the love of money, I'm giving lead showers
> Stop screaming, you know the demon said it's best to die
> And even if Jehovah witness, bet he'll never testify.[51]

Without ambiguity, the character of this song has fully embraced nihilism and has given his soul to the devil: "I never prayed to God, I prayed to

Gotti," he brags. Though the rap chronicles the nefarious choices of the protagonist, it is clearly a mistake to confuse the character in the song with the rapper as narrator. If anything, the rap is a sharp, biting denunciation of the evil embraced by this young gangster, a portrait of someone who has gained the whole world—power, cars, diamonds—and lost his soul. Once a pleasant guy, he has been irreparably corrupted by the love of money and power. The song's opening line, "This shit is wicked on these mean streets," draws a cold picture of this environment, as if the streets are thoroughly under the mafia-like control of the devil and his mobsters. The main character has been beaten down by the D'Evils and has become, to quote Jay-Z again, "a raging, money-obsessed sociopath." Unequivocally, the song stands in judgment of this character and cautions the listener—in the ghetto or on Wall Street—about the slippery slope to perdition when money becomes one's lord and master.

We find a similar account in Immortal Technique's eerie and frightening song "Dance with the Devil." A gentle, plaintive piano rhythm dances lightly over powerful, hammering beats, and the combination, mixed with the rapper's poetic gifts and hard delivery, gives the song an incantatory power like few others. In this arresting, unsettling song, Immortal Technique perfectly sculpts the sound of the song to match the dark story, about a boy so eager to become a hardened gangster that he does the devil's bidding at whatever cost:

> He fiended for props like addicts with pipes and needles
> So he felt he had to prove to everyone he was evil
> A feeble-minded young man with infinite potential
> The product of a ghetto-bred capitalist mental
> Coincidentally dropped out of school to sell weed
> Dancing with the devil, smoked until his eyes would bleed
> But he was sick of selling trees and gave in to his greed.[52]

In his "fiending" for props, power, and material possessions, the boy escalates his criminal activity, begins selling crack, and then is asked to rape and murder a woman in order to "guarantee a spot in the crew." He follows these commands, but just before he pulls the trigger on the beaten woman, he starts to cringe and shudder as the image of his mother suddenly flashes before his eyes, and he recoils in utter fright and horror. "He turned away from the mother that had given him birth":

> And crying out to the sky 'cause he was lonely and scared
> But only the devil responded, 'cause God wasn't there
> And right there he knew what it was to be empty and cold
> And so he jumped off the roof and died with no soul.

In order to make the moral of the story as clear as possible, the verses that follow define in clear terms the devil's nefarious plot:

> The devil grows inside the hearts of the selfish and wicked
> White, brown, yellow and black, color is not restricted.

Though the tale is disturbing and dreadful, it contains a glaring moral message, with a warning the size of a Las Vegas neon sign about the consequences of making any pact with the devil. Nothing is hidden about the terms and conditions therein; there aren't any refunds in this transaction, as J. Cole puts it in a related song.[53] In bold and plain letters, we are told about the devil's bloody, vile business, about his phony, tawdry hustle. We are told about the spiritual costs of greed, violence, and hate, and how these evils infect and warp every human soul, regardless of skin color. We are told about the dark side of capitalism, the way it can fudge and make fraudulent its ledgers, allowing greed and violence to trump the values of the soul. This theme is developed more in another Immortal Technique song, "Industrial Revolution":

> The bling-bling era was cute but it's about to be done
> I leave you full eclipse like the moon blocking the sun
> My metaphors are dirty like herpes but harder to catch
> Like an escape tunnel in prison I started from scratch. . . .
>
> Technique is chemically unstable, set to explode
> Foretold by the Dead Sea scrolls, written in codes
> So if your message ain't shit, fuck the records you sold
> Cause if you go platinum, it's got nothing to do with luck
> Just means that a million people are stupid as fuck
> Stuck in the underground in general and rose to the limit
> Without distribution managers, a deal, or gimmick.[54]

With one hand hammering at excessive materialism ("the bling-bling era," the "ghetto-bred capitalist mental"), the rapper's other hand enters the battle in classic hip-hop style, brandishing and swinging his fists against his opponents and telling them that, for all their record sales, they ain't shit.[55] He's the moon that eclipses their sun, the chemically unstable lyricist who discharges "clips" at their trite and spent narratives about cars, jewels, and the like. And he does all of this, he reminds us, by remaining in the underground, without the big record companies. Like John's denunciations of Roman elites for their adornments of gold, jewels, and pearls, Immortal Technique unsheathes his tongue and uses it like a sharp, two-edged sword to malign and indict the effects of capitalism on hip-hop. He takes his place in a respected tradition of hip-hop that clings tightly to the prophetic traditions of black religion, artists in the mold of KRS-One, Grandmaster Flash and the Furious Five, Rakim, the Poor Righteous Teachers, Gang Starr, Common, Black Star, Digable Planets, Lupe Fiasco, and numerous others.

When exploring the apocalyptic landscape of hip-hop, it should become obvious that nihilism lurks around every corner, ready to explode in one's soul like a land mine. As though these rappers are careening on the edge of a black hole and the abyss, their survival comes across as a careful balancing act that could end in disaster if not for their grace and grit. With all the threats to one's body and soul, survival entails a constant effort to "protect ya neck" and to move with the reflexes of a Shaolin artist, mastering the lessons and the shadow-like moves, practicing the art of living in a world, to quote Revelation again, "where Satan's throne is" (Rev. 2:13, 12:7–9). Under these conditions, close to the heat of Satan's throne, life burns and bruises, and various injustices occur with impunity: "Do not fear what you are about to suffer. Beware, the devil is about to throw some of you in prison" (Rev. 2:10).

Like a page out of Revelation, Snoop Dogg's classic rap "Murder Was the Case" tells the story of a young man tossed into prison after various entanglements with the devil. The song opens with the young man in a coma after being shot, staring at the sky, and all he can see is demons. In Faust-like fashion, the devil enters the picture and offers him limitless rewards and enticements. They are irresistible, and the man enters into a villainous pact with the devil, getting everything he's ever wanted, "living like a baller loc, havin' money, and blowin' hella chronic smoke."[56] But despite all the promises and material rewards ("I bought my Boo-Boo a Jag, I bought my momma a Benz, and now I'm rollin' in a nine-trizzay El Do-Rad"), the young man ends up stripped of his freedom and thrown into prison. He's been betrayed by the devil's glittering promises. Given these brutal consequences, the main character has his regrets, and he subsequently pleads with God in the course of the song's catastrophic episodes: "Dear God, I wonder can ya save me. . . . I pray the Lord, my soul to keep."

Here again the song carries an implicit moral warning about the wages of sin and evil. In the spirit of Shakespeare's *Macbeth*—a play about the dire consequences of Macbeth's association with necromancy, witches, and devils—Snoop's song is a cautionary tale of negotiations and conspiracies with hell.[57] It shows the pact with the devil to be misguided, a conjuring that lacks beauty and grace and that will prevent someone of his ilk from turning his life into art. It's impossible, in this light, to read the song as advocacy on behalf of the pleasures of nihilism, since the main character ends up in total ruin, with his homeboy "shanked" and himself behind bars. The character of the story surrenders his soul to the forces of evil around him, but the rapper as narrator does not follow the same path. He surveys the fray and tragedy with a degree of omniscience, as if Snoop Dogg has learned from these sorts of temptations and has chosen to make poetry and music instead of succumbing to the life of a drug dealer.

In each of these songs, to speak in literary terms, the rapper has adopted the dramatic voice. As Adam Bradley has written on these cases, it's a mistake to simply equate the voice of the rapper with the character of the story.[58] While rap frequently uses the narrative voice— in which the rapper speaks in the first person out of his or her own lived experience—it's also common for the narrator to adopt a fictional persona and mask, as in the examples above. By severing the bond between the rapper's personal life and the character in the drama, the rapper is now free to explore dimensions of experience—often harrowing and macabre—that are outside the boundaries of the rapper's own life. The dramatic voice or mask liberates the narrator to speak with a boldness and daring on themes—incest, pride, violence, vengeance, dark spirits, the divine, justice—that seem to match the darkest moments of Greek tragedy and are equally terrifying to the established social order.

In spite of these dramatizations of gangster life, then, the "baddest" rapper is neither a criminal nor a pimp, but someone who has managed to transform the inelegant babble of human speech into eloquent and witty displays of oratory. As a form of competitive poetry (again reminiscent of the competitive spirit of lyric poetry or tragic drama in ancient Greece), rap crowns the artist with the best lyrics, music, story, and performative skill. When battling the forces of nihilism, the rapper uses his tongue as a sword, and in the process slices and carves up his enemy with rhetorical ripostes. Even apart from the lyrics in "Murder Was the Case," anyhow, Snoop's cool, smooth, "dro'ed out," Karo-syrup drawl is bursting with enough soul and rhythm to produce sweetness and pleasure in the listener's ear, to produce catharsis in the listener's emotions. Whether in the throbbing exuberance of the music and beats or the poetic delivery and performance of the rapper, so much of hip-hop is life-affirming in this way and a danger to anything that represses the joy of human life.

APOCALYPTIC CITYSCAPES

To insist that hip-hop is life-affirming and pleasurable does not, of course, deny its moments of pathos; the two experiences are artfully combined in hip-hop, making for wild juxtapositions. I'm reminded of Frederick Douglass's comments about the slave spirituals: "They would sometimes sing the most pathetic sentiment in the most rapturous tone, and the most rapturous sentiment in the most pathetic tone."[59] Since it came of age in the 1970s in the Bronx—a city that became a nationally known symbol of urban ruin and decay—it is natural that hip-hop would adopt the sound of pathos. As capital, commerce, and tax revenues increasingly left the inner cities for the suburbs and developing countries, the city left behind fell into a deep pothole of decline, with underfunded schools, burned-out tenements, and drug-infested projects. The inner city became synonymous with poverty, violence, danger, and moral degeneracy.[60] In response, federal and state governments intensified their methods of policing and punishment, fattening their budgets for both law enforcement and prison facilities while slashing funding for social services and welfare programs. Between 1970 and 2000 the prison population grew to gluttonous proportions, increasing by as much as 500 percent. If we add to these factors the mushrooming rates of unemployment; the introduction of crack cocaine; the creation of an urban police state; and the availability of Uzis, German Glocks, and assault rifles in the hood, we can guess why the mix turned unstable and volatile.[61]

At its best, rap music raised its voice in protest against these factors; at its worst, it added fuel to the burning problems of the city by delighting in the possession of guns, drugs, and expensive cars. In the latter case, rap took pleasure in any taste of success, however achieved, however fleeting, however at odds with spiritual flourishing. "The go-go capitalism of Reagan's America," Nelson George writes, "flowed down to the streets stripped of its jingoistic patriotism and fake piety. The unfettered free market of crack generated millions and stoked a voracious appetite for 'goods,' not good."[62] When hip-hop mimicked the worst appetites of Reagan's America, fantasies of material excess accumulated to fill in spiritual cavities, but the solution was cheap and superficial, like trying to treat a dental cavity with a filling of sugar. Needless to say, the root problems were not addressed.

One might argue, moreover, that the responses of some religious communities were equally superficial and sentimental, offering sugary consolations and fantasies like so many pies in the sky. And in the meantime, shit was going down; in the meantime, to quote Ta-Nehisi Coates on the circumstances of his Baltimore, "hundreds of kids were slain every year from gunshots and bricks to the skull and every other undignified means to their end."[63] If the religious communities weren't directly responsible, at the very least many of them failed to diagnose these wounds in urban America, committing sins of omission if not commission. As a result, the youth of the hip-hop generation found themselves left without spiritual and communal support. The apocalyptic landscape had started to erode many of the spiritual pillars of earlier days, making for shaky, tenuous religious convictions. The earlier cosmos of African American traditions was increasingly released from its orbit, leading to widespread feelings of disorientation and dizziness among many black residents of the ghetto. Though God would remain alluring to many rappers in this new world order, he was now seen through a dark cloud or black haze hanging over the projects, through a glass darkly.

The religious notes in hip-hop are thus heavily burdened by anxiety and existential dread, as if they have looted the apocalyptic imagination in a postmodern vein. The hip-hop generation superimposed an urban, tattooed look on ancient torments, on the timeless question of theodicy.[64] If theodicy was as inscrutable to the rappers as it had been to earlier generations, this did not stop them from trying their own hands at solving the riddle, like a DJ remixing a classic record. Naturally the enigma of suffering proved too much to solve in any theoretical manner, but their efforts suggested that the question of God was still of value, still precious. And this effort alone, this interrogation of and clutching onto God, kept the relentless forces of nihilism at bay. The desperate appetite for God in hip-hop often prevented the house of hip-hop from being swallowed by the abyss like the house of Usher in Edgar Allan Poe's frightening tale.

Again, Tupac is a classic case: His own persistent, writhing struggle with God saves his music from the death of meaning and purpose. Even at his most profane and raunchy, Tupac remains haunted and hounded by God, and he frequently interrupts his songs with prayers, supplications, wails, and protests unto God (e.g., "Hail Mary," "I Ain't Mad at Cha," "Thugz Mansion," "Shed So Many Tears," "Ghetto Gospel," "Black Jesus," "I Wonder if Heaven's Got a Ghetto," "Only God Can Judge Me," "Are You Still Down?"). God appears so frequently in Tupac's work because the threat of the devil is so real, so dangerously close to snuffing out his soul.

As in Job, Jeremiah, or Jonah, there is an existential blackness to Tupac's music, uneasy and defiant, but it is hardly equivalent to a state of unbelief or atheism. If anything, the seeming permanence of Tupac's "dark night of the soul" gave him a desperate affection for God. And it added a certain silhouette or hue of blackness to his image of God. By contesting white portraits of the divine, distant, and indifferent to ghetto struggles, Tupac gave his listeners a God who is deeply immersed in the tragedies of human history. If Tupac's God is black, it is because he saw God as incarnate in the darkest circumstances of human life. "Black Jesus, give me a reason to survive in this earthly hell, 'cause I swear, they're trying to break my well. I'm on the edge lookin' down at this volatile pit. Will it matter if I cease to exist, black Jesus? . . . Trapped, black, scarred and barred. Searching for truth where it's hard to find God. My black Jesus, walk through this valley with me."[65] As Michael Dyson notes, Tupac's vision of God is an offspring of a theology of the cross, a vision that looks for potential revelations in unsuspecting and afflicted locations, in the careworn face of a beggar, migrant, prostitute, pregnant twelve-year-old girl, or prisoner.[66] More than a redefinition of Jesus in terms of skin color, Tupac's black Jesus here is someone who accompanies him through the treacherous valleys of the ghetto, someone who comes to set free "all the young thugs, raised on drugs and guns, slaves to the slums." Tupac's Jesus is brother to outcasts and outlaws, father of orphaned ghetto children, defender of the poor and hopeless. He embraces and identifies with those enslaved by the slums or caught in a cycle of poverty and addiction, the ones whom many others, including Christians, turn away from in fear and loathing. Tupac's Jesus resembles the tortured figure in Mark's narrative, crying out in desperation to God the Father. His Jesus knows the demons of despair, the traps and snares of the streets, the dreams of a Kingdom to come.

While there is a particular level of intensity in Tupac's search for God, he was not alone in designing a spirituality for the ghettos of the world. As hip-hop grappled with the diseases of urban life, it often turned to various religions and spiritualities for therapeutic relief. In some cases, treatment was sought in traditional religious communities, but more frequently unorthodox resources were used, like turning to a witch doctor as a last-ditch effort to survive. Food for their souls was sought elsewhere, even if they displeased the Christian orthodoxy of the "religious right" or the traditional black church. Instead of fighting the system with the angels of their better nature, as the civil rights generation had done, rappers turned to other, meaner, badder, more devilish models. Black oral traditions of the "bad man" or the trickster were used to "destabilize norms, undermine authority, and upend power structures," as Ebony Utley describes it.[67] Theatrical antics were used as strategic tactics.

A LITERATURE OF NEGATION

In the tradition of the "bad-man" folklore, then, we might say that there is another scenario concerning the Faustian bargain, something less heinous than we have seen in the songs of Jay-Z, Immortal Technique, and Snoop. In this second scenario, the Faustian bargain is a trope of rebellion or defiance, similar to Huck Finn's willingness to go to hell to save his slave friend, Jim. (And for Mark Twain, this meant opposing a Christianity that advertised slave auctions on church bulletin boards.)[68] In this construction, hip-hop's solidarity with Jim's descendants in today's outlaws, fugitives, and agitators is a protest against a prevailing order—religious or secular—that protects and even blesses prejudice, intolerance, and injustice. Like Huck's waywardness or a Promethean storming of the heavens, it uses acts of insubordination and insolence to denounce the "sivilizing piety" (Huck's spelling) and jingoistic patriotism of the Christian Right, and it does so with couplets that match the booming, talking beats of a drum. If the antiquated idols and fossilized gods of religion prove too old and rigid to respond to the life and death situations in the ghettos of the world, then they must be replaced. James Baldwin put it this way long before the phoenix of hip-hop arose from the ashes: "If the concept of God has any validity or any use, it can only be to make us larger, freer, and more loving. If God cannot do this, then it is time we got rid of him."[69] Along these lines, hip-hop drags all the false gods through the apocalyptic fires of hell in order to forge a more inclusive God, purified of all the prejudicial contaminants in American history.

Nelson George puts his finger on another dimension of hip-hop, besides its cleansing of theology of graven images, when considering some of the most troubled rebels in the game, like Tupac and Biggie: namely, its bold probing of the most frightening and shady parts of the human psyche:

> Ultimately, Tupac and Biggie, like most of the controversial and best rappers who came after Public Enemy's political spiels, were both poets of negation, a stance that always upsets official cultural gatekeepers and God-fearing folks within black America. African-Americans have always been conflicted by art that explores the psychologically complex, even evil aspects of their

existence, feeling it plays into the agenda of white oppression. . . . Yet, Tupac and Biggie were artists who look[ed] at the worst things in their world and reveled in describing their meanest dreams and grossest nightmares.[70]

In George's assessment, the best rappers are "poets of negation," wordsmiths who explore the most forbidden and chilling jungles of the human psyche. While other artists have kept their sights on the positive and uplifting dimensions of human experience, rappers take their listeners to the underground of the soul and dredge up from its rank bottom the meanest dreams and fantasies, fears and nightmares. Like Robert Johnson's devilish Delta blues, Miles Davis's bebop, or Garcia Lorca's demonic-inspired poetry, their music has given us life at its most sweaty, funky, dirty, hot, frightening, joyful, resplendent, and sartorial. Though they run the risk of playing into the fears and stereotypes of white prejudice, their music identifies and articulates, more than glorifies, the savage violence and morally twisted hearts of every human person after the Fall ("Twisted-ass mind, got a pretzel for a brain," in Eminem's words).[71]

As a literary analogue, one can discern a similar inclination in nineteenth-century literature, among what David Reynolds calls the "dark or subversive reformers." These writers exploited the public's fascination with criminal underclasses and flamboyant pariahs, and they outraged genteel readers in the process. They boldly explored psychopathic states: the haunted mind of criminals, nightmare visions, the hypocrisy and depravity of authority figures, eroticism, savage violence, broken homes, and the collapse of romantic ideals.[72] Among the most politically inclined writers, poverty was sketched in the likeness of a quagmire, entangling and engulfing many of its victims, a breeding ground for crime and vice. Instead of targeting the working classes and unemployed for vice, though, their barbs and reproaches focused on the hidden vices of the social, religious, and economic elites. The upshot of these critiques was a growing identification with the plight faced by many criminals and pariahs in nineteenth-century America. And speaking philosophically, the upshot was a more complicated understanding of morality, in which sin was seen as entangled with virtue and just as likely to appear among the respectable citizens of the world as among the poor and desperate. Melville called it "ruthless democracy": "It is but nature to be shy of a mortal," he wrote about himself, "who boldly declares that a thief is as honorable a personage as General George Washington."[73] If Melville had the audacity to dethrone George Washington from his pedestal in American life and elevate a criminal, then all other sacrosanct idols associated with respectable power and riches were at risk in this "ruthless democracy."

While this salute to the coarse and plebeian in American literature sometimes indulged in gratuitous violence, amorality, and sensationalism (like the worst of hip-hop), the best writers resisted these temptations and raised the "subversive imagination"—a focus on tabooed desires, social militancy, urban poverty, and likable criminals—to aesthetic, moral, and spiritual heights. In essence, they exploded the moral and sanctimonious principles of the age in the interest of a higher morality: honest, ruthless, compassionate, loving, and just. In a world where bombast, deception, and duplicity are veils to cover crimes that would disgrace a nation of savages (in Frederick Douglass's words), to be an infidel or a thug might be the most righteous act possible; it might be synonymous with sheltering the outcast, freeing the oppressed, and feeding the hungry.[74] No wonder that James Baldwin counted the black preacher—a voice of freedom and equality—among the first "warriors, terrorists, and guerrillas" in black history, an "Original G."[75]

I am suggesting that something similar exists in the culture of hip-hop. If there are instances when rappers adopt the dark side as an identifying mask—as Miles Davis did with his epithet, the "Prince of Darkness"—it is usually in a theatrical form of dissent and rebellion, a smashing of moralistic myths and sacred idols. We see this in the preference for the hoodlum figure in rap over the humble and subservient figure of Uncle Tom. Though Uncle Tom is morally righteous, he is dissed and mocked by hip-hop culture, as someone who would not have the smarts and nerve to survive the mean streets of modern urban America. Instead of the conventional, pious figure of Uncle Tom, hip-hop prefers the dangerous ruffian and lawbreaker, a Nat Turner or Malcolm X; instead of the tender and warm figure of Jesus—the lamb of God—hip-hop prefers the lion of Judah, fierce and proud, untamed and smooth, teeth so sharp they could cut with a touch, hair tight as Bob Marley's dreads. Though we surely need both images of Jesus, I understand hip-hop's regard for the latter: it represents a revelation of the whole wilderness of the soul, the dangers and terrors as much as the more tender dispositions—and it represents all facets of Jesus's life in the Gospels: the subversive, threatening features in addition to the gentle, humble ones.

Contrary to appearances, then, the Faustian bargain in hip-hop does not amount to the renunciation of morality or God; in lieu of nihilistic conclusions, hip-hop employs tones of defiance and distress as a way of preserving the integrity of soul as it is threatened by deadly forces or rigid piety. In these acts of spiritual resistance, hip-hop rescues many kids from the grind and agony of life and provides them with a medium in which to sweat out their worries through music and poetry.

SIGNIFYING GOD

Although the apocalyptic imagination has been the anthem of our times and has found a receptive host in the culture of hip-hop, we would do a disservice to rap if we neglected the elation and exuberance obvious in so much of it. Though the portrait of life in rap lyrics is frequently painted with the blackest of hues, there is also bursting color and radiance in the music that can make the darkest of ghetto colors shine warmly and brightly. Even when the gaping jaws of death and despair seem to engulf the music, what strikes most fans of hip-hop is the feverish hunger for life that prevails over the gloom. Although I have emphasized the dark and infernal ambience of hip-hop, therefore, it is wrong to simply equate the beats and rhymes with tolling bells and funeral laments.

Rap's inclination to brood over the problems of ghetto life, or in more existential terms, the problems of death and suffering, is part of the tragic greatness of hip-hop, but it is surely not the only note in the music; comedy is also there, like the antiphony in a chorus, introducing a rich palette of sound that lightens the tragic vision with a spirit of celebration. Whether in the aptitude for verbal inventions and spiritual triumphs, or in the Viola loops and "garbled voice samples flying in from impossible angles," to summon Ta-Nehisi Coates again, hip-hop steals beauty from the scorched, Hades-like terrain of urban life.[76] It puts together jams and joints for a festive purpose.

I maintain, nonetheless, that we can only appreciate the comedy, play, and merriment of hip-hop when we stare, unflinchingly, at the dark sun of ghetto life. Consider the case of RZA and the Wu-Tang Clan, beginning with the fascinating account of RZA's life in *The Tao of Wu:*

> I've lived in at least ten different projects in New York—Van Dyke in Brown-ville, Marcus Garvey in East New York, Park Hill and Stapleton in Staten Island—and they all taught me something, even if they were lessons no one would choose. . . . I now see it for what it was: hell—hell of violence, addiction, misery, and humiliation. These forces were even in the air and water; in times of heavy rain, human excrement floated by under our basement-level bedroom, where me and my five brothers slept on two twin beds. No one chooses to live like that, but I now see that even that experience was a source of precious wisdom.[77]

It's impossible to read those lines and not be struck by the repressive darkness of the projects, their facility for snuffing out the sparks of light among their inhabitants. In telling the story of Wu-Tang's rise out of the tenements and basements of America, RZA begins with these sordid facts of ghetto life: the humiliating gravitas of poverty, the fetid rain, putrid air, and soiled streets.[78] With these foul actualities assaulting one's body and senses (famously described in Grandmaster Flash's "The Message"), it takes a farsighted, visionary soul to discern beauty behind sordid appearances, to extract so much joy and creativity out of such forlorn conditions. (Hawthorne's formula for poetic insight, by the way.)[79]

And this is what is so noteworthy about hip-hop: its refusal to remain buried in the tombs of the ghetto, its success in mining beauty and joy out of the squalor of urban struggles. Hip-hop's achievements are evidence of the remarkable agility of soul, its ability to flex, bend, and expand even under constrained circumstances. In RZA's case, musical training and religious instruction gradually gave him this ability, an aptitude for seeing the projects differently, as a "source of precious wisdom." For a kid who felt unfit for life in America, it came as a startling revelation that he was, as his cousin GZA insisted, sacred at his deepest core (a teaching of the Nation of Gods and Earths): "GZA was the first one that I heard talk about God inside, instead of looking up into the sky. That snapped a revelation inside my head."[80] Needless to say, this revelation opened up new vistas of possibility, enabling RZA to see farther than the ghetto would allow, as if he could now navigate his life by the stars far above the low-hanging ceilings of the projects.

RZA's life story is also the story of hip-hop: it is a tale of surprising moments of spiritual fullness, even in the context of material deprivation. If there is a certain infernal, morbid trait in rap's analysis of the modern world, there is also an ebullient aspect, a comic greatness. And if I have insisted on anything in this book, it is that soul is somewhere on the border between tragedy and comedy, in those places where sublimity manages to burst through the repressive forces of despair and darkness. In the alchemy of hip-hop, base and ignoble conditions are transformed into golden jewels of sound, and prison bars, to borrow the quip of Sohail Daulatzai, are converted into music bars.[81] If we only focus on misery, the soul of hip-hop is lost; if we only focus on misery, we will miss "the beautifully constructed word portraits, lyrical wonderment, and rhythmic timing that define the genre at its best," as Eddie Glaude says.[82] We will miss the way the artists exorcize gloom with the help of lyrical spells and talisman-like rhymes, the way ill beats, mad drumming, and verbal wit can undo the devil's lasso (as Nas says). In hip-hop, grace may come by sweat and tears, but when it comes, it comes with great surges of energy and eloquence, words shimmying and dancing together, creating mad static and voltage, creating the vigor needed to beat the blues down until they relent and say your name.

I suggest in this final section of the chapter that we pay attention to these spiritual feats in the cryptic clues that dot the landscape of hip-hop, that simultaneously reveal and hide these redemptive motifs. For outsiders to the music, the lyrics may seem dark and despairing or ridiculous and frivolous, and they may be all these things, but in the best cases, there is something else at work, some deeper meaning that can only be cracked by a special street knowledge. RZA describes it this way: "We refer to the first task in any situation as 'doing the knowledge,' which means to look, listen, and observe. The power of the Lessons didn't just come from the information they provided; it also came from their actual vocabulary and cadence."[83] As a theologian might say, the creeds of a religious tradition are more than a set of propositions to be affirmed or denied; the substance of faith requires prayer, observance, discipline, thought, and action. (Aquinas, for example, called the object of his studies *sacra doctrina,* "sacred instruction," in order to distinguish it from a purely speculative investigation; it aims for *sapientia* more than *scientia*.)[84] For RZA, too, the pursuit of wisdom is a comprehensive calling, requiring intellectual, artistic, and spiritual training, whether in the mysteries of religion or the principles and cadences of music.[85]

This is to say that there is an art to spiritual discovery. Whether in the recondite customs of hip-hop or in the apocalyptic traditions of Christianity, the human soul must learn how to read and crack the codes of wisdom before the scales will begin to fall from its eyes. If we succeed in seeing past the plain meaning of biblical or rap narratives, important discoveries may materialize. To return to the book of Revelation, consider the way certain truths suddenly appear when the text is read, to use Walter Benjamin's language, as an "allegory of ruins," written in the rubble of Rome's destruction of Jerusalem.[86] The text simultaneously hides and reveals these circumstances: the dragon represents Satan and the forces of evil; the seven-headed beast is Rome (the number 7 here represents the number of emperors from the time of Augustus until the author's time); another beast, indicated by 666, is likely the Emperor Nero; the woman clothed with the sun is Israel and her child, Jesus; the four horsemen represent war, violence, famine, and death; and so forth. In addition to these symbols, there is a very intriguing reference in

Revelation to a special community, 144,000 in number: according to Adela Collins, they are the first individuals to die at the hands of Rome, victims of violent death.[87] For sharing this experience of oppression, they are granted special knowledge, represented in this case by the cryptic hymn that they intone, a hymn forbidden to outsiders (Rev. 14:1–5). If they are privileged, it is by virtue of what they have suffered and endured, by virtue of their ability, it seems to me, to continue to sing in tumultuous and repressive times.

Taken figuratively, of course, we can see this "special community" as something like the purists of hip-hop, the insiders of the culture who cry out on behalf of the victims of untimely deaths. Like jazz and modernist literature, hip-hop has always taken delight in Gnostic encryptions of this sort. If puns, allusions and slang are plentiful in rap, it is to celebrate the art of camouflaged communication, according to Adam Bradley: "Slang is born of the desire to find new and compelling ways to speak about familiar things but it also emerges out of the desire for coded communication."[88] And Imani Perry makes a similar observation: "Multiple tiers of understanding and subtextual discourse hide in some of the music and they only reveal themselves to those who know where and how to look."[89]

In describing hip-hop as like a palimpsest, with certain scripts buried under the plain surface of a text, Bradley and Perry make it clear that there is a subtle and sophisticated process of simultaneously unveiling and veiling in rap music. As in the apocalyptic tradition, including the Gospel of Mark, certain things are said in code or parable to confound outsiders, on the one hand, and to impart a secret wisdom to the lowly and despised of the world, on the other. By using irony, circumlocution, indirection, obfuscation, and satire, rappers often say one thing and mean something else entirely, speaking with a forked tongue to mislead the casual listener ("so that they may see but not perceive, hear and listen but not understand"; Mark 4:12).[90] By testing the metaphorical flexibility and range of words, they employ allusive strategies—hooded words, cloaked meanings, and esoteric images—in order to upset or reverse situations of unequal power. Only the initiated disciple will know the true meaning, as Frederick Douglass noted about the slave spirituals: "Slave song was sung, as a chorus, to words which to many would seem unmeaning jargon, but which, nevertheless, were full of meaning to themselves."[91] Whether this was an early form of scatting—in which the sound conveyed meaning without words—or simply a form of song rich in allusion and allegory, Douglass describes the spirituals as confusing and mystifying to outsiders. The plain meaning—seemingly innocuous or unintelligible—concealed a dangerous underground meaning, full of explosive cries for justice and endless promises of hope.

In the scrolls of hip-hop, "unmeaning jargon" is used to similar ends, with the hieroglyphs, stories, and noises jammed with spiritual and aesthetical significance. This is certainly true, at least, among the majority of rappers inspired by Christianity or Islam, like Public Enemy, Rakim, Ice Cube, Brand Nubian, Big Daddy Kane, X-Clan, Poor Righteous Teachers, Tribe Called Quest, Black Star, the Roots, Gang Starr, Big Pun, Wu-Tang, Brother Ali, Lupe Fiasco, Common, Kendrick Lamar, Chance the Rapper, and many others. Most of these artists will use certain codes to speak about the jewels of knowledge, the divine nature of humanity, or the path of righteousness. In some cases, theirs raps are turned into mystical treatises on numbers, letters, and the names of God.[92] With the rapper playing the part of the seer, mystical wisdom is broken open for everyone, especially for the poor and needy. In the words of Rakim Allah, one of the very best in this tradition: "God by nature, mind raised in Asia / since you was tricked, I have to raise ya / from the cradle to the grave / but remember you're not a slave / 'cause we were put here to be much more than that / but we couldn't see because our mind was trapped / But I'm here to break away the chains, take away the pains / remake the brains, rebuild my name / . . . Lyrics of fury / my third eye makes me shine like jewelry."[93] Like some kind of spiritual master, with his third eye of wisdom and lyrics of fury, Rakim imparts the jewels of understanding to his disciples. Rakim is here to liberate his listeners from the grave, break away their chains, and educate them in the knowledge of their divine origins.

We find many of these same themes in Wu-Tang's classic song "C.R.E.A.M."[94] When I'm teaching my class on hip-hop at the University of Arizona, "Rap, Culture, and God," almost everyone can identify the acronym as meaning "cash rules everything around me"; almost no one, however, catches the underlying spiritual world of the song. Though "cream" can, in fact, mean money, the narrative of the song suggests another possibility from the Nation of Islam: the black man is the "cream" of planet Earth and participates in the divine nature. Keeping this principle in mind, we find that the song abounds in a spiritual significance entirely lost on someone who sticks to the surface, literal meaning. The rap speaks in the first person and follows the life of a young kid raised on the "crime side" of New York. He once had a dream of making a lot of cream and turned to the drug game to make it happen, but he failed:

"I went to jail at the age of 15." As he grows in age and experience, his mind becomes cynical after seeing so many kids in his neighborhood struggling in poverty, locked up in prison, or dead: "Life is hell, living in the world, no different than a cell." He almost loses all hope, until he turns to the "Old Earth" for advice (an older woman in the "Nation of Gods and Earths"). She subsequently instructs him in the ways of the world, and the knowledge proves transformative, even redemptive. Now the narrator describes an older, wiser, more thoughtful man who surveys the landscape of the ghetto and embraces the responsibility of educating young, misguided kids: "Leave it up to me while I be living proof, to kick the truth to the young black youth. But shorty's running wild, smokin' sess, drinkin' beer, and ain't trying to hear what I'm kickin' in his ear."[95]

In this spiritually inflected rap, the narrator finds a beacon of light, and this proves enough to help him "maintain, to learn to overcome the heart-aches and pain." While the song ends on a note of pessimism concerning the appropriation of the deeper message (they ain't trying to hear it), the tale is a testimony to the more soulful side of hip-hop. As Rakim's song did, this rap speaks of the emancipating experience of knowledge and spiritual understanding; it speaks of the power of poetry, music, and spirituality to keep the human soul in balance when it is tumbling and sinking under the pressures of the streets; and it speaks of the ability of the soul to extract wisdom from dehydrated conditions, to make cream out of the bitter herbs of ghetto life.

In countless cases, hip-hop has been this kind of life force in the United States and throughout the globe, the voice of those who have felt the weight of Plymouth Rock on their bodies and souls. In sampling the religious resources of various traditions, hip-hop has warded off spiritual ruin with esoteric strategies and lyrical geometries, creating new shapes and sounds that have all the mystery of a Pythagorean theorem to the uninitiated, but can be revelatory for those trained in the "higher sciences."

Though this deeper spiritual trope seems marginal and weak in hip-hop's most garish forms broadcast on radio and television, it remains a strong, beating pulse, the heart that sends blood and oxygen to the rest of the body of hip-hop. In some ways, hip-hop keeps this dimension close to its body, under wraps, for fear that the music will be misappropriated and exoticized. When this happens, rap music, like the blues or jazz before it, becomes synonymous with a prurient delight in difference.[96] When that happens, exoticism gratifies the heart's desire for otherness while hindering participation in the struggle for recognition, equality, and justice. If anything is true about the search for soul, as we have seen, it entails a willingness to risk one's security in an effort, following RZA's instruction, to contemplate, meditate, and act on behalf of the most threatened communities of our world.[97] This is the deeper meaning of hip-hop's garbled ciphers, the soul of its contorted word-play and dance moves.

7

Afro-Latin Soul and Hip-Hop

Only in his music has the black man been able to tell his story.
—James Baldwin[1]

With his murals, Rivera fashioned a vision of the outsized
humanity pulsing within the common Mexican laborer. . . .
What the world needs now is a rapper who can do for the
common man and woman verbally what Diego Rivera was
able to do with a paint brush and a blank wall.[2]

James Baldwin's famous remark about music in black history largely
holds true for Latin American cultures as well: music has been the central platform for their display of personality, style, and aesthetical character. "Is it even remotely clear to most students of English," writes
music critic Timothy Brennan, "that African-based popular music plays
a similar role in Latin America and the Caribbean that literature does in
Europe and the United States? Is it appreciated that the popular and
national sense of self is bound up with musical expertise, musical style,
the power of exerting musical influence that seems to be every bit as
strong as the urge for political dominance, scientific prowess, or literary
skill?"[3] If it's true that musical prowess has been a defining feature of
Latin American and Caribbean identities, any study of these traditions
should begin by listening to their musical signatures. In letting music act
as our guide, we might catch certain themes and sonorities often overlooked by standard European accounts of the New World, certain pulses
that give us an alternative history of the Americas, told at a sonic level in
the beats of a drum, a base line, a chant, or a grunt. As Gustavo Perez
Firmat once said about the mambo, there can be greatness and eloquence
in a simple grunt, a whole record of human experiences and beliefs

contained in such compacted sounds.[4] To the right ear, noises that seem like so much babble can represent untold stories of cultural life and can reveal truths that are only available through the beauty of sound.

The great Cuban novelist, musician, and architect of magical realism Alejo Carpentier clearly understood the revelatory importance of music in Latin America: His classic study *Music in Cuba* puts the theme of music in Latin American cultures front and center, as a necessary prelude to any opus dealing with the Americas. In his telling, music has not only shaped many of the distinctive patterns of culture in the New World; it has also prefigured the future when it comes to race relations, as if it were a blind seer compelled by sounds and stories more than by colors of skin.[5] As early as the sixteenth century, music in Hispaniola outran the other arts and sciences when it came to cooperation and intermingling among Africans, American Indians, and Europeans, with oppressed groups experiencing spaces of freedom here while they were still corralled and caged elsewhere.[6] In these open plains of musical creativity, *mestizaje* (cultural miscegenation) came alive in the New World like a new breed of the human species, blending different rituals and sounds into a thick, curvaceous aesthetics of culture.

In the following centuries the mix thickened, as festivals such as Día de los Reyes and Corpus Christi added African "native tongues"— Yoruba hymns, sacred drums, and ritual dances—to Catholic processions to produce a distinctly American and baroque extravaganza of ritual, music, dance, and sexuality. One can see why Carpentier, or more recently Jacques Attali, considers music a harbinger of change and subversion.[7] As an auditory revelation, felt in the sinews and muscles of the body, or deeper in the rhythmic contractions of the heart, music has proven to be far more supple and sinuous than some of the other arts, changing and whirling with the times and venturing into forbidden regions of experience. In some cases, when music has been attuned to the gusts of the spirit in history, it has breached the repressive barriers of society like a hurricane, leaving not only shards and debris in its wake, but also the opportunity for a fresh start. Unlike in other arts, especially those with the authority of the written word, many of the breakthroughs in American music have come from the bottom rungs and peripheries of the modern world, from those cultures on the margins of the literary and political centers of Western power. In emerging from the cracks and fissures of the modern world, many of the greatest achievements in American music have subtly but undeniably challenged prejudices that consigned non-European traditions to a cultural backwater. In too many cases to count, as David Tracy has written, the West used the custody of writing as a sign of cultural superiority and consequently demeaned, if not silenced altogether, nonliterate and nonalphabetic traditions, considering them stagnant inlets of history, with no current or flow.[8] The ability to manipulate the sacred aura of writing often allowed the educated and lettered classes of Europe and America—the *letrados* in Latin American societies—to use grammatology as an instrument of empire, especially in largely illiterate contexts. (Aptly put, Nebrija's classic book of grammar, *Gramática sobre la lengua castellana* [1492], called written language "the companion of empire.")[9]

In this tired narrative of Western evolutionary development, with the proprietors of the written word at the apogee of culture and politics, the study of music, folklore, dance, ritual, or ceremony has the potential to alter, even overthrow, these glaring biases. With their surging, rocking, cresting sonic waves, the blues, jazz, rock and roll, soul, hip-hop, *son*, salsa, and so many other American sounds are proof of a riotous potential that can batter and break many of our barriers of prejudice.[10] In terms of race relations in the New World specifically, music has frequently been the occasion for an exchange of ideas and sounds that has brought together various cultures, transforming conflicting and clashing relations into harmonious streams of sound. Among the many examples of such synthesizing arrangements, African and Spanish fusions have a venerable history. For Ted Gioia, these fusions have been so plentiful and fecund in the Americas that he imagines a lasting and haunting influence from the Moorish age in Spain: "Indeed, in the area of music alone, the number of successful African and Latin hybrids (including salsa, calypso, samba, and cumbia, to name a few) is so great that one can only speculate that these two cultures retain a residual magnetic attraction, a lingering affinity due to this original cross-fertilization."[11] According to Gioia, lingering affinities from medieval Al-Andalus have been the inspiration for African and Spanish conjunctions and collaborations in modern times and have resulted in novel, hybrid inventions, everything from salsa and samba to funk and hip-hop. Before considering hip-hop in particular, I take a quick look at the cultural soil of Latin America to appreciate the roots and branches of African and Spanish blends in the New World.

THE CATHOLIC BAROQUE IN THE AMERICAS

Catholicism played a key role in the baroque culture of the New World. When contrasting the respective roles of Protestantism and Catholicism in the Americas, it is fair to say that each had its own logic and aesthetic values. At the very least, we can say that their evangelization proceeded in different ways, with Iberian and Catholic cultures assuming a more accommodating stance when it came to African and Native peoples, and North American Protestantism generally practicing a policy of separation and segregation, keeping non-Christian cultures at a greater distance. Each had its own glaring, titanic sins, colossal in scale, when it came to the African slave trade or treatment of Native peoples, but the Catholic baroque model—with its penchant for visual excess, folkloric richness, and indulgent syncretism—seems to have been better able to acclimatize its mind to the strange new myths, gods, and narratives that it encountered in the Americas. Even in the face of official warnings and censures, the Latin baroque soul swelled and expanded to make room for the pantheon of gods and cultures in the New World. By "baptizing" American "pagan" traditions, a new Catholic baroque was created, *el indio barroco*, which brought together various religious and cultural fragments—African, European, and indigenous—into a fresh concert of sound, flavor, and belief specifically for the Indies: a *concierto barroco* (incidentally, the title of one of Carpentier's novels).[12] Faced with improbable juxtapositions and fantastic combinations, Latin American dictionaries and vocabularies reeled in the effort to name the creatures of this hitherto unmapped world. A ravishing lexicon of brownness was the result, as Richard Rodriguez has observed: "Mexico has for centuries compiled a ravishing lexicon of brown because in Mexico race is capricious as history is capricious. For the colonial era, the verbal glamour of Mexico has been to entertain a spectrum of brown—of impurity—as rich and as wet as a Hollander palette: *mestizo, castizo, alvina, chino, negro torno atras, morisco, canbujo, albarrasado, tente en el aire, canpa mulato, coyote, vorsino, lobo.*"[13] Like the arabesque lines of a baroque church, or the verbal abundance of baroque rhetoric, words multiplied and proliferated to find the right adjectives and descriptions for the dizzying variety of New World identities. In this restless odyssey searching for the right word, the lexicon of the Indies has a way of overwhelming the human mind's compulsion to define and classify, reminding us of the sheer incommensurability of human identity. Racial nomenclature in Latin America accordingly has been a profusion of metaphors and anthropomorphisms, thick with nuances, gradations, accents, and puzzles. As the names of God in mystical traditions did, metaphors and labels have multiplied, if only to remind us that human identity, like God, is wholly other. In lieu of emptiness as metaphor, the baroque piled together confused, frenetic, and vertiginous lines and images, with borders that gyrated and zig-zagged, crisscrossed and meandered in search of the perfect design that would encapsulate the wonder of the world. If we contrast this "Hollander palette" of identity with North American categories for race, the latter come across as unusually thin and pale, especially when conceived in black and white, with straight lines and stark borders separating them, as if the categories mimicked the simple lines of a Shaker table.

For the purposes of this book, we can see and hear evidence of the baroque imagination in the music of the Americas, all the way up to the hip-hop scene. The music of Latin America is proof of the carnival-like identity of Latin America, with African and indigenous cultures surviving and even thriving in the Caribbean and Latin America, while largely disappearing from Protestant North America. In Cuba, Haiti, and Brazil, African cultures transplanted themselves and put down deep roots, eventually becoming part of Latin America's religious and musical soil. African cultural and religious traditions in the United States, by contrast, rarely survived the violence of the Middle Passage, falling on hard, rocky soil when they came ashore, or worse, encountering concerted efforts to uproot and exterminate any traces of these traditions.[14]

Of course there are many explanations for the survival of African culture in the Caribbean and Latin America—especially given the greater number of first-generation slaves in those settings—but certainly one factor was the part played by the Catholic theater of saints, martyrs, festivals, and theologies in keeping African memories and rituals alive.[15] In the words of Albert Raboteau, "The nature of Catholic piety with its venerations of saints, use of sacramental and organization of religious fraternities among the slaves offered a supportive context for the continuity of African religious elements in recognizable forms."[16] The color and religious bars were more unclear and malleable in Latin America, so Catholicism and African religions entered into secret pacts and covenants, resulting in a version of soul that was a colorful mask of heterogeneity, animated by a multitude of spirits. While many U.S. evangelical Protestants regarded such unions as evidence of Catholic promiscuity, debauchery, and the idol-making faculty of the Catholic mind, Catholic thought assumed that grace was generously and universally diffused in the diverse array of human cultures. Seen through eyes aided by grace, all tribal ancestors and graven images—say, Quetzalcoatl and Tonantzin in Mexico, or Elegua and Shango in Cuba—had sacramental value and were worthy of communion with Christian belief and practice.

AFRO-LATIN SOUL IN THE AMERICAS: THE *SON*

Many of these features of Catholicism in the New World are evident in the development of Afro-Latin religion and music. On the stage of the eccentric world of the Americas, religion underwent a metamorphosis as startling as anything else that occurred on the continent. After making contact with African and indigenous traditions, Catholicism would not be the same. Evangelization worked both ways, injecting African and Native religions with a Christian element while converting Old World Catholicism into a new American variety, replete with pagan rites, gods, and stories. As Carpentier sees it, in this way American cultures added exotic colors and flavors to an already rich rainbow in baroque Catholicism. "The altars, the accessories surrounding the cult of worship, the images, the religious garments, were crafted to seduce souls strongly attracted by a sumptuous world of rites and mysteries. Deep down, of course, it did not mean that the ancient gods of Africa were renounced. Ogún, Changó, Eleguá, Obatalá, and many others continued thriving in the hearts of many."[17] Catholicism's "sumptuous world of rites" found a place for these gods even if they were unofficially recognized and concealed under the façade of Catholic icons, saints, and festivals. Wedded to these Catholic figures, African deities continued to thrive in the hearts of many and reappeared in countless fiestas and ceremonies.

Music and dance in particular were conduits for these appearances of the Orishas (African ancestors and deities), bursting into time and space through the charged, throbbing currents of the drums. In the language of vibrations and beats, only intelligible to the initiates, the African *batá* drums would summon the Orishas and plead for their intercession in the lives of the people. With the repetition of certain words, or the precise sequence of beats alone, the Orishas would descend into the participants and take possession of their bodies and spirits. (The expressions *bajar al santo*, "to make the saint descend," and *subirse el santo*, "to have the saint rise through you," describe these experiences.)[18] When these percussive qualities were joined with Spanish and Arabic musical legacies, a ravishing symbiosis of New World religion and sound was created—the Cuban *son* was one of these products, a child of these synchronicities.

As a result of the migration of African slaves to Cuba from San Domingo in the 1790s in the aftermath of the Haitian revolution, African-based rhythms arrived in force, seducing and converting more and more Cubans. Suddenly the sediments of Haitian French traditions filtered into the wide river of Spanish-Arabic music from Andalusia and

Cuba. Unlike the *contradanza*, a French salon dance and musical style performed with an orchestra, the *son* developed in the lowest strata of Cuban society, among Spanish settlers, freed slaves, mulattos, and *cimarrones* (runaway slaves).[19] Some critics trace its origins to the eastern mountain regions of Cuba around 1860, where greater permissiveness seemed to prevail in relations among settlers from Spain, freed slaves (many Bantu and Dahomeyan), and mulattos. (The term *son montuno*, "son of the mountain," reveals its rural origins.)[20] Carpentier, however, traces the roots of the *son*, particularly its narrative and poetic components, back further into the mists of time, to the slum songs of the eighteenth century that delighted in puns, humor, and libidinous allusions (derived from the *chuchumbé*).[21] Whatever its exact origins, the *son* supplemented the Spanish *canción* and other European melodies with a battery of African percussion, thus creating a prototypical Afro-Latin genre. (The *son* usually was played in an ensemble of the guitar, tres, güiro, bongos, marímbula, maracas, and claves.)[22]

In this vein, Samuel Feijóo speaks of the *son* as "heated-up rhythm, with its percussion section of neo-African instruments and its extraordinary folkloric literary sense."[23] For our purposes, the folkloric sense of the *son* is important, as it introduced popular ballads, social satire, political commentary, and religious hymns and incantations to the remarkable variety of African drums. If we add the music of the carnival parades *(comparsas),* with their totemic echoes of Yoruba gods and hymns as well as invocations to the Virgin and the saints, we get an idea of the various currents and waves of emotion and rhythm that inundated the island like a tropical storm. Because the *son* traversed a wide spectrum, it disturbed artificial categories of the sacred and profane. In this respect, *son*'s polyrhythm—its signal achievement in Carpentier's view—represents in music the wider spiritual and cultural climate of Afro-Latin America.[24] In its rhythmic variation and spontaneity, *son* gave voice to the vibrant, vertiginous *mestizaje* of the New World just as jazz would later articulate key principles of North American culture.

As *son* infiltrated forbidden domains, however, it acquired detractors among the ruling white elites in Cuba, the zealots of a monotone version of Cuba. For Jory Farr, *son* has a subversive history: "As it spread across the island, it became a dangerous music, a shout of defiance, a fluming of raw, mixed-race sensuality that disrupted the tight controls enforced by Cuba's light-skinned ruling class. The early history of *son* has tales of repression and harassment, of police destroying instruments and jailing 'lewd' musicians."[25] Accusations of its diabolical character emerged as an index of its perceived danger from those fearing an outbreak of wild poly-rhythm, uncontrolled polyphony, and cultural miscegenation. Just as the blues, jazz, soul, and hip-hop have been sullied and demeaned with indict-ments of their devilish character, *son* faced similar charges, accused of prodigality and sensual extravagance. Heedless of high and low cultural boundaries, or sacred and profane classifications, *son* borrowed from dis-parate sources and produced sounds that brought together classes, races, and religions into a bacchanalia of jubilation. Like the *zarabanda* of the sixteenth and seventeenth centuries, *son* had lowly and disreputable ori-gins but would eventually prove delicious and irresistible to cultured elites. Fernando Ortiz makes this point about the *zarabanda:* "But there is also the art born below that climbs from class to class, from the puddles to the mountain tops, adjusting itself to the atmosphere at every level, until it finally converts itself, thanks to its beauty, into an art whose gesta-tion and early upbringing are utterly forgotten. . . . This was true of the *zarabanda,* that sprang to life in a scandalous and diabolical impropriety among black conjurers and witchdoctors of the Congo, and then, with the passing of time, was danced at the royal courts."[26]

In the case of *son,* not unlike the *zarabanda,* its origins are impossible to disentangle from the circumstances of slavery. One song in this tradi-tion, related to the *nengón,* is a plaintive, haunting lament about the plight of a slave. Like the blues in North America, the *son* could swing low and strike notes of sorrow and anguish, and then, just as suddenly, become jubilant and humorous; tragedy and festivity are hardly irrecon-cilable in the music. When channeling a bolero, *son* is typically mournful; when approximating the mambo, a later development of the *son,* it can be fast-paced, aggressive, and lascivious. Gustavo Perez-Firmat puts it this way: "The bolero is a medium for bemoaning unhappiness in love, for questioning the injustice of fate. If the mambo is about conquest, the bolero is about loss. If the mambo is copulative, the bolero is disjunctive. The mambo grunts, the bolero moans."[27]

Grunts and moans, conquests and losses, copulations and disjunc-tions: everything from the wide world of human experience can appear in the sublime cathedral of emotion known as *son.* Following is a well-known *son,* "Cajón de Muerto":

Solo ambicion de fatiga yerto
Cansado ya de fatiga guerras
Y al acostarme en mi cajón de muerto
Dormir en paz debajo de la tierra.

My only ambition, exhausted
and tired of the enduring war,
is to lie down in my box of death,
to sleep in peace underneath the earth.[28]

Like a bolero, the song bemoans the relentless banality of war and pleads for eternal peace beneath the earth. The plain meaning of the song is obvious here, but since the reference to *cajón,* coffin, can also be to the wooden boxes used in Afro-Cuban music and religion (used as percussion, for calling the Orishas), there is a hidden religious meaning as well. The singer thus spreads out his emotions in various directions, aiming at the sacred as much as the profane, at the sky as much as the earth.

At the table of this spacious imagination, Cuban musicians often find a place for the sacred even in moments of sensual indulgence. For such artists, the beats of the *batá* drum strike chords much deeper than the pleasures of the body. The beats may trigger the quivering vibrations of the flesh, the rush of the blood through the veins, and the gloss of sweat on the body, but they also stimulate spiritual faculties and mystical chords of memory. They can represent the thunderous sound of the coming of Shangó/Santa Barbara or the passage of Eleguá/San Antonio into the crossroads of the world. The drums invoke the ancestors in Afro-Cuban music the way ancient Greek poets and musicians invoked the muses with the lyre. When describing these revels in Cuban music and religion, Jory Farr offers this testimony: "At a jazz club in Havana one night, explosions of bebop horns and electric guitars, all building into climax after shuddering climax, suddenly gave way to chants of the Abakuá, a men's secret leopard society, and the sacred rhythms of the *batá* drums. At Casa de la Música, I saw the lead singer of Cuba's all-girl, twelve-member Chicas del Son go from a lusty bump-and-grind to the rapturous ritual dance of her *Orisha,* suggesting that sex, rhythm, harmony, and divine resonance were one and the same."[29] In these examples, music plays loosely with a wide range of ecstasies, sacred and secular alike. Whether in sacred rhythms or profane climaxes, these ceremonies charge the body electric with spiritual and physical energies and enrapture the listener with music "heard so deeply that it is not heard at all, but you are the music while the music lasts."[30]

Transports and elevations of this kind are of course abundant in African American music of the United States, as we have seen in previous chapters, but the echoes of African and Latin traditions grow fainter in the North American context and recede into the background of mainstream music. It becomes more difficult to determine the sources of the sound, to identify what role African ancestors or Latin rhythms played in the evolution of black music. The average listener to hip-hop knows very little, if anything, of fusions and collaborations among African and Latin traditions.

On the eve of hip-hop's delivery into the Bronx in the 1960s, however, Afro-Latin alliances were palpable parts of the atmosphere, setting the stage for musical innovation. Juan Flores calls attention to one case, the movement known as "Afro-Latin soul," sometimes called the boogaloo: "The bawdiness, the strong presence of funk and soul music, the abrupt break with some tradition-bound conventions of Latin style, all figure centrally in most boogaloo and point more clearly to the musical influences that set the stage for that brief yet dramatic transition in Latin music of the mid-1960s period."[31] Afro-Latin soul emerged with the Latin-funk fusions of the 1960s in North America and soon gave way to hip-hop. Though there was already a long tradition of interplay between jazz and Latin music in North America, the decades of the 1960s–1970s took the affiliations of Afro-Latin and Afro-American styles in new directions, especially with the rising tidal waves of R & B, soul, and funk.[32] The symbolic rapport of black and Latin revelry continued in these decades, but increasingly picked up new sensibilities, becoming harder, grittier, and funkier, a reflection of the brutal exigencies of American ghettos. Since Latinos and blacks often shared the beleaguered spaces of U.S. ghettos (Puerto Ricans in New York, Mexicans in Southern California, Haitians and Cubans in New Orleans and Florida), it was natural for them to cooperate in the production of new styles and sounds. Hip-hop is a product of these interactions, as Afrika Bambaataa once said: "Wherever hip hop was, and the Blacks were, the Puerto Ricans, and other Latinos were, too."[33]

AFRO-LATIN HIP-HOP IN THE AMERICAS

Besides the well-known contributions of Latinos in the areas of breakdancing and graffiti, it is clear that Latinos contributed greatly to the music of hip-hop. In particular, it is well established that hip-hop copped the percussion beats from Afro-Latin music (a descendant of the *batá* drums).[34] One of the pioneers of hip-hop beats, Jimmy Castor, is a case in point: "From watching or hearing records of Latin musicians like Tito Puente, Chan Pozo and Cal Tjader," writes David Toop, "he learned to incorporate authentic Afro-Cuban rhythms and percussion, adding timbales to his vocal and multi-instrumental abilities."[35] Besides appropriating some of these rhythms (as in his "Block Party," 1972), Castor introduced the dozens and jive talk into his music with songs like "Hey Leroy, Your Mama's Callin'," "Say Leroy, the Creature from the Black Lagoon Is Your Father," and "Dracula." At a minimum, he is a bridge figure who straddles the world of soul, funk, and Latin music, on the one hand, and the budding rap game, on the other.

Beyond the example of Jimmy Castor, the close encounters between Latin and African American music in New York in the 1960s–1970s created a climate that was positively saturated with hybrid sounds and styles; Castor was a microcosm of a larger, multicolored cosmos that included contributions from Latin America, the Caribbean, and elsewhere. (The Caribbean roots of some of the founding figures of hip-hop, like DJ Kool Herc and Afrika Bambaataa, have long been acknowledged.) At this stage in hip-hop studies, appreciation for the pluralistic history of rap's origins seems well established, but it is worth recalling the transnational and intercultural influences that coalesced, condensed, and heated up to produce the big bang explosion of hip-hop. Because so many North Americans think of the U.S.–Mexican border as a mental wall as much as a political demarcation, this recognition of a common musical heritage throughout the Americas is frequently overlooked and even denied.[36] Whether in musical theory or cultural studies, the building of insurmountable fences between various nation-states or ethnic nationalities has a way of obscuring the mad combinations and riotous arrays of musical and cultural influences that produced black music in the Americas. And this holds true in hip-hop studies, in which so many voices, rhythms, and loops are echoed, sampled, faded in and out, and scratched over, as much as in anything else.

It is equally true, however, that rap music created something authentically new in the Bronx, something quite different from Latin musical conventions. Though there were many forerunners of rap in Latin America—*decimas* (dueling and mocking verses); *plenas* and *corridos* (news reports and folk stories chanted or sung); and carnival conventions of satire, parody, obscenity, and saturnalia—there is no doubt that rap music in North America reconfigured and remixed various sources into a unique and singular creation.[37] Without denying the importance of the creole complexity of New York in the 1970s, hip-hop was surely a breakthrough of African American youth, as Imani Perry has maintained.[38] Though African American youth drew from a crazy variety of musical heritages, they emerged from the laboratory of invention with a previously unheard style, fresh and original.

Many Latinos who were in earshot of this new sound greeted hip-hop like a newly discovered truth, with a shock of recognition, like falling in love. Because of this new beloved, Latinos in the United States saw the traditions of their ancestors interrupted and amplified by African American styles and flows, making for new identities for these Latinos in the diaspora. In my case, the mariachi music that my parents adored was passed on to me in the milk of my mother, but I was also nursed on the music of Grandmaster Flash, the Gap Band, Run DMC, Rakim, Tupac, Nas, and others. As Gustavo Perez Firmat once said about mambos, mariachi music will not be forever.[39] And the fact that mambos and *corridos* have given way to hip-hop for many Cuban and Mexican youths only illustrates the inevitability of change for Latinos dispersed in this "first world" America. In both the United States and Latin America, hip-hop has challenged traditional Latin music for the right to speak for the barrios.[40]

And yet at the same time the converse is true: Latino hip-hop has also challenged the mainstream scene in the United States. By adding their own intonations and themes to North American rap, many Latin rappers indigenize their music with a *sabor Latino,* inserting their own piquancy and kick into the soul food of hip-hop. For this reason alone, the relationship of Latino hip-hop with U.S. rap is usually dialogical rather than simply mimetic, a critical exchange rather than plain imitation. While U.S. hip-hop has clearly worked its magic on these cultures, Latin America has also spoken back with some of its own charms.

In the remainder of this chapter I consider some of the distinctive themes in Latin hip-hop throughout the Americas, assessing first its "third world" context, then its sampling of African religion, and finally its connection with indigenous histories.[41]

The "Third World" Context of Afro-Latin Hip-Hop

As I discussed in chapter 6, one of the great MCs of hip-hop, Chuck D, used his furious, apocalyptic-inspired tongue to decry American-sponsored violence against blacks in the United States. However, I neglected to mention that he can be equally tough on the state of the hip-hop industry today. As a key witness to the rise and success of hip-hop, Chuck D has expressed deep concern about how it has aged: a child once so fresh and so clean, a child of endless promise, it is now in danger of losing its soul, "talkin about popping locks, servin rocks and hittin switches, now she's a gangsta rollin with gangsta bitches, always smokin blunts and gettin drunk."[42] Though Common penned these lines, Chuck D has long been warning the hip-hop nation of these dangers, of the ruinous incursions of venal materialism and crass hedonism in the soul of the rap game.

Besides changing the message of hip-hop—preferring the themes of booty, blunts, and bling over prophetic indictments of grinding poverty, racist legacies, and spiritual emptiness—more recent developments in the business of hip-hop have had the effect of severely shrinking the range of its voices and perspectives. Now an artist must secure a corporate imprimatur in order to get any play, and this process has clearly blunted the prophetic edge. As in biblical prophecy, when a prophet works for the king and is a part of the courtly retinue, he becomes the voice of the king, not the voice of God. Something like this, according to Chuck D, has happened in hip-hop: "In the first ten to twelve years of rap recordings," he states, "rappers rapped for the people, and they rapped against the elite establishment. In the last ten or so years, rappers rap for their companies and their contracts, and they're part of the establishment now. It's two diametrically opposed ideas."[43] Because of this sea change in hip-hop, the tides have frequently turned against the most artistic and dissident voices. We are left, as Immortal Technique, Chuck D, and Brother Ali suggest, with a civil war for the soul of the nation of hip-hop.[44]

Given these concerns about hip-hop's survival in a culture of self-gratification, Chuck D began to look to other parts of the world for alternatives to U.S. rap. During a visit to South Africa in 2011, he spoke with excitement about what he was experiencing there, as if he had traveled through a wormhole and returned to the state of hip-hop in its "livest" infancy. "The world has parity now," he wrote, "and has surpassed the USA in all of the basic fundamentals of hip hop."[45] For those disenchanted with the current status of hip-hop in the United States, voices from the global periphery offer refreshing alternatives; they are more urgent, more timely, and more relevant to the convulsions and distresses of communities throughout the world. These voices give us glimpses of hip-hop at its most resourceful and cunning, in which beats and rhymes are diamonds mined out of the ruins of poverty and social crisis, and a concern with "ends" runs deeper than "money, hos, and clothes." Instead of eliding or reinforcing the massive inequalities of the global capitalist order, these rappers raise their voices against the powers that benefit from this discriminatory state of affairs. And when necessary, they target all those in hip-hop who are untroubled and complacent about these realities, all the perpetrators of hip-hop, those too faded on chronic to notice the depths of global suffering.

The study of hip-hop's global dispersion has other benefits as well. I see it as decentering and challenging the North American ego about supremacy in art and culture, reminding us of the unconscious (and sometimes blatantly conscious) prejudices that elevate this ego like a sacred chalice at the moment of consecration. As Paul Gilroy insists, there is a glaring "American-centrism" in a lot of hip-hop, and when this attitude prevails, it tends to be silent about the struggles of anyone outside the United States, whether south of the border, across the Atlantic, or throughout the African continent.[46] When turning our attention to the global underground, not only do we get a different spin on hip-hop, but we are also exposed to a more heterogeneous and chameleon-like version of "blackness" than portraits in the United States, "blackness" as the color of pariahs and outcasts, as a symbol of various stripes and hues of oppression.[47] Since the majority of blacks in the western hemisphere reside in Latin America (approximately 37 percent live in the United States), by expanding our field of vision in hip-hop studies, we encounter a new vista of the African diaspora, one that can shed light on the unions, blends, and combinations between Africa and various Spanish and Portuguese cultures, the Afro-Latin hybrids. True to the spirit of hip-hop, when we flip the script on the prevailing state of hip-hop in the United States, we may begin to see things with fresh eyes, fixing our sight on previously unseen things.

Many Cuban hip-hop artists, I argue, embody this construction of faith, in which the poor of their country are suddenly made visible and their voices are given a hearing. Consider EPG's simple description of their mission: "We rap about the conditions of our lives, the fact that our people, the poor, continue to get poorer while the rich get richer."[48] Or Anónimo Consejo on a similar note: "Rap is something that is born here in your heart, with the idea of combatting injustice perpetrated by the government against immigrants, African Americans and Latinos."[49] For many Cuban rap groups—add Obsesión, Hermanos de Causa, Gente de Zona, Daymé Arocena, and the Orishas to this list—hip-hop remains a revolutionary struggle, a voice of protest and peace. This engaged vision of hip-hop comes up a lot among Latin American rap groups, as if they feel obliged to mark their territory with a distinct demarcation from the commercially popular rap of North America, more in keeping with a pedagogy of the oppressed than a pedagogy of ballin'. In one of their raps, "Tengo," Hermanos de Causa describe their griefs and grievances as follows:

Tengo una palmera, un mapa sin tesoro
Tengo aspiraciones sin tener lo que hace falta. . . .
Tengo una raza oscura y discriminada
Tengo una jornada que me exige y no da nada
Tengo tantas cosas que no puedo ni tocarlas
Tengo instalaciones que no puedo ni pisarlas
Tengo libertad entre un parenthesis de hierro
Tengo tantos derechos sin provechos, que me encierro
Tengo lo que tengo sin tener lo que he tenido.

I've got a palm tree, a map without a treasure
I've got aspirations without having what I need. . . .
I've got discrimination because I'm black
I've got a job that demands and gives nothing
I've got so many things that I can't even touch
I've got all these places I can't even step foot in
I've got freedom in a parentheses of iron
I've got so many rights without any benefit that I feel confined
I've got what I have without having what I've had.[50]

As Alan West-Durán and Sujatha Fernandes note about this song, it is riffing on the classic poem by Nicolás Guillén, "Tengo" ("I Have"), about many of the achievements of the Cuban Revolution of the 1950s: "Tengo que ya tengo donde trabajar y ganar lo que me tengo que comer. / Tengo, vamos a ver, tengo lo que tenía que tener." (I have, now, a place to work and I can earn what I have to eat. / I have, let's see, I have, what was coming to me.)[51] In adopting this trope from the Cuban Revolution, Guillén cast his lot with the promises and dreams of the new regime. Typical of the hip-hop generation, however, this song by Hermanos de Causa interrupts complacency about the revolution's noble ideals with a disillusioned note of complaint, protest, and dissent. In line after line the song accumulates these gripes until the regime appears deficient and defective, fragmented by the weight of these social problems, humbled by the conspicuous cracks that appear in the façade of Cuba's state apparatus. By using irreverent parody and ridicule in their raps, Hermanos de Causa hold the revolution accountable for not making good on its promises, for writing checks with no bullion in the bank (the attitude of U.S. rappers toward "civil rights" is similar). Though this attitude does not lead the group to disown the revolution, they also refuse to muzzle their barking at the poverty and racism that continue to hound Afro-Cubans.

In the same manner, the song targets material and consumer values: "No confundas tener más con tener cualidades" (Don't confuse having more with being better), or "Mientras más tienes más quieres y siempre más querrás. / Mientras más tú tengas más ridículo serás" (The more you have, the more and more you want. / The more you have, the more ridiculous you'll be). The group uses the Cuban style of *choteo*—a style of signifying—as a way of censuring and "dissing" anything that presumes innocence and sanctity, anything that claims for itself an infallible eminence, be it socialism, capitalism, or any other triumphal ideology.[52]

It's important to note here that Guillén's poetry was inspired by the rhythms and flows of Afro-Cuban *son;* therefore, what appears in Hermanos de Causa's rap is the *son* remixed for the hip-hop generation. (In a very interesting example of black and Latin exchanges, according to Arnold Rampersad, it was Langston Hughes who first encouraged Guillén to make use of *son* in his poetry, as Hughes had done with the blues.)[53] Many of the group's songs rework the *son* in this manner, such as in another rap, "Lagrimas Negras" ("Black Tears," the title of a classic *son* by the famous composer Miguel Matamoros). The persistence of racism in Cuba is its topic:

> Siento odio profunda por tu racismo
> Ya no me confundo con tu ironía
> Y lloro sin que sepas que el llanto mío
> Tiene lágrimas negras como mi vida.

> I feel profound hate for your racism
> I am no longer confused by your irony
> And I cry without you knowing that my cry
> Has black tears like my life.[54]

In this rap, the group has changed its focus from romantic abandonment and mourning, in Trio Matamoros's original version, to the legacy of racism. The song follows the plaintive and gentle tone of Matamoros's song (true to a classic Cuban bolero), but the lyrics are delivered with the anger and edginess of a hip-hop activist, someone who has simmered and simmered until finally reaching a boiling point. The black tears represent so much more than the agony of love; they are traces and symptoms of centuries of dishonorable behavior toward Afro-Cubans, tears that have calcified into rage and distrust.

In the Brazilian hip-hop scene, also, many of these themes—race, religion, poverty, and violence—are almost always the scaffoldings on which musicians build their houses of language and music. Derek Pardue suggests that the youth movements of the late twentieth century in Brazil—responses to the military dictatorship that ruled from 1964 to 1985—were used in these ways and infused rap music in Brazil with a revolutionary spirit.[55] In Pardue's account, hip-hop is the voice of the *periferia,* the voice of slums and abandoned neighborhoods, in which outlaws and the destitute live together in a common struggle. Brazilians use the perfectly apt term *quebradas,* broken or cracked, to designate these communities, as if everything here is inoperative, wrecked, and failed, as if there is a fissure or fault line running through their hoods, ready to swallow them. One of the best known hip-hop groups in Brazil, Racionais MCs, raps about life in these dilapidated and broken circumstances. In their early work in a compilation titled *Consciência Black,* and in the subsequent albums *Holocausto Urbano* (Urban Holocaust, 1990), and *Sobrevivendo no Inferno* (Surviving in Hell, 1997), they present harrowing portraits of life in the *periferia,* with lyrics laced with both distress and determination, lyrics that are threads of light guiding the listener through the mazes of their hoods. "Diaro de um detento" is a song about the smothering darkness of prison life, from the album *Sobrevivendo no Inferno:*

> Hoje, tá difícil, não saiu o sol
> Hoje não tem visita, não tem futebol. . . .
> Gracias a Deus e á Virgem Maria
> Faltam só um ano, três meses e uns dias.
> Tem uma cela lá em cima fechada
> Desde terça-feira ninguém abre pra nada
> Só o cheiro de morte e Pinho Sol.

> It's hard today, the sun has not come out
> There is no visitation, there is no soccer. . . .
> Thank God and the Virgin Mary,
> There is only one year, three months and some days left.
> There's a cell block upstairs that is closed.
> Since Tuesday, nobody opens it.
> There is only the smell of death and Pine Sol.[56]

In this song and others by this group, the raps move freely between the sacred and the profane, the spiritual and the social, stitching together a composite quilt of many emotions and concerns. As if they are wringing from their souls bitter poisons that would sink them in despair if they were held in, the group's appeals to God and the Virgin Mary give them strength and grace to face the darkness without succumbing to the self-destructive temptations of drugs, violence, and nihilism. The reference here to Mary is particularly noteworthy given the importance of Marian devotion in the Caribbean and Latin America (associated with Yemanjá in Brazil and Yemayá in Cuba). Like a touch of tenderness in an otherwise hard and violent life, the image of Mary is an enlivening presence in the song, the smell of roses in an environment that reeks of death and Pine Sol.

It seems to me that these songs, in a world far from the Bronx, are true to the original spirit of hip-hop that once broke loose and electrified the ghettos of the world. While the form and flow of the rap—the distinctive lyrical cadence, timbre, timing, tone, poetry, rhythm—are as essential to the music as the content and substance of what is said, I nevertheless insist that the dominant beat of Latin American hip-hop is meant to match the tough and impoverished predicaments of urban life, and that it's meant to be, to quote K'naan, "the new poor people's weapon."[57] In Latin American hip-hop's efforts to produce music that summarizes the cultures, spirituality, and social injustices of the global periphery, it has the potential of being the refrain and requiem for our postmodern age, reminding us of the desperate need in our world today for sounds and lyrics that are attuned to the ghettos of the world, for music that rides low and close to the streets, a music that has a steely, asphalt edge to it, a music with the metallic polish of a lowrider.

Afro-Latin Religion and Hip-Hop

The sampling of African religion has been an essential feature of Latin American music and culture, thanks in no small part to the Catholic societies and guilds *(cabildos)*. Almost from the beginning of their arrival on the shores of the Americas, the *cabildos* coupled African beliefs, music, and dance with Catholic rites to produce a new flavor of belief, a rich, polyglot gumbo of religion and culture. Though they existed in fifteenth-century Seville (there were *cabildos* for gypsies, African slaves, and many other groups in Spain), those of the New World surpassed in number the Old World guilds and increasingly acquired African features, with secret ceremonies, hermetic languages, and special musical signatures. "Isuama's *cabildo*," one researcher remarks, "preserved the chants, songs, and dances of the original Carabalí slaves."[58] It is remarkable that these guilds could conserve such fragile treasures in oral and fleshly forms, passing on these rites in many cases without written records. Like curators of a dazzling heritage of sound, the *cabildos* built living museums to these memories and styles and had an impact on the entire history of music in the Americas. The *cabildos* did nothing less than ransom the spirits of the ancestors so that they could continue to live, dance, and sing in a new land, an example of the surprising, indomitable capacity of uprooted cultures to thrive in oppressive and inhospitable circumstances.

In the cases of *son* and salsa, incantations to African gods and ancestors were frequent themes. We see this in *cantos* to the Orishas by Roberto Fonseca, Chucho Valdés, Celina González, Machito, Mercedes Valdez, Willie Rosario, Tommy Olivencia, Los Van Van, and numerous others. In Olivencia's version of "Chango 'ta Beni" (Shango is coming), for example, the sound and lyrics capture the threatening, apocalyptic expectations of Shango, a dream that once fired the Haitian revolution:

Chango 'ta beni, Chango 'ta beni, Chango 'ta beni.
Con el machete en la mano, mundo va acabar, tierra va temblar.

Shango is coming, Shango is coming, Shango is coming.
With a machete in his hands, the world is coming to an end,
The world will tremble. [the rhyming words acabar/temblar don't quite
work in English][59]

Like the mysterious writing on the wall of the Babylonian palace in the book of Daniel—hieroglyphic words that spelled doom for the arrogance of empire—the rhymes and incantations here are highly charged with political significance and spell the end to all empires built on the backs of slaves and the poor. The desperate pleas for Shango here, repeated like a liturgical chant, strike an apocalyptic tone and are ill omens for the masters of history. Replete with warning and eschatological expectation, the song combines threat and promise, envisaging a transformation that will redeem the lives of the degraded and disenfranchised.

For many Afro-Latinos, hip-hop continues this legacy. With the dead still haunting the young votaries of hip-hop, music becomes an idiom of rebellion and a portent of danger. The retrieval of the past is a subversive act, taking the community forward, not backward. Consider one of EPG's raps: "We are creating hip hop using our roots. / Giving you these ancestral rhythms, uncovering your mind with my fountain, showing you clearly that on my island there is a branch of hip hop that rises like a stairwell."[60] For EPG, hip-hop surely represents a break with older generations, but there is a stronger note of continuity with the past than in much of U.S. rap, a resolve to constantly renew one's homage to "ancestral rhythms." In group after group, we encounter similar attitudes, such as in the song "Muralla," by the Cuban rap group Cuarta Imagen: "Entiendan que la voz de siete rayos ya llegó / Yoruba soy Yoruba lucumí / Desde Cuba suba mi llanto Yoruba / que suba el alegre llanto / Yoruba que sale de mí." (Understand, the voice of Nsasi has arrived / I'm Yoruba, Yoruba lucumí / may my Yoruba tears rise up from Cuba / may the joyful Yoruba weeping rise out of me).[61] In addition to the heartfelt description of joy and sadness in this song ("joyful weeping"), the rapper joins his voice with the chorus of the gods from the Palo religious traditions of the Congo (the reference to the Nsasi is from the Reglas de Palo). His rap is thus a link in a far-reaching chain that reverses the direction of the Middle Passage and takes his listeners back to Africa, hoping to be a remedy for the maladies of cultural loss and forgetfulness. Rap in this conscious vein is a reproach to all "booty-ass, no grass-roots-having-ass MCs," as Bahamadia puts it, and a prime instance of her claim that the "divine beings got the true sound of hip-hop."[62]

As their name suggests, the most famous Cuban rap group, the Orishas, also join these refrains. In their song "Represent," reference is made to the rich blend of musical and religious heritages in Cuba: "Ven que te quiero cantar de corazón así / la historia de mis raíces / rumba, son, y guaguancó, todo mezclado . . . . / Represento a mis ancestros." (You'll see that I want to sing from my heart the history of my roots, rumba, son, and guaguancó, all blended together . . . . / I represent my ancestors.) This song ends with a litany of praise: "Hey bro Elegua, Changó, Obatalá, Yemayá, Ochún . . . que mi canto suba pa' la gente de mi Cuba, mis ancestros, todos mis muerto, todo eso represento." (Hey bro Elegua, Changó, Obatalá, Yemayá, Ochún . . . I pray that my song will rise and represent the people of my Cuba, my ancestors and all the dead.)[63]

It should be obvious that in this sacred hymn, African gods, largely dead to U.S. rappers, remain alive among this new generation of Latin American youth, as if they refuse the promises of the future if pursuing them means betraying the spirits of the past. If Protestant North America belongs to the future, and Latin America to the Catholic past, hip-hop in Latin America is a curious negotiation between or conciliation of the two, bearing truths and beats that are simultaneously ancient and yet new. Among the Cuban rap groups that I have noted, these truths are multicultural and multicolored, like light seen through a stained-glass window; the cult of the saints, the black Madonna, and African spirits all shine through the mosaic patterns of their music. In one of the most explicit examples, a song by the Orishas, "Canto a Elewa y Changó" (Chant to Elewa/Elegua y Shango), highlights these religious themes:

Hijo Elewa, mi santo Elewa, mi vida Elewa
Mafareo, el rey de los caminos
La ley de mi destino, rojo y negro como el tinto vino
Quien me abre los caminos con su garabato. . . .

Yo como un rayo digo loco lo que siento
Mi voz que ruge como el viento
Blanco y rojo represiento
Changó virtuoso gordete como un oso.

Bien perezoso, jocoso, fogoso,
Santa Bárbara bendita es tu Changó
Guía por el bien camino a tus hijos como yo
Dale la luz señora de virtud. . . .

Tonada para los Orishas
Que llevo en el corazón con amor
Pido que me den salúd e inspiración
Y también la bendición. . . .

Recordarás mi voz, antes que reces,
Antes que reces, reces.

Son Elegua, my saint Elegua, my life Elegua,
All power to you, king of the (cross)roads
The law of my destiny, red and black like red wine
Who opens every road for me with his cane. . . .

Like the lightning, I say madly what I feel
My voice roars like the wind.
I represent white and red
Shango, masterful and powerful like a bear.
Indolent, playful, passionate.
Holy Saint Barbara is your Shango
Guide your children, like me, on the right track.
Give them light, Lady of Virtue. . . .

A melody for the Orishas
That I carry in my heart with love
I ask that they give me health and inspiration
And their blessings as well. . . .

You'll remember my voice before you pray,
Before you pray, pray.[64]

First, note the reference to the union of Shango and Santa Barbara; the song takes for granted their shared identity and bond. (Their feast day is celebrated together on December 4, one of the most important festivals of the year in Cuba.) As the master of lightning and fire, master of percussion-driven ritual and music, and master of dance and passion, Shango is the epitome of the flashy lover of life, the exuberant performer and artist.[65] Upon first glance, it seems peculiar that he would be associated with a Catholic female saint, but if we consider the ways in which Santa Barbara was celebrated in Spanish traditions—in fiery, rapturous, reveling festivity—the connection is not so remote. During the feast day of Santa Barbara and Shango the two figures converge in carnivals of dance and music, with certain jerky, fulgurating dance moves simulating the path of lightning from heaven to earth characteristic of both Shango and Santa Barbara. (Santa Barbara was the patroness of those who worked with explosives, those who harnessed the power of lightning.)[66] The fantastic legend of Santa Barbara—a faithful Christian woman who met a martyr's death but was eventually avenged by a bolt of lightning—seems to have been perfectly arranged to turn these figures into strange bedfellows, with Shango's command of lightning now given credit for avenging Santa Barbara's death, as if Shango would assail with his lightning and fire anyone who would do her harm. In connubial embraces, with Santa Barbara and Shango rubbing, clutching, and dancing with each other, it becomes difficult to tell the two apart, an allegory perhaps of a wider process of cultural eroticism and syncretism. Whatever the case, the product of this union is an eccentric, quixotic marriage of ideas and beliefs, the meeting of Yoruba and Catholic traditions at the crossroads of Hispaniola.

As I mentioned previously, such cross-cultural encounters inevitably affect each tradition brought into the mix: the cultures of master and slave, colonizer and colonized. With oblique allusions to Christian ideas and virtues in this song—the triad of faith, hope, and love is mentioned—it is clear that Christianity steals up on African culture here, changing its cast of mind to include biblical values and virtues. Given this transfiguration, the revolution that is being broadcast by the Orishas is primarily an upheaval of values rather than anything political, perhaps something in the spirit of W. E. B. Du Bois when he claimed that the stranglehold of poverty and injustice would be broken "not so much by violence and revolution, which is only the outward distortion of an inner fact, but by the ancient cardinal virtues: individual prudence, courage, temperance, and justice, and the more modern faith, hope, and love."[67] I suggest that this vision of revolution, cultural more than political, rings true for a great number of rappers throughout the Americas.

Perhaps more striking about this song, however, is that Shango is plainly feminized by his contact with his other half in Santa Barbara. Now Shango is colored with the virtues associated with the goddess traditions of Catholicism. In his female avatar, in other words, he is the "Lady of Virtue," a term that is unmistakably related to the female saints and of course to the Virgin Mary in her many apparitions in the Americas.

At the same time, the influence of the African side is also obvious. After her contact with Shango, Santa Barbara emerges from the ashes of her death as a liberator of African slaves, a fabulous and spectacular metamorphosis to say the least. As Roger Bastide has argued about the Brazilian case, Catholic saints underwent something like a transvaluation in the New World: they became confidants, protectors, and liberators of Africans.[68] Similar to the way in which Guadalupe was indigenized in Mexico, Santa Barbara became a patroness of many Afro-Cubans, lending her protection to the important guild Sociedad de Socorros Mutuos Nación Lucumí de Santa Barbara. Whether St. Benedict the Moor in Salvador, Bahia; or St. James the Elder in Haiti; or the Virgin of Regla (associated with Yemayá), the Virgin of El Cobre (associated with Ochún), the Virgin of Mercy (associated with Obatalá), and Saint Barbara, all in Cuba, the Catholic saints underwent an apotheosis that enthroned them on every Afro-Cuban altar that was dedicated to the struggle for humanity and justice in the Americas.

With Shango's features superimposed on Santa Barbara, furthermore, it is clear that both males and females can wield power. Hence another line in the song appeals to the sword of Santa Barbara, cutting through the obstacles and obscurities of life to light the path of virtue. In this construction, she is strong and brave, a shield and safeguard for weary workers and downtrodden communities; she is anything but a submissive, timid figure. Even with her beatific, feminine countenance, she appears in this tradition as a thunderous threat to the status quo, a lightning bolt against injustice; she appears as a figure of human rights, deft with the sword, perhaps something like the biblical Judith (who famously wields the sword against Holofernes): "For thy power stands not in multitude nor thy might in strong men," Judith prays, "for thou art a God of the afflicted, a helper of the oppressed, an upholder of the weak, a protector of the forlorn, a savior of them that are without hope" (Jth. 9:11).

In this betrothal of Santa Barbara and Shango, then, a religious imagination dedicated to the oppressed and forlorn is fashioned out of the crosscurrents of African religion and Catholicism. Even when Cuban rappers are summoning the Orishas in their raps, calling on them with a ritual-like cadence, the acoustics of their world are clearly Catholic, and this creates a fusion of sound and image that could be the sound track of the New World. This encounter is like a vibrant painting in watercolor, suddenly sodden with rain so that there are smudged borders, blended pigments, amalgamated colors, jumbled images, dripping dyes, and puddled paints. In this postdiluvian view of culture, the original image is irretrievable, but what remains is nonetheless resplendent.

Considering these Afro-Cuban religious influences on the rap scene in Cuba, I suggest in summary that Cuban *raperos* know when to play the trickster, á la Elegua; when to channel Shango's fiery dances and percussion-driven hymns; when to add Spanish and Arabic flourishes; and finally, when to engage and battle with North American sounds. In playing with such combinations, the best of these artists create a feast of meaning that combines the sacred and the profane, the spiritual and the political. Alan West-Durán nicely sums up these various themes in his reading of the Hermanos de Causa song "Tengo." His exegesis concerns the following lines: "Tengo de elemento, tengo de conciente, tengo fundamento." (I've got some funky elements, but I don't scare, I'm politically aware, I've got the initiation, got the foundation.) West-Durán writes: "Both *conciente* and *fundamento* have philosophical, educational, and political meanings, with *conciente* referring to political or social consciousness and *fundamento*, speaking not only to foundations of knowledge, but also of being a *santero*. Hence, in three short lines, Hermanos de Causa reveal their situated knowledge: they 'drop science' from street experience, from their educational training, their politico-philosophical background and their religious dialogue with the Orishas."[69] In claiming *conciente* and *fundamento*, Hermanos de Causa embrace a higher order of knowledge in which there is no contradiction among street smarts, social consciousness, and spiritual wisdom—each plays its part in this science of the soul.[70]

Exile and Indigenous Motifs

When compensating for the relative invisibility of indigenous struggles in U.S. rap, Latin American rappers tend to give considerable, even primary, weight to American Indian voices. Especially in parts of Latin America where the indigenous presence is most conspicuous, hip-hop has frequently modified its accent and cadence to resonate with Native histories and beliefs. In bringing these communities into bold relief, Latin hip-hop exhibits a constant preoccupation, almost an obsession, with the subjects of mass displacement, exile, and migration ("Latin hip-hop" here is inclusive of Latin Americans and U.S. Latinos). Music is transformed into a site of aesthetical experimentation in the face of social traumas and disturbances: violence and conflict, poverty and inequality, oppression and incarceration, migration and diaspora, and so forth.[71] Among U.S. Latinos in particular, hip-hop has been the medium for many immigrants and their children to verbalize feelings of disaffection and alienation in the promised land of North America. In making so much of these themes, Latin rappers often wrap themselves around their countries of origin like a flag worn to a soccer game and transform their music into a network of identification and alliance with slum dwellers south of the border. With their music spinning on an axis of cultural nationalism—interrupted by the scratches, breaks, and ruptures of life in the United States—rap in the Latin style often seems frenzied in its compulsion to find a sense of belonging to center their disoriented souls. A connection with American Indian histories has often been a remedy in this regard, a balm to ease the disorientation.

Given the prominence of indigenous themes in Mexican history and culture, it should not be surprising that many rappers in this tradition travel across the U.S.–Mexican border in search of native roots. The names of some of these groups demonstrate the connection: the Funky Aztecs, Kinto Sol (an Aztec reference to the fifth sun), Ñengo el Quetzal, Aztlan Underground, the Mexakinz, and Ozomatli (Aztec god of dance, fire, and music). And whether or not they have such names, many Latin groups appeal to the indigenous heritage of Latin America as a symbol of solidarity with colonized communities. This is certainly true for Immortal Technique, the Peruvian-American rapper and self-identifying "Zapatista," and for Jaas, the Mapuche *mestiza* from Chile, and for Mare, the wonderful Zapotecan rapper from Oaxaca, and for Cypress Hill in their "Los Grandes Éxitos en Enspañol." Almost without exception, these musicians employ hip-hop as a medium for narrating indigenous memories and struggles and for "transnationalizing" the hip-hop community.[72]

For Kinto Sol, for example, these themes are pervasive. One song, "Hecho in Mexico," radiates indigenous pride: "Soy Azteca, Chichimeca, Zapoteca, (y adentro) soy Indio, Yaqui, Tarasco, y Maya."[73] The Spanish legacy of Kinto Sol's Mexican identity is hardly acknowledged in this song, as the group gives the listener a roll call of tribal filiations. In prioritizing Indian blood in this way, the group strikes a rebellious pose and derides middle-class and elite Mexicans who claim Spanish ancestors while ignoring or downplaying their native roots. Kinto Sol mocks this legacy, calling these types *malinchistas* after La Malinche, the famous interpreter and mistress of Hernán Cortés. There is of course plenty of hyperbole in this attitude (the group consists of *mestizos,* after all, the children of La Malinche *and* Cortés), but the rhetorical excess in the song is a response to centuries of tortured memories and violent histories that have consistently belittled Indian blood. If the group's position is inflated and overstated in this identification with Native America, it is clearly for a prophetic purpose, scathing in the manner of Bartolomé de Las Casas (himself notoriously profligate with words).

In this same signifying, mocking tone, a song by the Funky Aztecs, "Prop 187," ridicules those Mexican-Americans who suddenly become super-patriotic when it comes to the influx of new undocumented immigrants, largely comprised of the poorest and most indigenous of Latin Americans. In solidarity with the stranger and the vulnerable, the group berates the prevailing racism in North American society, so widespread that it creeps into the hearts of every person regardless of color. With Mexicans cast in the role of illegal alien, dope-dealer, rapist, or gang member (descriptions widely used in the election of Donald Trump), the song "Prop 187" castigates everyone active or complicit in the racism:

> A message to the coconut: no matter how much you switch,
> here is what they think about you:
> cactus frying, long distance running,
> soccer playing, shank having, tortilla flipping,
> refried beans eating, border crossing, fruit picking,
> piñata breaking, lowrider driving, dope dealing,
> Tres Flores wearing, green card having, illiterate gang-member,
> go the fuck back to Mexico.[74]

Proposition 187 in California would have denied citizenship to U.S.-born children of undocumented immigrants, as well as access to health services, public schools, and other public services. In this song the Funky Aztecs unroll a long scroll of grievances about this proposition and similar initiatives, leading up to a witty collection of racist epithets that have been hurled at Mexicans and other Latinos.

In another cut by Kinto Sol, "Los hijos del Maiz" (Children of maize), these themes continue, but now with a relentless mantra that adds up the agonies and atrocities endured by Native peoples, until the hymn slowly seeps into the listener's blood. Since the narrative relates many of the hardships of the poor and tries to extract meaning out of the misfortunes endured by the common Mexican laborer, it's not surprising that the group resorts to myth as a means of grappling with the perplexities of life. When the mind and spirit have reached an impasse, when reason is at a loss to explain or justify tribulation, myth is often the most creative means for producing order out of chaos, and in this case for bestowing dignity on the "children of corn."[75] In combining poetry, prophecy, and myth, Kinto Sol's rap does verbally "what Diego Rivera was able to do with a paint brush and blank wall" (cited in the epigraph to this chapter).

In this particular song, the lyrics swing between a prophetic demand for action and social change on the one hand and a more tragic sense of disappointment and despondency on the other. (The melancholic guitar chords and the refrain of women's voices, in particular, give the song a dirge-like feel.) Just as the group's name has apocalyptic echoes (like the four preceding ages, the age of the fifth sun appears to be coming to a catastrophic end), this particular song is mournful and nostalgic, dejected and eschatological. The rap bleeds with aggrieved memories, from the painful struggle for survival of the rapper's Tarascan grandfather in Mexico to the plight of all *hijos del maize* in diaspora:

> Esclavo del hambre, miseria, violencia,
> Trabajos no hay, dinero esta escaso
> Politicos con feria no nos hacen caso
> Esto es un fracaso cada día que paso
> Un nuevo partido es otro madrazo
> Le llaman democracia, me causa gracia
> Pero mas dolor y me deja un mal sabor
> Yo a la muerte le he perdido el temor
> No se si morir sea el remedio major
> Nuevas caras nuevas leyes, falsas ilusiones
> He pasado tanto tiempo que he llegado a conclusions
> Atencion los hijos del maize.
>
> 500 años escondida la verdad
> 5 generaciones en la oscuridad
> Llego la luz termino la tempestad
> El gigante dormido vuelve a despertar
> El alma del Che me aconseja
> Villa me dice mochales la oreja
> Por fin esta lucha se encuentra pareja
> Con gusto termino con toda la nobleza. . . .
> Llego la estapa spiritual.
>
> Slave of hunger, poverty and violence,
> There are no jobs, money is scarce
> Politicians with money don't pay us any attention
> Every day that passes is a disaster
> A new political party is another blow
> They call it democracy, makes me laugh
> More pain, and it leaves me with a bad taste in my mouth
> I've lost all fear of death,
> Perhaps dying is a better solution
> New faces, new laws, false illusions
> It's been a long time since I've had any answers
> Listen to me, children of maize.

For 500 years, the truth has been hidden
5 ages in darkness
The light has arrived, the storm has ended
The sleeping giant will awaken again
The soul of Che guides me
Villa advises me to slash ears
Finally this struggle is fair
I will finish it with nobility. . . .
The spiritual era has arrived.[76]

The song covers a broad spectrum of emotions, seeming despairing at one end and then suddenly inspired at the other. At one moment the rapper seems resigned and melancholic, ready to commit his spirit to the earth, but then the light of Che Guevara and Pancho Villa comes to him and rallies his flagging spirit. In this valley of dry bones on earth, he suddenly visualizes a renewal and promise of justice, with the wounds of the conquest healed and equality bestowed on the children of the sun, with the same superabundance of the sun over the Sonoran desert.

As buoyant as hope appears in the song, it hardly obviates the tragic motifs. Unlike the prophetic vision, in which hope remains in the capacity for social reform, here the tragic attests to the losses and troubles that haunt every human effort. As I suggested in chapter 6, this tragic sensibility is present in much of hip-hop, marking the movement's distance from the prophetic orientation of the civil rights generation. In this specific case, Kinto Sol assumes this tragic mood, in which poverty seems ineradicable, ignorance and darkness are pervasive, and death is a "better solution." Like a nightmare in which one is running and going nowhere, history seems to be running to stand still, beset on all sides by forces that impede advancement. With its invocation of Villa and Che, Kinto Sol wants to believe that the revolution can drive the "locomotive of history" forward (Marx's famous metaphor) and wants to believe in a spiritual age that will flood the world with a light of parity and truth. The conflict in the song, however, is between what the rapper's mind perceives about history—that it is a stalled locomotive going nowhere—and a mythological dream of a more just and humane future. The rap moves across these various borders of thought, starting with the tragic, where misery seems crushing and falls on Native peoples like a leaden, winter sky, and then suddenly, when things seem bleakest, the heavens open up and let in rainbows of light that illuminate the earth with brilliant, colorful rays.

Notice that the dream of revolution is described here in spiritual terms, not as political acts of violence. The war waged against racism and colonialism is understood to be a war of words, a strategy of music, poetry, dance, art, and prayer. More like a modern shaman than a modern politician, Kinto Sol uses mythical images, tight loops, bass lines, and spell-like words to restore its patients to their lost dignity, allowing the ceremony to wash over them like a cleansing rain and rumbling thunderstorm. If we recall that the shaman, at least for many romantics, was a poet, myth-reciter, and performance artist, Kinto Sol nicely fits the description.[77] With the rapper playing the role of shaman and soul artist, Kinto Sol and others in this tradition call upon myth, poetry, religion, and music in the struggle to preserve the defeated memories of the past. The group Anonimo Consejo also strikes this note: "Here I go: silencing mouths of jealous people who want us to change. I know what I have to do. We feel the support of our dear people. In the footsteps of the Taino. . . . America, discovered by our indigenous people, who suffered three hard blows of the New World. When Columbus arrived, slaughter, slavery and oppression also arrived. Kokino is here though you forgot me, honoring study like Don Fernando Ortiz."[78] In addition to this intriguing reference to the pioneering scholar of Afro-Cuban culture and music Fernando Ortiz, the group leaves no doubt that it is following the trails of tears and long walks taken by many black and indigenous communities throughout the Americas, and that rap music is bread and wine for the journey, a new shamanistic medium for an ancient struggle.

For Anonimo Consejo and many others, hip-hop is a return to the sweaty and sublime roots of soul. In preserving the sacred and profane inflections of soul, rap in this tradition does its part to counter the modern dilution and thinning of soul. By considering the needs and trials of the soul from the perspective of ghetto dwellers, migrants, and colored folks—the way the soul is constantly migrating, shifting, adapting, amalgamating, scattering, hiding, fleeing, and doing whatever it takes to carry on—hip-hop gives expression to the ills of time (to recall Nas again) and to the many travails that the soul must endure in the wastelands of the modern world.

But hip-hop also resists these ills. In the forms we have examined, the music mixes bitterness with sweetness, adding the taste of anguish when needed and the taste of solace and joy when the former is overpowering. Religion, myth, and folklore play a key role in endowing the music with this balance and harmony of contrasts. By embracing religious and mythical ligatures that bind them to an ancient past, Latin rappers work with an understanding of myth that is older and richer than what appeared in the Age of Reason, that is even older than Plato and is closer to Homer and Hesiod. In their retrieval of myths from Yoruba, Aztec, Taino, and other indigenous traditions, rappers employ an understanding of *mythos* that is a vehicle of *alethea* (truth), a truth that is a gift of the divine. "In the *Odyssey*," writes Talal Asad, "Odysseus praises poetry—asserting that it is truthful, that it affects the emotions of its audience, that it is able to reconcile differences—and he concludes his poetic narration by declaring that he has recounted a *mythos*."[79] For many of the rappers whom I have discussed, the same is true: myth provides them with a poetic language that reconciles the contradictions of their lives and touches some deep part of truth that eludes the purview of scientific knowledge, some deep part of themselves, some deep part of this astonishing universe. Far from being a lie, myth lights the path of human quests for truth, sometimes in small doses like "matches struck unexpectedly in the dark," and at other times in glaring, raging illuminations.[80] For many of these rappers, myth and religion are employed to deconstruct the dogmas that modern men and women ascribe to the free market, progress, reason, science, and European civilization; they use *mythos* as an alternative narrative to the standard portrait of European hegemony, and they use *mythos* as a way of shoring up the soul against the ruinous and oppressive conditions of modern history.

One might say, borrowing from Aristotle on tragic poetry, that rap music effects a catharsis of artist and listener in this regard, a metamorphosis of pain into pleasure, whereby the drops or even torrents of suffering are channeled into tributaries that can nourish the soul and prevent it from corroding and rusting. As dire and distraught as some of these rap songs seem, the sheer act of composition, the pure creative achievement in making this music, is surely an act of resistance against the demons of destruction, a spell against the most fatal curses. However hip-hop expresses this resistance—in bombast or boast, mourning or festivity—what consistently beats through it all is the ever-resilient pulse of life, the throbbing, flowing movement of blood through the veins. In riding the wave of these sounds and surfs, hip-hop robs death of its tyranny, as joy and love prove stronger than the abyss, more powerful than the grave. When this happens, the music offers the listener a high that is far more profound and lasting than anything a blunt can provide: dope beats, tight lyrics, and spiritual feelings so intoxicating that they allow us to lose ourselves and gain something bigger and better. Something like this happens in Ozomatli's exuberant, boisterous song, "Cumbia de los muertos" (The dance of the dead). Though the lyrics do very little to convey the richness of the song—which requires full band sound of percussion and horns, guitars and accordions, Latin cajónes and tablas, and hip-hop mixers and flows—a small piece of the song is caught in the words that follow:

> Aqui no existe la tristeza, sole existe la alegrias
> El baile de los queridos, de los queridos del pasado
> Mira como baile mi mama, bailando con mi hermano del pasado
> Sus espiritus se juntan bailando, lleno de alegria y gozando.

> Here, sadness doesn't exist, only joy
> The dance of loved ones, the loved ones of the past
> Look how my mother dances, dancing with my dead brother
> Their spirits joined in dance, filled with joy and delight.[81]

For this East L.A. rap group, hip-hop celebrates an impossible, spiritual vision, in which music finds the still point of the turning world and binds us—in the ancient sense of *religare*—to the community of the dead: "At the still point of the turning world. Neither flesh nor fleshless, neither from nor towards; at the still point, there the dance is."[82]

Notes

INTRODUCTION

1. Wallace Stevens, "Two Figures in Dense Violet Night," in *Wallace Stevens: The Collected Poems*, ed. Chris Beyers and John N. Serio (New York: Vintage Books, 1990), 86.

2. Quoted in Alfred Kazin, *Native Grounds* (New York: Mariner Books, 1995), 316.

3. Jonathan Lear, *Open-Minded: Working Out the Logic of Soul* (Cambridge, MA: Harvard University Press, 1998), 27.

4. James McBride, *Kill 'Em and Leave: Searching for James Brown and the American Soul* (New York: Spiegel and Grau, 2016), 25.

5. Lauryn Hill, "Final Hour," on *The Miseducation of Lauryn Hill,* Ruffhouse/ Columbia, 1998.

6. On a related topic, see Mark Edmundson, *Self and Soul: A Defense of Ideals* (Cambridge, MA: Harvard University Press, 2015).

7. Throughout this study I use the term *Latin* as inclusive of Spanish, Latin American, and Latino/a traditions.

8. For a good discussion of this theme, see Stuart Hall, "What Is This 'Black' in Black Popular Culture," in *Black Popular Culture*, ed. Gina Dent (New York: The New Press, 1998), 29.

9. See Tracy Fessenden, *Culture and Redemption: Religion, the Secular and American Literature* (Princeton, NJ: Princeton University Press, 2013), 113–14, 122–23, 131–34.

10. On the subject of romantic racialism, see the excellent book by Curtis Evans, *The Burden of Black Religion* (Oxford: Oxford University Press, 2008).

11. Robin D. G. Kelley describes "soul" in these terms: "Soul is a discourse through which African Americans claimed ownership of the symbols and practices of their own imagined community." "Lookin' for the 'Real' Nigga: Social

Scientists Construct the Ghetto," in *That's the Joint: The Hip Hop Studies Reader,* ed. Murray Foreman and Mark Anthony Neal (London: Routledge, 2011), 140.

12. Robert Alter, *The World of Biblical Literature* (New York: Basics Books, 1992), 204.

13. Quoted by George Steiner in *George Steiner: A Reader* (Oxford: Oxford University Press, 1987), 36.

14. See Leslie Stainton, *Lorca: A Dream of Life* (New York: Farrar, Straus and Giroux, 1999), 48, 64.

15. Michael Eric Dyson, *Holler If You Hear Me: Searching for Tupac Shakur* (New York: Civitas Books, 2006).

16. Lin-Manuel Miranda, "My Shot," on *Hamilton Musical,* Atlantic, 2015.

17. The "Sirens" chapter in *Ulysses* is modeled, in fact, on the eight-part structure of a fugue. The opening is bewildering because the writing plays with the pure sound of words apart from their meaning.

18. Gang Starr, "Moment of Truth," on *Moment of Truth,* Noo Trybe, Virgin, 1998; and Jay Z, "Moment of Clarity," on *The Black Album,* Roc-A-Fella, Def Jam, 2003.

19. Nas, "N.Y. State of Mind," on *Illmatic,* Columbia Records, 1994.

20. Eric B. and Rakim, "I Know You Got Soul," on *Paid in Full,* 4th and B'way, 1987.

CHAPTER 1: IN SEARCH OF SOUL

1. Virginia Woolf, *The Common Reader* (New York: Harcourt Books, 1925), 63.

2. William Butler Yeats, "A Dialogue of Self and Soul," in *The Yeats Reader,* ed. Richard Finneran (New York: Scribner Poetry, 1997), 110.

3. Quoted in Kevin Birmingham, *The Most Dangerous Book: The Battle for James Joyce's Ulysses* (New York: Penguin Books, 2015), 17.

4. I'm paraphrasing here verses from Led Zeppelin, "Ramble On," on *Led Zeppelin II,* Atlantic Records, 1969. Regarding the "new atheists," I'm thinking of the work of Christopher Hitchens, Richard Dawkins, Daniel Dennett, and Sam Harris.

5. See Martin Luther King Jr., "A Christmas Sermon for Peace," in *A Testament of Hope: The Essential Writings and Speeches of Martin Luther King, Jr.,* ed. James M. Washington (New York: HarperOne, 2003).

6. In this sense, my book parallels Andrew Delbanco's study *The Death of Satan.* As he tracks the approach of modernity with the fall of the devil into invisibility and insignificance, I follow a similar path with the idea of the soul. See Andrew Delbanco, *The Death of Satan: How Americans Have Lost the Sense of Evil* (New York: Farrar, Straus, and Giroux, 1995).

7. Woolf, *Common Reader,* 178.

8. Ibid., 178–79.

9. Ibid., 174–75.

10. John Keats, "Letter to the George Keatses," in *John Keats: The Complete Poems,* ed. John Barnard (New York: Penguin Books, 1973), 550.

11. Quoted in Richard Kearney, *Anatheism: Returning to God after God* (New York: Columbia University Press, 2010), 135.

12. Quoted in ibid., 133.

13. Ibid., 141.

14. As many contemporary critics have argued, the terms I am using here, "sacred" and "profane," have a rather recent genealogy. Talal Asad, for one, argues that the term "sacred," conceived as a universal essence, only developed with modern anthropology (in particular, with Émile Durkheim) and paralleled the creation of other universal categories like "religion" and "nature," all concepts that came on the heels of European encounters with the non-European world. See Asad, *Formations of the Secular: Christianity, Islam, Modernity* (Stanford, CA: Stanford University Press, 2003), 33–35.

15. The scholarship of George Lipsitz is another instance of this, in which the metaphor of the crossroads is used to describe these indeterminate zones, where danger dwells for those insisting on rigid boundaries to their own advantage. See Lipsitz, *Dangerous Crossroads: Popular Music, Postmodernism, and the Poetics of Place* (London: Verso Books, 1994), 7–8.

16. Gustavo Perez Firmat, *Life on the Hyphen: The Cuban-American Way* (Austin: University of Texas Press, 1994), 83.

17. Ibid., 81.

18. See Mark Ribowsky, *Dreams to Remember: Otis Redding, Stax Records and the Transformation of Southern Soul* (New York: Liveright, 2015), 43.

19. See Peter Guralnick, *Sweet Soul Music: Rhythm and Blues and the Southern Dream of Freedom* (New York: Little, Brown, 1986), 25–27.

20. See *Meister Eckhart: The Essential Sermons, Commentaries, Treatises and Defense*, trans. Edmund Colledge and Bernard McGinn (New York: Paulist Press, 1981), 60.

21. John Keats, "Letter to Richard Woodhouse," in *John Keats: The Complete Poems*, ed. John Barnard (New York: Penguin Books, 1973), 547.

22. Paul Gilroy, "It's a Family Affair," in *Black Popular Culture*, ed. Gina Dent (Seattle: Bay Press, 1992), 315.

23. Adilifu Nama, "It Was Signified: The Genesis," in *Born to Use Mics: Reading Nas's Illmatic*, ed. Michael Eric Dyson and Sohail Daulatzai (New York: Basic Civitas Books, 2010).

24. See W.B. Yeats, "The Circus Animals' Desertion," in *The Yeats Reader*, ed. Richard Finneran (New York: Scribner Poetry, 1997), 151.

25. Richard Kearney describes the meaning of "persona" in these terms. See Kearney, *The God Who May Be: A Hermeneutics of Religion* (Bloomington: Indiana University Press, 2001).

26. Quoted in Jean-Luc Marion, *In the Self's Place: The Approach of St. Augustine*, trans. Jeffrey Kosky (Stanford, CA: Stanford University Press, 2012), 259.

27. Ibid., 259.

28. Augustine, *Confessions*, IV.14.

29. Ibid., X.33.

30. Ibid., X.8.

31. Ibid.

32. Ibid., X.16.

33. For these reasons, Martin Heidegger was right to challenge the reading of Augustine by Descartes, right to emphasize the abyss that separates their modes of introspection: "Descartes blurred Augustine's thoughts," Heidegger wrote. "Self certainty and the self-possession in the sense of Augustine are entirely different from the Cartesian evidence of the cogito." See Marion, *In the Self's Place*, 62, 240–42.

34. Virginia Woolf, *Mr. Bennett and Mrs. Brown: The Hogarth Essays* (London: Hogarth Press, 1924), 3.

35. Nicholas of Cusa, *On Learned Ignorance,* ch. 1, in *Nicholas of Cusa: Selected Spiritual Writings,* ed. H. Lawrence Bond (New York: Paulist Press, 2005). See also David Bentley Hart, *The Beauty of the Infinite: The Aesthetics of Christian Truth* (Grand Rapids, MI: William Eerdmans, 2003), 254.

36. This Navajo chant serves as the title of N. Scott Momaday's book, *House Made of Dawn* (New York: Harper and Row, 1968).

37. Hart, *Beauty of the Infinite,* 138.

38. The philosopher Charles Taylor speaks of the soul as being "porous" in this paradigm. See Taylor, *A Secular Age* (Cambridge, MA: Harvard University Press, 2007), 152.

39. Hart, *Beauty of the Infinite,* 275.

40. See James O'Donnell, *Augustine: A New Biography* (New York: Harper-Collins, 2005), 76.

41. Ibid., 76.

42. Michel de Certeau argues that music is a hermeneutical key in Teresa's most famous work, *The Interior Castle*. In his view, it is arranged as a musical score or symphony, with each dwelling striking a particular string or melody, and notes that rise in a crescendo until the final coda, when amazement turns the tongue into stone and the soul is undone in ecstasy. See Teresa of Àvila, *The Interior Castle,* trans. Kieran Kavanaugh and Otilio Rodriguez (New York: Paulist Press, 1979), 38. See also Michel de Certeau, *The Mystic Fable: The Sixteenth and Seventeenth Centuries,* trans. Michael Smith (Chicago: University of Chicago Press, 1992), 190–95.

43. Walt Whitman, "Song of Myself," in *Leaves of Grass* [1855] (New York: Viking Press, 1959), 29.

44. Friedrich Nietzsche, *The Birth of Tragedy: Out of the Spirit of Music* [1872], trans. Shaun Whiteside (New York: Penguin Books, 1994).

45. Friedrich Nietzsche, *The Will to Power,* trans. Walter Kaufmann and R.J. Hollingdale (New York: Vintage Books, 1968), 428.

46. On this theme in Aquinas, see Bernard McGinn, *Thomas Aquinas's Summa Theologiae: A Biography* (Princeton, NJ: Princeton University Press, 2014). For Nietzsche and his relationship with music, see M.S. Silk and J.P. Stern, *Nietzsche and Tragedy* (Cambridge, UK: Cambridge University Press, 2016), 299–302.

47. Biggie, "Hypnotize," on *Life After Death,* Puff Daddy Records, 1997; Eminem, "Lose Yourself," on *From the Motion Picture 8 Mile,* Shady, Aftermath, Interscope, 2002; Master P, "Make 'Em Say Uhhh!" on *Ghetto D,* No Limits Records/Priority, 1997; T.S. Eliot, "The Dry Salvages," in *The Four Quartets* (New York: Harcourt Books, 1943).

48. Taylor, *Secular Age;* Louis Dupre, *Passage to Modernity: An Essay in the Hermeneutics of Nature and Culture* (New Haven, CT: Yale University Press, 1993).

49. Taylor, *Secular Age,* 106–10.

50. Ibid., 131.

51. W. E. B. Du Bois, *The Souls of Black Folk* (New York: Penguin Books, 1989), 155.

52. I'm paraphrasing here Sacvan Bercovitch, *Rites of Assent: Transformations in the Symbolic Construction of America* (London: Routledge, 1992), 40.

53. Brad Gregory, *The Unintended Reformation: How a Religious Revolution Secularized Society* (Cambridge, MA: Harvard University Press, 2012), 261, 288.

54. Karl Marx also seemed concerned about the fate of the soul in the modern world. In some writings he sounded a lot like a classic Jewish prophet, such as when he denounced the way the bourgeoisie "creates a world after its own image" and thereby substitutes love of capital for ineffable goods like love, intelligence, beauty, and honesty. Quoted in Wendy Brown, "The Sacred, the Secular, and the Profane: Charles Taylor and Karl Marx," in *Varieties of Secularism in a Secular Age,* ed. Michael Warner, Jonathan Vanantwerpen, and Craig Calhoun (Cambridge, MA: Harvard University Press, 2010), 93–94, 99.

55. See Soren Kierkegaard, *Practice in Christianity,* ed. and trans. Howard Hong and Edna Hong (Princeton, NJ: Princeton University Press, 1991).

56. Quoted in Bercovitch, *Rites of Assent,* 31–32.

57. Ibid., 50.

58. Ibid., 53.

59. See Kierkegaard, *Practice in Christianity,* 215.

60. Michel Foucault, *Discipline and Punishment: The Birth of the Prison,* trans. Alan Sheridan (New York: Vintage Books, 1979), 275–78.

61. Ibid., 76–77, 274. In Britain and the United States, between 1829 and 1878 more than two hundred new laws were passed to expand police powers, creating more criminals and the need for a larger police force.

62. Ibid., 275.

63. Ibid., 137.

64. See Andrés Reséndez, *The Other Slavery: The Uncovered Story of Indian Enslavement in America* (New York: Harcourt Books, 2016), 2.

65. Foucault, *Discipline and Punish,* 199.

66. Delbanco, *Death of Satan,* 106.

67. S. C. Gwynne, *Empire of the Summer Moon: Quanah Parker and the Rise and Fall of the Comanches* (New York: Scribner Books, 2011), 20.

68. See Benjamin Madley, *An American Genocide: The United States and the California Indian Catastrophe, 1846–1873* (New Haven, CT: Yale University Press, 2016); see also Roxanne Dunbar-Ortiz, *An Indigenous Peoples' History of the United States* (Boston: Beacon Press, 2015), 129ff.

69. Herman Melville, "The Quarter Deck," in *Moby Dick* (New York: Penguin Books, 2010).

70. See Leigh Eric Schmidt, *Restless Souls: The Making of American Spirituality* (Berkeley: University of California, 2012), 30.

71. Quoted in Delbanco, *Death of Satan,* 101.

72. Quoted in Bercovitch, *Rites of Assent,* 46.

73. Herman Melville, "The Castaway," in *Moby Dick, or the Whale* (New York: Penguin Books, 1992).

74. F. Scott Fitzgerald, *The Great Gatsby,* ch. 6 (New York: Scribner Books, 2004).

75. Fitzgerald quoted in Marius Bewley, "Fitzgerald and the Collapse of the American Dream," in *Modern Critical Views: F. Scott Fitzgerald,* ed. Harold Bloom (New York: Chelsea House Publisher, 1985), 46, 69.

76. See ibid., 46, 69.

77. F. Scott Fitzgerald, *This Side of Paradise* (New York: Simon and Schuster, 1998), 14.

78. Ibid., 242.

79. Arnold Rampersad, *The Art and Imagination of W.E.B. Du Bois* (New York: Schocken Books, 1990), 86.

80. W. E. B. Du Bois, *The Souls of Black Folk* (New York: Penguin Books 1989), 10.

81. Quoted in Rampersad, *Art and Imagination of W.E.B. Du Bois,* 62.

82. Du Bois, *Souls of Black Folk,* 38.

83. Gerard Manley Hopkins, "God's Grandeur," in *Gerard Manley Hopkins: A Selection* ed. Catherine Phillips (Oxford: Oxford University Press, 1995), 114.

84. Quoted in Rampersad, *Art and Imagination of W.E.B. Du Bois,* 121.

85. Kwame Anthony Appiah, *Lines of Dissent: W.E.B. Du Bois and the Emergence of Identity* (Cambridge, MA: Harvard University Press, 2014), 58.

86. See Angel Rama, *The Lettered City,* trans. John Charles Chasteen (Durham, NC: Duke University Press, 1996), 79.

87. Bruce Lincoln, *Theorizing Myth: Narrative, Ideology and Scholarship* (Chicago: University of Chicago Press, 1999), 50–51.

88. James Joyce, *A Portrait of the Artist as a Young Man* (New York: Penguin Books, 2003).

89. Lincoln, *Theorizing Myth,* 27.

90. Ibid., 38.

91. Du Bois, *Souls of Black Folk,* 10–11.

92. Ibid., 5.

93. On the influence of preachers and popular revivalists on the American Renaissance, see David Reynolds, *Beneath the American Renaissance: The Subversive Imagination in the Age of Emerson and Melville* (Cambridge, MA: Harvard University Press, 1989).

94. Du Bois, *Souls of Black Folk,* 205.

95. Ibid., 207–10.

96. For the debate on the spirituals, see the essay by Eddie Glaude Jr., "Of the Black Church and the Making of the Black Public," in *African American Religious Thought,* ed. Cornel West and Eddie Glaude (Louisville, KY: Westminster John Knox Press, 2003), 338–65. See also Albert Raboteau, "The Black Experience in American Evangelicalism: The Meaning of Slavery," in *African-*

American Religion: Interpretative Essays in History and Culture, ed. Timothy Fulop and Albert Raboteau (New York: Routledge, 1997), 99–102.

97. I'm following Terry Eagleton on this reading of Herder and the Enlightenment. See Eagleton, *Culture and the Death of God* (New Haven, CT: Yale University Press, 2014), 89.

98. Ibid., 89.

99. See J. G. Herder, "Treatise on the Origin of Language," in *Herder: Philosophical Writings,* ed. Michael Forster (Cambridge, UK: Cambridge University Press, 2002), 65–164.

100. See George Fredrickson, *Racism: A Short History* (Princeton, NJ: Princeton University Press, 2002), 70ff.

101. Ibid., 75.

102. Eagleton, *Culture and the Death of God,* 117.

103. Richard Ellmann, *The Identity of Yeats* (Oxford: Oxford University Press, 1964), 14–16.

104. I'm following Bruce Lincoln on these themes. See Lincoln, *Theorizing Myth,* 25.

105. "From this it follows," Fiedler writes, "that the writer's duty is to say, Nay!: to deny the easy affirmation by which most men live, and to expose the blackness of life most men try deliberately to ignore. For tragic humanists, it is the function of art not to console or sustain, much less to entertain, but to *disturb* by telling a truth which is always unwelcome; and they consequently find it easy to view themselves in Faustian terms, to think of dangerous vocations as a bargain with the Devil." See Leslie Fiedler, *Love and Death in the American Novel* (New York: Criterion Books, 1960), 418.

106. Gerard Manley Hopkins, "Pied Beauty," in *Gerard Manley Hopkins: The Major Works,* ed. Catherine Phillips (Oxford: Oxford University Press, 2009).

107. Quoted in F. O. Matthiessen, *American Renaissance* (New York: Barnes and Noble Books, 2009), 406–7.

108. Herman Melville, "His Mark," and "A Bosom Friend," in *Moby Dick* (New York: Penguin Books, 1992).

109. In the case of Twain, how can we forget Huckleberry Finn's infamous entanglements with wickedness in his own decision to ally himself with a dark-skinned heathen and slave? In his alliance with his beloved slave friend Jim, he makes himself into an exile and fugitive from the Christian south and from all that is good and holy. Huck's power of blackness is thus manifest in his capacity for mutiny against the Christianity of his culture, in his willingness to face the gates of hell out of loyalty to and affection for his endangered friend.

110. Quoted in Ribowsky, *Dreams to Remember,* 116.

111. This expression is from William Jelani Cobb, quoted in Adam Bradley, *The Book of Rhymes: The Poetics of Hip Hop* (New York: Basic Civitas Books, 2009), 87.

112. Bradley, *Book of Rhymes,* 125.

113. This episode is narrated in the *Homeric Hymns to Hermes.* See Lincoln, *Theorizing Myth,* 9. Lincoln discusses numerous cases in which logoi are associated with cunning, lies, and dissimulation. To mention one other case: in

Hesiod, Hermes is portrayed as instilling in Pandora's breast falsehoods, seductive logoi, and a wily character. Whether among the young, women, or the weak, logoi seem to be related to the tactics of the powerless.

114. S. Craig Watkins, *Hip Hop Matters: Politics, Pop Culture and the Struggle for the Soul of a Movement* (Boston: Beacon Press, 2006), 234.

115. J. Cole, "Dead Presidents 2," on *The Warm Up,* Roc Nation, 2009.

116. The first quote is from "Vocab" by the Fugees, on *Blunted on Reality,* Ruffhouse, 1992. The second quote is from "Lost Ones," by Lauryn Hill, on *Miseducation of Lauryn Hill,* Ruffhouse, Columbia Records, 1997.

117. Imani Perry, *Prophets of the Hood: Politics and Poetics in Hip Hop* (Durham, NC: Duke University Press, 2004), 52.

118. Stuart Hall has a fine description of the virtue of these components of black popular culture: "In its expressivity, its musicality, its orality, in its rich, deep, and varied attention to speech, in its inflections toward the vernacular and the local, in its rich production of counter-narratives, and above all, in its metaphorical use of the musical vocabulary, black popular culture has enabled the surfacing . . . of other traditions of representation." See Stuart Hall, "What Is This 'Black' in Black Popular Culture," in *Black Popular Culture,* ed. Gina Dent (Seattle: Bay Press, 1992), 27.

119. Quoted in Bradley, *Book of Rhymes,* 193.

120. W. B. Yeats, "Ideas of Good and Evil," in *The Yeats Reader,* ed. Richard Finneran (New York: Scribner Poetry, 1997), 363–69.

121. Melville, *Moby Dick,* ch. 119, "The Candles." For the reference to Ralph Waldo Emerson's line, see Emerson, "Self Reliance," in *The Essential Writings of Ralph Waldo Emerson,* ed. Larzer Ziff (New York: Penguin Books, 1982), 175–203.

122. See Simone Weil, *Waiting for God* (New York: Harper Books, 1973), 69.

123. Louis Armstrong, "Aunt Hagar's Blues." Quoted in Stanley Crouch, *Considering Genius: Writings on Jazz* (New York: Basic Civitas Books, 2007), 80.

CHAPTER 2: ON HEBREW SOUL: *DE ELOQUENTIA VULGARIA*

1. Quoted by Ilan Stavans in the epilogue to *The Poetry of Pablo Neruda,* ed. Ilan Stavans (New York: Farrar, Straus and Giroux, 2003).

2. Eric Auerbach, *Mimesis: The Representation of Reality in Western Literature,* trans. Willard Trask (Princeton, NJ: Princeton University Press, 1968).

3. Robert Alter, *The World of Biblical Literature* (New York: Basic Books, 1992), 160.

4. See Robert Alter, "Psalms," in *The Literary Guide to the Bible,* ed. Robert Alter and Frank Kermode (Cambridge, MA: Harvard University Press, 1987), 248.

5. See Alfred Tennyson, "Ulysses," *Tennyson: Poems,* ed. Peter Washington (New York: Everyman's Library, 2004).

6. See André Wénin, "Heart," in *Encyclopedia of Christian Theology,* ed. Jean-Yves Lacoste (London: Routledge Books, 2004), 3:1496–97.

7. The Melodians, "Rivers of Babylon," on *The Harder They Come,* Mango Records, 1972.

8. Bob Marley and the Wailers, *Soul Rebels,* Trojan Records, 1970.

9. The revolutionary nature of his project was only intensified by his historical context: he was a German Jew removed from his teaching post in Marburg and forced into exile by the Nazis in 1935. See James Porter, Introduction to *Selected Essays of Erich Auerbach: Time, History and Literature,* ed. James Porter (Princeton, NJ: Princeton University Press, 2014), x.

10. Eric Auerbach, *Mimesis: The Representation of Reality in Western Literature,* trans. Willard Trask (Princeton, NJ: Princeton University Press, 1968), 8.

11. See Herbert Schneidau, *Sacred Discontent: The Bible and Western Tradition* (Baton Rouge: Louisiana State University Press, 1976), 30.

12. See Jon Levenson, *The Death and Resurrection of the Beloved Son: The Transformation of Child Sacrifice in Judaism and Christianity* (New Haven, CT: Yale University Press, 1993), 138.

13. In speaking of the silence of Genesis concerning some of the details about Isaac (his age or physical features), Jon Levenson writes: "As is usual when the biblical text exhibits a gap of such significance, the midrash fills it in." In his reading of the "binding," Levenson offers many wonderful examples of midrash. See ibid., 133.

14. This is a paraphrase of a line by Thomas Wentworth Higginson, quoted in David Reynolds, *Beneath the American Renaissance: The Subversive Imagination in the Age of Emerson and Melville* (Cambridge, MA: Harvard University Press, 1989), 33.

15. For a discussion of Queequeg's tattoos in *Moby Dick,* see Birgit Brander Rasmussen, *Queequeg's Coffin: Indigenous Literacies and Early American Literature* (Durham, NC: Duke University Press, 2012).

16. Quoted in Harold Bloom, *The Daemon Knows: Literary Greatness and the American Sublime* (New York: Spiegel and Grau, 2015), 156.

17. See Robert Alter, *The Art of Biblical Narrative* (New York: Basic Books, 2011), 158.

18. See Levenson, *Death and Resurrection of the Beloved Son,* 53.

19. I'm following Ted Gioia's brilliant portrait of the blues in *Delta Blues: The Life and Times of the Mississippi Masters Who Revolutionized American Music* (New York: W. W. Norton and Company, 2009), 136ff.

20. Alter, *Art of Biblical Narrative,* 159.

21. See James Wood, *How Fiction Works* (New York: Picador Books, 2009), 141ff.

22. Levenson, *Death and Resurrection of the Beloved Son,* 168.

23. Miguel Cervantes, *Don Quixote,* trans. John Rutherford (New York: Penguin Books, 2000), pt. I, ch.9, 76.

24. As many theologians have noted, Heidegger's understanding of Being's self-disclosure in time is clearly indebted to Jewish and Christian understandings of revelation. For a good discussion of this, see George Steiner, *Martin Heidegger* (Chicago: University of Chicago Press, 1991); see also Ryan Coyne, *Heidegger's Confessions: The Remains of Saint Augustine in Being and Time* (Chicago: University of Chicago Press, 2016).

25. For a good discussion of this literary revolution, see Schneidau, *Sacred Discontent,* 31.

26. Alter, *Art of Biblical Narrative,* 192.

27. Hans Frei defines literary realism as followings: "The term realistic I take also to imply that the narrative depiction is of that peculiar sort in which characters or individual persons, in their internal depth or subjectivity as well as in their capacity as doers and sufferers of actions or events, are firmly and significantly set in the context of the external environment, natural but more particularly social. See *The Eclipse of Biblical Narrative: A Study in Eighteenth and Nineteenth Century Hermeneutics* (New Haven, CT: Yale University Press, 1974), 13.

28. Alter, *Art of Biblical Narrative,* 28.

29. Quoted in Johann Baptist Metz, *A Passion for God: The Mystical-Political Dimensions of Christianity,* ed. and trans. J. Matthew Ashley (New York: Paulist Press, 1998), 81.

30. Schneidau, *Sacred Discontent,* 16–17.

31. One might say that there is something originally misbegotten about the city since Cain was the first city-builder (Gen. 4:17). Through Cain's murder of his shepherd brother Abel and his subsequent founding of the city, the history of violence and injustice is foreseen like a dark omen. In Philo of Alexandria's interpretation, Cain is thus an allegory of "possession because he thinks he possesses all things," and Abel represents dispossession, "one who refers all things to God." Needless to say, the Bible advocates the way of Abel, his ethic of dispossession, because it proved the better parable of Israel's experiences of bondage, diaspora, and exile. See Gerald Bruns, "Midrash and Allegory: The Beginnings of Scriptural Interpretation," in *The Literary Guide to the Bible,* ed. Robert Alter and Frank Kermode (Cambridge, MA: Harvard University Press, 1987), 639. Augustine, too, followed Philo on this and gave it an individual signature in his *City of God.* See Peter Brown, *Augustine of Hippo: A Biography* (Berkeley: University of California Press, 1967), 320.

32. In the case of Isaac, as with Abraham earlier, instructions are given to follow the path that God will establish. The instruction—"settle in the land I shall show you"—recalls the summons to Abraham when he was still in Ur (Gen. 12:1), as well as the (vague) directions given about the binding of Isaac (Gen. 22:2). In each case, obedience merits God's blessing: "I will make your offspring as numerous as the stars of heaven" (Gen. 12:1–2, 22:17, 26:4).

33. The practice of reading the Hebrew Bible as a whole, linking the Pentateuch with the prophets and the writings, was a fundamental theme in midrashic exegesis. See Bruns, "Midrash and Allegory," 627.

34. Richard Rodriguez, *Darling: A Spiritual Autobiography* (New York: Viking Press, 2013), 66, 77.

35. Skip James, "Devil Got My Woman," on *Devil Got My Woman,* Vanguard, 1968.

36. See Joseph Blenkinsopp, *The Pentateuch: An Introduction to the First Five Books of the Bible* (New York: Doubleday, 1992), 35.

37. Joseph Blenkinsopp describes the formation of the Pentateuch in these terms: "The fivefold arrangement of the early history of humanity and the history of the ancestors looks like a well-planned narrative continuum from creation into the descent into Egypt. . . . I have suggested that this structure inscribes

or encodes into the narrative the theme of exile and return, near extinction and survival as an interpretative clue of literally central importance." *Pentateuch,* 108.

38. Richard Elliott Friedman, *Who Wrote the Bible?* (New York: Harper-Collins, 1987), 151.

39. See Daniel Smith-Christopher, *A Biblical Theology of Exile* (Minneapolis, MN: Augsburg Fortress, 2002), 45–52.

40. Historical critics, as one might guess, read such passages as postexilic insertions into the older narratives of Deuteronomy. For them, there is something like a school of scribes stitching together disparate stories and creating a unified artwork out of many fragments and scraps. And in this case, they edited Deuteronomy to include numerous references and prophecies about their own historical moment of crisis, thus creating a history of calamity, past and present. Richard Elliot Friedman has a fascinating take on how the editing and writing of the Deuteronomic history may have happened (including the book of Jeremiah). See Friedman, *Who Wrote the Bible?,* 146–49.

41. Walter Brueggmann, "The Book of Jeremiah: Portrait of the Prophet," in *Interpreting the Prophets,* ed. James Luther Mays and Paul Achtemeier (Philadelphia: Fortress Press, 1987), 115.

42. This line comes from James Muilenberg's essay on Jeremiah, "Jeremiah the Prophet," in *The Interpreter's Dictionary of the Bible* (New York: Abingdon Press, 1962), 2:824.

43. See Joseph Blenkinsopp, *A History of Prophecy in Israel* (Philadelphia: Westminster Press, 1983), 168.

44. See Joel Rosenberg, "Jeremiah and Ezekiel," in *The Literary Guide to the Bible,* ed. Robert Alter and Frank Kermode (Cambridge, MA: Harvard University Press, 1987), 194.

45. Ibid.

46. There's a powerful midrash on these texts in which mother Rachel sings dirges and laments on behalf of the children of Israel. In addition to the clarity and force of Rachel's argument on the matter of idolatry and the fact that it takes a woman and mother to reach God, we should also notice something else about this remarkable dialogue/trial: Rachel persuades God by the power of her haunting, moving lament, as if music alone, mixed with Rachel's tears, could have the power to arouse and stir God. See Tod Linafelt, *Surviving Lamentations: Catastrophe, Lament and Protest in the Afterlife of a Biblical Book* (Chicago: University of Chicago Press, 2000), 111.

47. See Ralph Ellison, *Shadow and Act* (New York: Vintage Books, 1995), 78–79.

48. Gioia, *Delta Blues,* 74.

49. Michael Walzer, *In God's Shadow: Politics in the Hebrew Bible* (New Haven, CT: Yale University Press, 2012), 80–81.

50. The prophet Elijah's incessant wandering is emblematic of this marginalization from the king's court and consequently of his fellowship with poor and ordinary folks. His peripatetic and nomadic lifestyle allows him to meet people where they live, in the barest and most meager circumstances. By his banishment from the royal court (for denouncing the idolatry of Ahab and Jezebel), he is put

in close contact with the lowliest of God's people and must make his way as his ancestors once did, as exiles (1 Kings 19:3).

51. He seems to have convinced slave owners to free their (debt) slaves to prevent the Babylonian conquest. When the Babylonian army was suddenly diverted by an Egyptian attack, however, slave owners reneged on this agreement and forced their slaves back into servitude (Jer. 34:11).

52. Walzer, *In God's Shadow*, 87.

53. Gioia, *Delta Blues*, 135.

CHAPTER 3: CHRISTIAN SOUL AND THE REVOLT OF THE SLAVE

1. W.B. Yeats, "Crazy Jane Talks with the Bishop," quoted by Richard Ellmann in *Yeats: the Man and the Masks* (New York: W.W. Norton, 1979), 272.

2. Friedrich Nietzsche, *Beyond Good and Evil*, trans. R.J. Hollingdale (New York: Vintage Books, 1973), 57.

3. See John Dominic Crossan, *Jesus: A Revolutionary Biography* (New York: HarperOne, 2009); see also Crossan, *How to Read the Bible and Still Be a Christian* (New York: HarperOne, 2016).

4. Friedrich Nietzsche, *On the Genealogy of Morals*, trans. Michael Scarpitti (New York: Penguin Books, 2013), 22.

5. Ibid., 17.

6. Since only fragments of Celsus's works survive, this quote is from Origen, *Contra Celsum*, 4.11. See Elaine Pagels, *Revelations: Visions, Prophecy, and Politics in the Book of Revelation* (New York: Penguin Books, 2012), 118. See also Wayne Meeks, *The First Urban Christians: The Social World of the Apostle Paul* (New Haven, CT: Yale University Press, 1983), 51.

7. Celsus remarks that Christianity is a religion of slaves and the foolish and uneducated, women, and little children. See *Celsus on the True Doctrine*, trans. R. Joseph Hoffman (New York: Oxford University Press, 1987), 73. See also Jaroslav Pelikan, *The Emergence of the Catholic Tradition (100–600)* (Chicago: University of Chicago Press, 1971), 29.

8. Quoted in Pagels, *Revelations*, 128.

9. Pelikan, *Emergence of the Catholic Tradition*, 30.

10. Pagels, *Revelations*, 129.

11. Tertullian, *De Testimonio Animae*, 1. See Pagels, *Revelations*, 129.

12. Tertullian, *De Testimonio Animae*, 6. See Pagels, *Revelations*, 129.

13. Friedrich Nietzsche, *Ecce Homo*, trans. Walter Kaufmann and R.J. Hollingdale (New York: Vintage Books, 1969), 272.

14. See "Soul-Heart-Body," in *The Encyclopedia of Christian Theology: Vol. 3*, ed. Jean-Yves Lacoste (London: Routledge Press, 2005), 1495.

15. Quoted in David Bentley Hart, *In the Aftermath: Provocations and Laments* (Grand Rapids, MI: Eerdmans, 2008), 130–31. For Emerson's line, see his essay, "The Over-Soul," in *Nature and Selected Essays*, ed. Larzer Ziff (New York: Penguin Books, 2003).

16. William Faulkner, *Absalom, Absalom* (New York: Vintage Books, 1990), 111–12.

17. Ralph Ellison, "Some Questions and Some Answers," in *Shadow and Act* (New York, Vintage Books, 1995), 263.

18. T. S. Eliot, *Prufrock and Other Observations* (New York: Scholars Choice, 2015).

19. This is from a stone inscription at Ephesus, 9 B.C.E. See John Dominic Crossan, *The Power of Parable* (New York: HarperCollins, 2012), 158. See also Crossan, *Jesus,* 3–4.

20. See David Rhoads, Joanna Dewey, and Donald Michie, *Mark as Story: An Introduction to the Narrative of a Gospel* (Minneapolis, MN: Fortress Press, 2012), 79.

21. Erich Auerbach, *Mimesis: The Representation of Reality in Western Literature,* trans. Willard Trask (Princeton, NJ: Princeton University Press, 1991), 45.

22. Ibid., 41–42.

23. Quoted in Paul Gilroy, *The Black Atlantic: Modernity and Double Consciousness* (Cambridge, MA: Harvard University Press, 1993).

24. Virginia Woolf, "Mr. Sassoon's Poems," in *Books and Portraits* (New York: Harcourt Brace Jovanovich, 1977), 100.

25. For this view of Jesus's riddles, see Rhoads, Dewey, and Michie, *Mark as Story,* 57.

26. The biblical scholar Jack Dean Kingsbury argues that because Mark's parables must be appropriated by the heart, the parables remain obscure to one who can only grasp the theoretical meaning. See Kingsbury, *The Christology of Mark's Gospel* (Minneapolis, MN: Fortress Press, 1983), 17.

27. I'm following Elizabeth Struthers Malbon here. See Malbon, "Narrative Criticism," in *Mark and Method: New Approaches in Biblical Studies,* ed. Janice Capel Anderson and Stephen Moore (Minneapolis, MN: Fortress Press, 2008), 53.

28. Eric B. and Rakim, "Follow the Leader," on *Follow the Leader,* Uni Records, 1988.

29. For a thoughtful reflection on this interpretation of "outsider" in Spanish America, see Ilan Stavans, *Borges, the Jew* (Albany: State University of New York Press, 2016).

30. Other possibilities include the sacrificial deaths of the righteous, such as the "suffering servant" of Isaiah and the Maccabean martyrs; their deaths are seen as "ransoms" on behalf of the oppressed and burdened. See Adela Collins, *The Beginning of the Gospel: Probings of Mark in Context* (Minneapolis, MN: Fortress Press, 1992), 69–70.

31. For a good discussion of the holiness codes of this period, see David Rhoads, "Social Criticism: Crossing Boundaries," in *Mark and Method: New Approaches in Biblical Studies,* ed. Janice Capel Anderson and Stephen D. Moore (Minneapolis, MN: Fortress Press, 2008), 145–79.

32. See Crossan, *Jesus,* 88–93.

33. See Thomas Powers, *The Killing of Crazy Horse* (New York: Vintage Books, 2011), 128.

34. See ibid., 97ff.

35. See Saidiya Hartman, *Lose Your Mother: A Journey Along the Atlantic Slave Route* (New York: Farrar, Straus and Giroux, 2007), 111–35.

36. Ibid., 115.

37. See Simone Weil, *Waiting for God* (New York: Harper Perennial, 2009).

38. See Richard Rodriguez, *Darling: A Spiritual Autobiography* (New York: Viking Books, 2013), 183ff.

39. Richard Cassidy, *John's Gospel in New Perspective* (Maryknoll, NY: Orbis Books, 1992), 33.

40. See Rhoads, Dewey and Michie, *Mark as Story*, 64.

41. See James Robinson, "The Gospels as Narrative," in *The Bible and Narrative Tradition*, ed. Frank McConnell (Oxford: Oxford University Press, 1986), 106ff. See also Graham Stanton, *The Gospels and Jesus* (Oxford: Oxford University Press, 2002), 40ff.

42. Gary Wills, *What Jesus Meant* (New York: Penguin Books, 2006), xxi.

43. See Tupac's song, "Still I Rise," on *Still I Rise,* Interscope Records, 1999, for a snapshot of this theme.

44. Quoted in Hartman, *Lose Your Mother,* 129.

45. See ibid., 129–30.

46. Tupac, "Trapped," on *2Pacalypse Now,* Interscope Records, 1991.

47. Wu-Tang Clan, "C.R.E.A.M.," on *Enter the Wu-Tang (36 Chambers),* Loud Records, 1994.

48. Skip James, "Hard Time Killing Floor Blues," on *Hard Times Killing Floor Blues,* Biograph, 2003.

49. Tupac, "Black Jesus," on *Still I Rise,* Interscope Records, 1999.

50. See Raymond Brown, *An Introduction to the New Testament* (New York: Doubleday Books, 1997), 157.

51. Quoted by Robert Ellsberg, *Blessed Among Us: Day by Day with Saintly Witnesses* (Collegeville, MN: Liturgical Press, 2016).

52. See Robert Gordon, *Respect Yourself: Stax Records and the Soul Explosion* (New York: Bloomsbury, 2015), 159–60.

53. Quoted in James Dunn, *Unity and Diversity in the New Testament: An Inquiry into the Character of Earliest Christianity* (London: SCM Press, 1990), 12.

54. The quote is from Aeschylus, *Agamemnon.* For the relationship of Mark and tragedy, see Louis Ruprecht, *The Tragic Gospel* (San Francisco: Wiley Books, 2008), 79–101. See also Stanton, *Gospels and Jesus* (Oxford: Oxford University Press, 2002), 40ff.; and Dennis MacDonald, *The Homeric Epics and the Gospel of Mark* (New Haven, CT: Yale University Press, 2000).

55. In the Gospel of Mark, for example, there are echoes of Jesus's fate on the cross in the baptism of Jesus and his followers. In Mark 10:38, baptism is paired with the cup of death that he will endure at Gethsemane: "Are you able to drink the cup that I drink," Jesus remarks, "or be baptized with the baptism that I am baptized with?"

56. I'm following Robert Alter here. See Alter, *The World of Biblical Literature* (New York: Basic Books, 1992), 22–23.

57. When Mark speaks of the blood of the covenant poured out for many, he is recalling Ps. 22:12, "I am poured out like water, and all my bones are out of joint"; Isa. 53:10–12, "My servant, the just one, shall justify the many, their iniquity he shall bear"; and the deaths of Jewish martyrs in 4 Macc. 17:21.

58. Melville, *Moby Dick*. Quoted in Robert Alter, *Pen of Iron: American Prose and the King James Bible* (Princeton, NJ: Princeton University Press, 2010).

59. Quoted in Alter, *Pen of Iron*, 50.

60. Cornel West, *The Cornel West Reader* (New York: Basic Civitas Books, 1999), 427, 435–36.

61. Emily Dickinson, "Hope Is the Thing with Feathers," in *The Complete Poems of Emily Dickinson*, ed. Thomas Johnson (New York: Basic Bay Books, 1976).

62. In Richard Wright's *White Man Listen!*, he borrows from Nietzsche to offer a very subtle and nuanced position on the threat of vengeance among the oppressed. He speaks of the ambivalence and "double vision" that inhere in the soul of the oppressed and combine hatred with a desire to copy and imitate. "A certain degree of hate combined with love (ambivalence) is always involved in this looking from below upward and the object against which the subject is measuring himself undergoes constant change." Quoted in Gilroy, *Black Atlantic*, 161.

63. This quote is from Saidiya Hartman, *Scenes of Subjection: Terror, Slavery, and Self-Making in Nineteenth-Century America* (Oxford: Oxford University Press, 1997), 72.

64. Indeed, in *Beyond Good and Evil*, in the section preceding his denunciation of the "god on the cross," Nietzsche tells us that his subject is nothing less than the frontiers of the human soul, "the entire history of the soul *hitherto* and its still unexhausted possibilities: this is the predestined hunting ground for a born psychologist and lover of the big-game hunt." See Nietzsche, *Beyond Good and Evil*, 56.

65. Lauryn Hill, "The Final Hour," on *The Miseducation of Lauryn Hill*, Ruffhouse, Columbia Records, 1998.

CHAPTER 4: IN SEARCH OF *DUENDE*: LORCA ON SPANISH SOUL

1. Edward Hirsch, *The Demon and the Angel: Searching for the Source of Artistic Inspiration* (New York: Harcourt Books, 2002), 196.

2. Czeslaw Milosz, "Ars Poetica?," in *Selected Poems*, ed. Seamus Heaney (New York: HarperCollins, 2004), 88.

3. Quoted in Ian Gibson, *Federico García Lorca: A Life* (New York: Pantheon Books, 1989), 29.

4. This accusation came from Ramón Ruiz Alonso, the man who arrested Lorca, and a member of Gil Robles's right-wing Coalition Party. Lorca was accused of having a clandestine radio to communicate with Soviet Communists. It is well known, however, that the real causes of the arrest were Lorca's anti-fascist statements to the press, his poetry and plays (especially the play *Yerma*, for its depiction of an Old Pagan Woman, who professes atheism), and his homosexuality. At first Lorca was taken to the civil government building; a few days later he was taken along the road to Alfacar and shot. Apparently the night before he had been told about the planned execution and requested a priest for confession. None was available, so he prayed with José Jover Tripaldi,

which according to Tripaldi's testimony calmed the terrified poet. See ibid., 454–67.

5. Ted Gioia, *Delta Blues: The Life and Times of the Mississippi Masters Who Revolutionized American Music* (New York: W. W. Norton, 2009), 377.

6. Walt Whitman, *Song of Myself* (New York: Penguin Books, 1996).

7. See Simon Gikandi, *Slavery and the Culture of Taste* (Princeton, NJ: Princeton University Press, 2011), 7.

8. For a good discussion of this topic, see Ryan Coyne, *Heidegger's Confessions: The Remains of St. Augustine in "Being and Time" and Beyond* (Chicago: University of Chicago Press, 2016), 6.

9. E. R. Dodds, *The Greeks and the Irrational* (Berkeley: University of California Press, 1951), 40.

10. Ibid., 42.

11. Ibid., 217.

12. Though Plato mentions four types of divine madness (the prophecy inspired by Apollo; the mystic madness of Dionysus; the poetic madness of the Muses; and the madness of love, inspired by Aphrodite and Eros), he speaks specifically of Eros as the most formidable daemon (*Symposium* 202E). See also *Phaedrus* 244A. I am assisted here by Luke Timothy Johnson's study, *Among the Gentiles: Greco-Roman Religion and Christianity* (New Haven, CT: Yale University Press, 2010), 39.

13. In *The Symposium,* in fact, one might read the mysterious figure of Diotima—the female seer who instructed Socrates on the art of love—as another manifestation of the daemon in the life of Socrates.

14. Robert Johnson, "Hellhound on My Trail," on *Vocalion,* 1937.

15. Dodds, *Greeks and the Irrational,* 41, 45.

16. He would conclude that we can only fear and adore this inscrutable aspect of God. See Luther, "The Bondage of the Will," in *Martin Luther: Selections from His Writings* (New York: Anchor Books, 1958).

17. David Tracy, "The Hidden God," *Cross Currents,* Spring 1996, 5–16.

18. Quoted in Giles Oakley, *The Devil's Music: A History of the Blues* (London: Da Capo Press, 1997), 94.

19. Son House, "Dry Spells Blues (Part 2)," Paramount Records, 1930.

20. In the blues, the guitar is surely a second voice. About the guitar playing of Charlie Patton, J. D. "Jelly Jaw" Short had this to say: "He used to play the guitar and he'd make the guitar say, 'Lord have mercy, Lord have mercy, pray, brother, pray, save poor me.'" See Oakley, *Devil's Music,* 55.

21. Timothy Mitchell, *Flamenco Deep Song* (New Haven, CT: Yale University Press, 1994), 64.

22. Ibid., 84.

23. Ibid., 88.

24. Ibid., 87. As an example of these songs, Mitchell mentions the *romances de matones,* the chronicles of underclass heroes. He gives an example from a seventeenth-century ballad collected by Francisco Rodríguez Marín, which portrays its hero in the following terms: "He was born in Córdoba of an innkeeper and a gitana. The 'chulo' grew up to become a 'valiente' among the underworld people of the Altozano, in Triana."

25. Quoted in Carlos Fuentes, *The Buried Mirror: Reflections on Spain and the New World* (New York: Mariner Books, 1999), 30.

26. In this description of lilies arising out of the mud, I'm reminded of Tupac Shakur's book of poems, *The Rose That Grew from Concrete* (New York: MTV Books, 2009).

27. Fuentes, *Buried Mirror*, 32.

28. Mitchell, *Flamenco Deep Song*, 101–2.

29. Ibid., 102.

30. Ibid., 139.

31. Ibid., 138.

32. Nietzsche, *Ecce Homo*, "Thus Spoke Zarathustra," section 3, in *The Genealogy of Morals and Ecce Homo*, trans. and ed. Walter Kaufmann (New York: Vintage Books, 1989), 300.

33. The Dionysian-inspired music, dance, and spirituality of Greek culture were special instances of "widely extended rhythms" for Nietzsche. "Indeed, it might also be historically demonstrable that every period rich in folk songs has been most violently stirred by Dionysian currents, which we must always consider the substratum and prerequisite of the folk song." See Nietzsche, *The Birth of Tragedy*, trans. Shaun Whiteside (New York: Penguin Books, 1994).

34. These lines appear in Lorca's early work, *Impressions and Landscapes*. Ian Gibson argues that they were inspired by Rubén Darío's poem "Divina Psiquis," in which he compares his soul to a butterfly flitting between pagan ruins and a cathedral (G, 69).

35. Ted Gioia, *The History of Jazz* (Oxford: Oxford University Press, 2011), 19.

36. Ibid., 7.

37. T. S. Eliot, *The Wasteland* in *Selected Poems* (New York: Harvest Books, 1964), 51.

38. In "The World Is Yours," on *Illmatic*, Columbia Records, 1994, Nas refers to NYC as the "rotten apple."

39. Grandmaster Flash and the Furious Five, "New York New York," Sugar Hill Records, 1982.

40. Lorca described the inspiration of his poem in these terms: "to make a poem of the black race in North America and to emphasize the pain that the blacks feel to be black in a contrary world" (DS, 95).

41. T. S. Eliot, "Little Gidding," in *The Four Quartets* (New York: Harvest Books, 1971), 57.

42. See Richard Predmore, *Lorca's New York Poetry: Social Injustice, Dark Love, Lost Faith* (Durham, NC: Duke University Press, 1980), 45.

CHAPTER 5: THE SOULS OF BLACK FOLK: RALPH ELLISON'S TRAGICOMIC PORTRAIT

1. Ralph Waldo Emerson, "The American Scholar," in *Ralph Waldo Emerson: Nature and Selected Essays*, ed. Larzer Ziff (New York: Penguin Books, 1982), 101–2.

2. Ted Gioia describes this modernist tendency, evident in the fascination for the blues and jazz in Paris and other modern cities, as the "primitivist myth."

See Gioia, *The Imperfect Art: Reflections on Jazz and Modern Culture* (Oxford: Oxford University Press, 1990), 19ff.

3. See David Reynolds, *Beneath the American Renaissance: The Subversive Imagination in the Age of Emerson and Melville* (Oxford: Oxford University Press, 2011), 93–94.

4. Angel Rama's work shows how the custody of writing and formal education—especially in the hands of the lettered classes—was used as an ideological tool to justify the racial and class hierarchies of Latin America. See *The Lettered City,* trans. John Charles Chasteen (Durham, NC: Duke University Press, 1996), 68.

5. See Edward Hirsch, *The Demon and the Angel: Searching for the Source of Artistic Inspiration* (New York: Harvest Books, 2003), 202.

6. Quoted in Adam Bradley, *Ralph Ellison in Progress* (New Haven, CT: Yale University Press, 2010), 76.

7. Walt Whitman, *Leaves of Grass: The First (1885) Edition,* ed. Malcolm Cowley (New York: Penguin Books, 1959), 41.

8. Houston Baker, *Blues, Ideology and Afro-American Literature* (Chicago: University of Chicago Press, 1984), 11.

9. The description of jazz as the "sound of surprise" comes from the music critic Whitney Balliett and is quoted by Nat Hentoff in *The Nat Hentoff Reader* (New York: Da Capo Press, 2001), 95.

10. Stanley Crouch, *Considering Genius: Writings on Jazz* (New York: Basic Civitas Books, 2006), 224.

11. Gary Wills, *Font of Life: Ambrose, Augustine, and the Mystery of Baptism* (Oxford: Oxford University Press, 2012).

12. See José Vasconcelos, *La raza cosmica/The Cosmic Race,* trans. Didier Jaén (Baltimore, MD: Johns Hopkins University Press, 1997).

13. Walt Whitman, "Crossing Brooklyn Ferry," in *Walt Whitman: The Complete Poems* (New York: Penguin Books, 2005).

14. Quoted in David Reynolds, *Beneath the American Renaissance: The Subversive Imagination in the Age of Emerson and Melville* (Oxford: Oxford University Press, 2011), 75.

15. Herman Melville, "Knights and Squires," in *Moby Dick* (New York: Penguin Books, 2009), 126–27.

16. See Reynolds, *Beneath the American Renaissance.*

17. Octavio Paz, *The Labyrinth of Solitude* (New York: Grove Press, 1994), 57.

18. Guralnick, *Sweet Soul Music,* 264.

19. "I have seen the moment of my greatness flicker / And I have seen the eternal Footman hold my coat, and snicker, / And in short, I was afraid." T.S. Eliot, "The Love Song of J. Alfred Prufrock," in *T.S. Eliot: Collected Poems, 1909–1962* (New York: Harcourt Brace Jovanovich, 1991).

20. See Peter Guralnick, *Feel Like Going Home: Portraits in Blues and Rock 'n' Roll* (New York: Little, Brown, 1999), 44.

21. See ibid., 54.

22. See Giles Oakley, *The Devil's Music: A History of the Blues* (New York: Da Capo Books, 1997), 198.

23. Little Brother Montgomery, "Goodbye Mister Blues," on *Little Brother Montgomery's State Street Swingers,* Delmark, 1976.

24. Ted Gioia, *Delta Blues: The Life and Times of the Mississippi Masters Who Revolutionized American Music* (New York: W. W. Norton, 2009), 13.

25. Toni Morrison, *The Bluest Eye* (New York: Plume Books, 1994), 26.

26. See Robert Alter, *The Art of Biblical Poetry* (New York: HarperCollins, 1985), 133. An analogy between the Psalms and the blues can also be suggested in this regard; both carry a very heavy emotional freight in simple, compact, and conventional verbal structures.

27. Cornel West, "Subversive Joy and Revolutionary Patience in Black Christianity," in *The Cornel West Reader* (New York: Basic Civitas Books, 1999), 436.

28. Albert Murray, *Stomping the Blues* (New York: Da Capo Press, 1976), 50–51.

29. Houston Baker emphasizes the origin of the blues in field hollers and work songs, even as far back as the slavery era. See Houston Baker, *Blues, Ideology and Afro-American Literature* (Chicago: University of Chicago Press, 1984), 188. Peter Guralnick emphasizes, as does Murray, the celebratory, drunken context for the emergence of the blues. See *Feel Like Going Home,* 47. It seems to me that Giles Oakley, in *The Devil's Music,* does justice to these various contexts.

30. Gioia, *Delta Blues,* 323.

31. Murray, *Stomping the Blues,* 27, 42.

32. Guralnick, *Feel Like Going Home,* 47.

33. See Bradley, *Ralph Ellison in Progress,* 45, for a discussion of the jazz-like construction of his second, unfinished novel.

34. Ibid., 116.

35. Abraham Joshua Heschel, *The Prophets: An Introduction,* vol. 1 (New York: Harper and Row, 1969).

36. T. S. Eliot, "Little Gidding," in *The Four Quartets* (New York: Harvest Books, 1971), 58. This theme of transcendence is also emphasized by Horace A. Porter in *Jazz Country: Ralph Ellison in America* (Iowa City: University of Iowa Press, 2001).

37. I'm drawing here from a comment of Stanley Crouch in *Considering Genius,* 189.

38. Ibid., 159.

39. Pascal, *Pensées,* 552, trans. A. J. Krailsheimer (New York: Penguin Books, 1995).

40. See Arnold Rampersad, *Ralph Ellison: A Biography* (New York: Alfred Knopf, 2007), 218.

41. Rampersad mentions Unamuno's *The Tragic Sense of Life* as influencing Ellison's understanding of tragedy. In particular, Ellison found valuable Unamuno's portrait of tragedy in Spanish traditions as related to the qualities of fatalism and passivity in African American culture. See ibid., 120.

42. "The Negroes of Africa," Kant writes, "have by nature no feeling that rises above the trifling." See Immanuel Kant, *Observations on the Feeling of the Sublime and Beautiful,* trans. John Goldthwait (Berkeley: University of

California Press, 2004), 120. See also Simon Gikandi, *Slavery and the Culture of Taste* (Princeton, NJ: Princeton University Press, 2011), 225.

43. Quoted in Bradley, *Ralph Ellison in Progress*, 165.

44. Robert Johnson, "Cross Road Blues," Vocalion, 1937.

45. In *Invisible Man*, the character Rinehart is a lot like the stereotypical rapper, a smooth-talking hustler, pimp, heartless thug, and even preacher (IM, 493–98). Adam Bradley has a very good description of Rinehart in *Invisible Man* and *Three Days Before the Shooting*. See Bradley, *Ralph Ellison in Progress*, 128ff.

46. In an essay on Harlem, for example, "Harlem Is Nowhere," he ruminates on the strange (dis)location of Harlem in the American imagination. To dwell in Harlem, he writes, is to endure life in the bowels of America, life in the labyrinthine dungeons and stenches of the urban landscape. Living in Harlem is a daily struggle, like walking through a battlefield littered with landmines or having to dodge stray gunshots on the way to school. In this world, "the crime side of New York" (Wu Tang), the air is so thick and congested with foreboding that one could suffocate in it.

CHAPTER 6: FROM SOUL TO HIP-HOP: THE RISE OF THE APOCALYPSE

1. Poor Righteous Teachers, "Ghetto We Love," on *Black Business*, Profile Records, 1993.

2. Jacques Derrida, *Specters of Marx: The State of Debt, the Work of Mourning, and the New International*, trans. Peggy Kamuf (London: Routledge Press, 1994), 14–15.

3. For a study of apocalypticism in Latin American literature, see Lois Parkinson Zamora, *Writing the Apocalypse: Historical Vision in Contemporary U.S. and Latin American Fiction* (Cambridge, UK: Cambridge University Press, 1993).

4. See Son House, "John the Revelator," on *The Legendary Son House: Father of Folk Blues*, Paramount, 1965. See also Ted Gioia, *Delta Blues: The Life and Times of the Mississippi Masters Who Revolutionized American Music* (New York: W. W. Norton, 2009), 378.

5. Alan Lomax, *The Land Where the Blues Began* (New York: The New Press, 2002), 58.

6. Nelson George, *Hip Hop America* (New York: Penguin Books, 1998), 1; and Anthony Mark Neal, *Soul Babies: Black Popular Culture and the Post-Soul Aesthetics* (London: Routledge Press, 2002).

7. Peter Guralnick, *Sweet Soul Music: Rhythm and Blues and the Southern Dream of Freedom* (New York: Little, Brown, 1986), 7.

8. Quoted in Andrew Delbanco, *The Death of Satan: How Americans Have Lost the Sense of Evil* (New York: Farrar, Straus and Giroux, 1995), 203.

9. I'm following here the description of soul's southern history by Mark Ribowsky, *Dreams to Remember: Otis Redding, Stax Records, and the Transformation of Southern Soul* (New York: Liveright Publishing, 2015), xxiii.

10. See Robert Gordon, *Respect Yourself: Stax Records and the Soul Explosion* (New York: Bloomsbury, 2015), 159–60.

11. Quoted in Ribowsky, *Dreams to Remember,* 152.

12. Solomon Burke, "I Wish I Knew (How It Would Feel to be Free)," on *I Wish I Knew,* Atlantic, 1968.

13. Toni Morrison uses this expression in *Beloved.* Adam Bradley makes reference to this motif in *The Book of Rhymes: The Poetics of Hip Hop* (New York: Basic Civitas Books, 2009).

14. Nas, "Represent," on *Illmatic,* Columbia Records, 1994.

15. Jay-Z, "Most Kingz," feat. Chris Martin, Roc-A-Fella Records, 2010.

16. Jay-Z, *Decoded* (New York: Spiegel and Grau, 2010), 95.

17. Afrika Bambaataa and the Soulsonic Force, "Renegades of Funk," on *Planet Rock: The Album,* Warner Bros. Records, 1986.

18. See Elaine Pagels, *Revelations: Visions, Prophecies, and Politics in the Book of Revelation* (New York: Penguin Books, 2012).

19. Adela Collins, *Crisis and Catharsis: The Power of the Apocalypse* (Philadelphia: Westminster Press, 1984), 99ff.

20. Ibid., 94–104.

21. Michael Eric Dyson, *Holler If You Hear Me: Searching for Tupac Shakur* (New York: Basic Civitas Books, 2001), 263.

22. Public Enemy, "Can't Truss It," on *Apocalypse 91: The Enemy Strikes Back,* Def Jam, Columbia Records, 1991.

23. Quoted in F. O. Matthiessen, *American Renaissance* (New York: Barnes and Noble, 2009), 429.

24. Olaudah Equiano, *The Interesting Narrative and Other Writings,* ed. Vincent Carretta (New York: Penguin Books, 2003), 85.

25. For a discussion of this theme in Revelation, see Collins, *Crisis and Catharsis,* 156–57. See also Richard Hays, *The Moral Vision of the New Testament* (New York: HarperCollins, 1996), 175.

26. Tupac Shakur, "Thugz Mansion," on *Better Dayz,* Amaru, 2002.

27. GZA, "Liquid Swords," on *Liquid Swords,* Geffen/MCA, 1995.

28. De La Soul, "The Bizness," on *Stakes Is High,* Tommy Boy, 1996.

29. Gang Starr, "Full Clip," on *Full Clip: A Decade of Gang Starr,* Virgin Records, 1999.

30. Boogie Down Productions, *Criminal Minded,* B-Boys Records, 1987; Ice-T, *Rhyme Pays,* Sire/Warner Bros., 1986; Schoolly D, "P.S.K.," on *Schoolly D,* Schoolly D Records, 1985.

31. Saidiya Hartman, *Lose Your Mother: A Journey Along the Atlantic Slave Route* (New York: Farrar, Straus, and Giroux, 2007), 39.

32. Quoted in David Blight, *Race and Reunion: The Civil War in American Memory* (Cambridge, MA: Harvard University Press, 2001), 5.

33. See Friedrich Nietzsche, "Attempt at Self-Criticism," preface [1886] to *The Birth of Tragedy, Or: Hellenism and Pessimism,* trans. Walter Kaufmann (New York: Vintage Books, 1967).

34. Tupac Shakur, "Brenda's Got a Baby," on *2Pacalypse Now,* Interscope, 1991.

35. Adam Bradley and Andrew DuBois contend that this simple style is central to the gangsta archetype in general, where the focus is on the gangsta's actions and not his speech. See Adam Bradley and Andrew DuBois, eds., *The Anthology of Rap* (New Haven, CT: Yale University Press, 2010), 127.

36. Quoted in Matthiessen, *American Renaissance,* 433. There's another related sentence in Melville's work: "Intrepid, unprincipled, reckless, predatory, with boundless ambition, civilized in externals but a savage at heart, America is, or may yet be, the Paul Jones of nations." Quoted in ibid., 482.

37. Ice Cube, "Dead Homiez," on *At Will,* Priority Records, 1990.

38. Tupac Shakur, "Trapped," on *2Pacalypse Now,* Interscope, 1991.

39. Michelle Alexander, *The New Jim Crow: Mass Incarceration in the Age of Colorblindness* (New York: The New Press, 2012).

40. Tricia Rose discusses these sorts of inversions as fundamental in hip-hop. See Rose, *Black Noise: Rap Music and Black Culture in Contemporary America* (Middletown, CT: Wesleyan University Press, 1994), 100–1.

41. Tupac Shakur, "Words of Wisdom," on *2Pacalypse Now,* Interscope, 1991.

42. Andrew Delbanco, *The Death of Satan: How Americans Have Lost the Sense of Evil* (New York: Farrar, Straus, and Giroux, 1995), 23.

43. Susan Sontag, *Regarding the Pain of Others* (New York: Picador Books, 2003), 114.

44. And even Ishmael, in the famous chapter on the "whiteness of the whale," will confess his own feelings of awe and terror at the phantom-like pallor of the white whale, symbolically associated, in his mind, with the infinite void and annihilating emptiness of the universe. See Herman Melville, "The Whiteness of the Whale," in *Moby Dick* (New York: Penguin Books, 1992), 204–12.

45. Melville, "Moby Dick," in *Moby Dick,* 200.

46. Delbanco, *Death of Satan,* 9.

47. Tupac Shakur, "Shed So Many Tears," on *Me Against the World,* Interscope, 1995.

48. Tupac Shakur, "Souljas," on *2Pacalypse Now,* Interscope, 1991.

49. See Ebony Utley, *Rap and Religion: Understanding the Gangsta's God* (Santa Barbara, CA: Praeger Books, 2012), 74. Though it does not concentrate its attention on apocalypticism, as in my discussion, this book has an excellent discussion of the role of the "devil" in hip-hop.

50. Jay-Z, *Decoded,* 17.

51. Jay-Z, "D'Evils," on *Reasonable Doubt,* Roc-A-Fella, Priority, 1996.

52. Immortal Technique, "Dance with the Devil," on *Revolutionary, Vol. 1,* Viper Records, 2001.

53. J. Cole, "Enchanted," on *Friday Night Lights,* Roc Nation, Columbia, Sony, 2010.

54. Immortal Technique, "Industrial Revolution," on *Revolutionary, Vol. 2,* Viper Records, 2003.

55. Adam Bradley discusses this song with a focus on its literary qualities. See *Book of Rhymes,* 100.

56. Snoop Doggy Dog, "Murder Was the Case," on *Murder Was the Case,* Death Row/Interscope, 1994.

57. See Gary Will's wonderful book on this subject, *Witches and Jesuits: Shakespeare's Macbeth* (New York: Oxford Paperbacks, 1996), 46, 73, 94–95.

58. Bradley, *Book of Rhymes,* 163–65.

59. Frederick Douglass, *Narrative of the Life of Frederick Douglass, an American Slave* (New York: Penguin Books, 1982).

60. There's a fine discussion of these changes in Sohail Daulatzai, *Black Star, Crescent Moon* (Minneapolis: University of Minnesota Press, 2012).

61. Jay-Z explains the crack epidemic in these terms: "The deeper causes of the crack explosion were in policies concocted by a government that was hostile to us, almost genocidally hostile when you thin[k] about how they aided or tolerated the unleashing of guns and drugs on poor communities, while at the same time cutting back on schools, housing, and assistance programs." See *Decoded*, 158.

62. George, *Hip Hop America*, 41.

63. Ta-Nehisi Coates, *The Beautiful Struggle* (New York: Spiegel and Grau, 2009), 97.

64. The question of theodicy has been a common theme in a lot of rap. For a few examples, see Ja Rule, "Father Forgive Me"; the Roots, "Dear God"; and Tupac, "Nothing to Lose," "Letter to My Unborn," and "Shed So Many Tears."

65. Tupac, "Black Jesus," on *Still I Rise*, Insomniac/Interscope Records, 1999.

66. Dyson, *Holler If You Hear Me*, 209.

67. Utley, *Rap and Religion*, 83.

68. See Tracy Fessenden, *Culture and Redemption: Religion, the Secular and American Literature* (Princeton, NJ: Princeton University Press, 2006).

69. James Baldwin, *The Fire Next Time* (New York: Vintage Books, 1992).

70. George, *Hip Hop Culture*, 47–48.

71. Nicki Minaj, feat. Eminem, "Roman's Revenge," on *Pink Friday*, Young Money, Cash Money, Universal, Motown, 2010.

72. David Reynolds discusses the work of George Lippard and George Thompson in this regard. See Reynolds, *Beneath the American Renaissance: The Subversive Imagination in the Age of Emerson and Melville* (Cambridge, MA: Harvard University Press, 1989), 59, 69, 106, 230.

73. Ibid., 278.

74. I'm paraphrasing a line from the 1844 issue of the reform newspaper *The Liberty Bell*. See Reynolds, *Beneath the American Renaissance*, 75, 88.

75. Quoted in William Jelani Cobb, *To the Break of Dawn: A Freestyle on the Hip Hop Aesthetic* (New York: New York University Press, 2008), 15.

76. Ta-Nehisi Coates, *A Beautiful Struggle* (New York: Spiegel and Grau, 2009), 101.

77. RZA, *The Tao of Wu* (New York: Riverhead Books, 2009), 1–3.

78. "The ghettos aren't designed for living," Saidiya Hartman remarks on a similar refrain, "the debris awash in the streets, the broken windows, and the stench of urine in the project elevators and stairwells are the signs of bare life." See Hartman, *Lose Your Mother*, 87.

79. "What is called poetic insight is the gift of discerning, in this sphere of strangely mingled elements, the beauty and majesty which are compelled to assume a garb so sordid." See Nathaniel Hawthorne, *The House of Seven Gables* (New York: Random House, 2001), 38.

80. RZA, *The Wu-Tang Manual* (New York: Penguin Books, 2005), 41.

81. Daulatzai, *Black Star, Crescent Moon,* xxvii.

82. Eddie Glaude, "Represent, Queensbridge, and the Art of Living," in *Born to Use Mics: Reading Nas's "Illmatic,"* ed. Michael Eric Dyson and Sohail Daulatzai (New York: Basic Civitas Books, 2010), 186.

83. RZA, *Tao of Wu,* 39.

84. See Bernard McGinn, *Thomas Aquinas's Summa Theologiae* (Princeton, NJ: Princeton University Press, 2014), 52.

85. RZA, *Tao of Wu,* 33.

86. For Benjamin's work on allegory and ruins, see Benjamin, *The Origin of German Tragic Drama* (London: Verso Books, 2009). For a study of these themes in the book of Revelation, see Elaine Pagels, *Revelations* (New York: Penguin Books, 2012), 1–35.

87. Collins, *Crisis and Catharsis,* 128.

88. Adam Bradley and Andrew Dubois, *The Anthology of Rap* (New Haven, CT: Yale University Press, 2010), xxxvi.

89. Imani Perry, *Prophets of the Hood: Politics and Poetics in Hip Hop* (Durham, NC: Duke University Press, 2004), 150.

90. See ibid., 61.

91. Douglass, *Narrative of the Life of Frederick Douglass,* 24.

92. For a study of the Nation of Islam, the Moorish Science Temple, and the Five Percenters, see Hisham Aidi's book, *Rebel Music: Race, Empire, and the New Muslim Youth Culture* (New York: Pantheon Books, 2014), esp. chs. 5 and 10. See also Michael Muhammad Knight, *The Five Percenters: Islam, Hip Hop and the Gods of New York* (Oxford: Oneworld, 2007).

93. Eric B. and Rakim, "Follow the Leader," on *Follow the Leader,* Uni Records, 1988.

94. For an explication of the numerology and meaning behind the group's individual names, see RZA, *Wu-Tang Manual.*

95. Wu-Tang Clan, "C.R.E.A.M.," on *Enter the Wu-Tang (36 Chambers),* Loud Records, 1994.

96. From public comments of Cornel West at the Hip Hop Symposium, Princeton University, 2006.

97. See RZA, *Tao of Wu,* 33, 98.

CHAPTER 7: AFRO-LATIN SOUL AND HIP-HOP

1. James Baldwin, "Many Thousands Gone," in *Notes of a Native Son* (Boston: Beacon Press, 1983), 24.

2. William Jelani Cobb, *To the Break of Dawn: A Freestyle on the Hip Hop Aesthetic* (New York: NYU Press, 2008), 35.

3. Timothy Brennan, *Secular Devotion: Afro-Latin Music and Imperial Jazz* (London: Verso Books, 2008), 9.

4. Gustavo Perez Firmat, *Life on the Hyphen: the Cuban-American Way* (Austin: University of Texas, 1994), 102.

5. Alejo Carpentier, *Music in Cuba,* trans. Alan West-Durán (Minneapolis: University of Minnesota Press, 2001), 95.

6. Ibid., 84.

7. Jacques Attali, *Noise: The Political Economy of Music*, trans. Brian Massumi (Minneapolis: University of Minnesota Press, 1985), 4–5.

8. David Tracy, "Writing," in *Critical Terms for Religious Studies*, ed. Mark C. Taylor (Chicago: University of Chicago Press, 1998), 391–92.

9. See Angel Rama, *The Lettered City*, trans. John Charles Chasteen (Durham, NC: Duke University Press, 1996), 24–25.

10. See Hisham Aidi, *Rebel Music: Race, Empire and the New Muslim Youth Culture* (New York: Pantheon Books, 2014), for a discussion of music in various anticolonial struggles across the globe.

11. Ted Gioia, *The History of Jazz* (Oxford: Oxford University Press, 1997), 6.

12. Alejo Carpentier, *Concierto Barroco* (Mexico City: Editorial Lectorum, 2003).

13. Richard Rodriguez, *Brown: The Last Discovery of America* (New York: Viking Books, 2002), 132.

14. The only exception to this would be among Afro-Latin Catholics of New Orleans and New York, who clearly brought Haitian vodou and Cuban *santería/lukumí* to North America, as Zora Neale Hurston shows in her classic study, *Mules and Men*. In part 2 of *Mules and Men*, Hurston travels to New Orleans for her study of voodoo in African American folk culture. As she notes, the vast majority of figures associated with voodoo continued to consider themselves Catholic. See *Mules and Men* (New York: Harper Perennial, 2008).

15. Many factors contributed to the loss of African culture in North America: the smaller number of African slaves in relation to white Americans in the United States allowed for tighter control and supervision over African customs than in Latin America; the emphasis on reproduction in North America versus importation in Latin America led to a larger number of second- and third-generation of slaves in the United States; and the greater number and concentration of free black communities in Latin America, organized in various guilds and *cabildos,* proved beneficial for the survival of African gods and customs. See George Reid Andrews, *Afro-Latin America: 1800–2000* (Oxford: Oxford University Press, 2004), 3, 13, 40.

16. Albert Raboteau, "Death of the Gods," in *African American Religious Thought: An Anthology,* ed. Cornel West and Eddie Glaude (Louisville, KY: Westminster John Knox Press, 2003), 274.

17. Carpentier, *Music in Cuba,* 81.

18. Ibid., 261–65.

19. "Once confined to the slave barracks and dilapidated rooming houses of the slums," writes Carpentier, "*son* eventually revealed its marvelous expressive resources, achieving universal status." See ibid., 228.

20. See Danilo Orozco, "El son: ¿ritmo, baile o reflejo de la personalidad cultura cubana?" *Santiago* 33 (March 1979): 87–113. See also Maya Roy, *Cuban Music,* trans. Denise Asfar and Gabriel Asfar (London: Markus Wiener, 2002), 120ff.

21. Carpentier, *Music in Cuba,* 155.

22. Similar to a guitar, the tres has three doubled strings; the güiro is made from a gourd or calabash and scratched with a stick; the marímbula is a bass instrument, consisting of metal strips arranged on a sounding board and mounted

on a box; the bongo is a drum of Bantu inspiration, held between the knees; the maracas is a pair of gourds, filled with seeds and shaken for rhythm; and the claves are small percussion instruments, made of small, cylindrical pieces of wood struck together.

23. Brennan, *Sacred Devotion*, 60.

24. Carpentier, *Music in Cuba*, 229.

25. Jory Farr, *Rites of Rhythm: The Music of Cuba* (New York: Regan Books, 2003), 31–32.

26. Brennan, *Sacred Devotion*, 101.

27. Firmat, *Life on the Hyphen*, 150–51.

28. Quoted in Farr, *Rites of Rhythm*, 39–40.

29. Ibid., 3.

30. T. S. Eliot, "The Dry Salvages," in *The Four Quartets* (New York: Mariner Books, 1968).

31. Juan Flores, *From Bomba to Hip Hop: Puerto Rican Culture and Latino Identity* (New York: Columbia University Press, 2000), 87.

32. As Juan Flores suggests, songs like "Danzón Boogaloo," "Guaguancó in Jazz," "Azucaré y Bongo," "Richie's Jala Jala," "Colombia's Boogaloo," and "Stop, Look and Listen" were examples of the rich sense of kinship of Afro-Cuban sounds with African American music. See Flores, *From Bomba to Hip Hop*, 84.

33. See Nelson George, "Hip Hop's Founding Fathers Speak the Truth," in *That's the Joint: Hip Hop Studies Reader*, ed. Murray Forman and Mark Anthony Neal (London: Routledge, 2012), 49.

34. "Many of the bass patterns heard in today's hip hop and classic funk were nicked from Afro-Cuban bands," writes Jory Farr in *Rites of Rhythm*, 7. And William Eric Perkins says the same thing in an early critical volume on hip-hop, *Droppin' Science: Critical Essays on Rap Music and Hip Hop Culture*: "I contend that the introduction of percussion beats in the dance music of the 1970s and in early hip hop were products of Latin music's powerful influence on New York and New Jersey popular culture." See Perkins, *Droppin' Science*, 6.

35. David Toop, *Rap Attack #3* (London: Serpent's Tail, 2000), 24.

36. Brennan, *Sacred Devotion*, 9.

37. In his study of Cuban festivals, Roberto González Echevarría explores the idioms and customs of carnival in Cuba: the mocking and satire of decorum, the insults and parodies of the ruling classes, the language games of *choteo*, and so forth. See Echevarría, *Cuban Fiestas* (New Haven, CT: Yale University Press, 2012).

38. Imani Perry, *Prophets of the Hood: Politics and Poetics in Hip Hop* (Durham, NC: Duke University Press, 2004) 13.

39. Firmat, *Life on the Hyphen*, 17.

40. In speaking of Brazil, Hisham Aidi argues that the hegemony of samba has been dethroned by hip-hop as the voice of the favelas. See Aidi, *Rebel Music*, 32–33.

41. For a discussion of Latin influences on hip-hop origins, see Flores, *From Bomba to Hip Hop*; Raquel Rivera, *New York Ricans from the Hip Hop Zone* (New York: Palgrave Macmillan, 2003); Pancho McFarland, *The Chican@ Hip*

Hop Nation: Politics of a New Millenial Mestizaje (Lansing: Michigan State University, 2013).

42. Common, "I Used to Love H.E.R.," on *Resurrection,* Relativity Records, 1994.

43. Quoted in S. Craig Watkins, *Hip Hop Matters: Politics, Pop Culture and the Struggle for the Soul of a Movement* (Boston: Beacon Books, 2005) 127.

44. S. Craig Watkins, *Hip Hop Matters: Politics, Pop Culture, and the Struggle for the Soul of a Movement* (Boston: Beacon Books, 2005), 137–38, 242. See Immortal Technique, feat. Brother Ali and Chuck D, "Civil War," on *The Martyr,* Viper Records, 2011.

45. See Aidi, *Rebel Music,* 255.

46. Paul Gilroy, "It's a Family Affair," in *Black Popular Culture,* ed. Gina Dent (Seattle: Bay Press, 1992), 307.

47. Manning Marable, "Race, Identity and Political Culture," in *Black Popular Culture,* ed. Gina Dent (Seattle: Bay Press, 1992), 302.

48. Quoted in the hip-hop documentary *Inventos: Hip Hop Cubano,* Eli Jacobs-Fantauzzi (Clenched Fist Productions, 2005). Quotes from this video are my translations.

49. Ibid.

50. Hermanos De Cause, "Tengo," Papaya Records, 2001.

51. Nicolás Guillén, *Yoruba from Cuba,* trans. Salvador Ortiz-Carboneres (Leeds: Peepal Tree, 2005), 122. See Alan West-Durán, "Rap's Diasporic Dialogue: Cuba's Redefinition of Blackness," *Journal of Popular Music Studies* 16 (2004): 20. See also Sujatha Fernandes, *Close to the Edge: In Search of the Global Hip Hop Generation* (London: Verso Books, 2011), 45.

52. See West-Durán, "Rap's Diasporic Dialogue," 20, for a good discussion of *choteo.*

53. This relationship between Langston Hughes and Guillén is discussed in Arnold Rampersad's biography, *The Life of Langston Hughes, Vol. 1, 1902–1941* (Oxford: Oxford University Press, 2002). See also Claudia Milan, *Latining America: Black-Brown Passages and the Coloring of Latino/a Studies* (Athens: University of Georgia Press, 2013), 90–91.

54. Hermanos de Causa, "Lagrimas Negras," Mixer Music, 2008.

55. See Derek Pardue, *Brazilian Hip Hoppers Speak from the Margins* (New York: Palgrave Macmillan, 2011), 39–43.

56. Racionais MCs, "Diaro de um detento," on *Sobrevivendo no Inferno,* Cosa Nostra Phonographic, 1997.

57. Quoted in Alastair Pennycock and Tony Mitchell, *Global Linguistic Flows,* ed. H. Samy Alim, Awad Ibrahim, and Alastair Pennycock (London: Routledge, 2008), 33.

58. See Farr, *Rites of Rhythm,* 215.

59. Quoted in Brennan, *Secular Devotion,* 114.

60. *Inventos.*

61. Cuarta Imagen, "La Muralla," High Times, 2005.

62. Bahamadia, "Spontaneity," and "Uknowhowwedu," on *Kollage,* Chrysalis/EMI Records, 1996.

63. Orishas, "Represent," on *A lo Cubano,* Universal Latino, 2000.

64. Orishas, "Canto Para Elewa y Chango," on *A Lo Cubano,* Universal Latino, 2000.

65. See David Brown, *Santería Enthroned: Art, Ritual, and Innovation in Afro-Cuban Religion* (Chicago: University of Chicago Press, 2003), 271, for an excellent discussion of Shango and other aspects of Afro-Cuban religion.

66. See ibid., 67.

67. W. E. B. Du Bois, *Black Folk, Then and Now* (Oxford: Oxford University Press, 2014), last page. See also Kwame Anthony Appiah, *Lines of Descent: W.E.B. Du Bois and the Emergence of Identity* (Cambridge, MA: Harvard University Press, 2014), 135.

68. See Roger Bastide, *The African Religions of Brazil: Toward a Sociology of the Interpenetration of Civilizations,* trans. Helen Sebba (Baltimore, MD: Johns Hopkins University Press, 1978), 114–16.

69. West-Durán, "Rap's Diasporic Dialogue," 24.

70. Another example of this is the previously mentioned group Obsesión. In their music, Yoruba chants are carefully layered with hip-hop beats and Afro-Cuban percussion, with an effect that seems contemporary and nostalgic, modern and traditional (such as in the song, "La llaman puta," in which Magia Lopez raps about the debasing and violent treatment of prostitutes in Cuba using a jazz vibe and Yoruba chant). In this group's case, it is clear that the barrio where the rap duo is from, Regla, has left its imprint on their music. Home of one of the very first secret Abakuá societies (a black male society with origins in Nigeria), Regla today remains a center for Afro-Cuban traditions and a very popular destination for Santería pilgrims, who go to visit La Santisima Virgen de Regla, the "black Madonna," in the town's colonial church.

71. George Lipsitz, *Dangerous Crossroads: Popular Music, Post-Modernism and the Poetics of Place* (London: Verso Books, 1994), 17.

72. Pancho McFarland, "Here Is Something You Can't Understand: Chicano Rap and the Critique of Globalization," in *Decolonial Voices,* ed. Arturo Aldama and Naomi Quiñonez (Bloomington: Indiana University Press, 2002), 308.

73. Kinto Sol, "Hecho en Mexico," on *Hecho en Mexico,* Disa, 2003.

74. Funky Aztecs, "Prop 187," on *Day of the Dead,* Raging Bull Records, 1995.

75. In speaking of the appeal of myth to literary modernists, specifically the Arab poet Adonis, Talal Asad expresses this exact point: "For Adonis, myth arises whenever human reason encounters perplexing questions about existence and attempts to answer them in what can only be a non-rational way, thus producing a combination of poetry, history and wonderment." See Asad, *Formations of the Secular: Christianity, Islam and Modernity* (Stanford, CA: Stanford University Press, 2003), 55. Sacvan Bercovitch also has a nice description of myth in *The American Jeremiad* (Madison: University of Wisconsin Press, 2012), xli.

76. Kinto Sol, "Los Hijos del Maize," on *Los Hijos del Maize,* Univision Records, 2006.

77. See Gloria Flaherty, *Shamanism and the Eighteenth Century* (Princeton, NJ: Princeton University Press, 1992), 74–75. In particular, writes Georgi, "the litany was one favored form because its rhythms and tones affected the body

directly, without appeal to the higher faculty of reason." See also Asad, *Formations of the Secular,* 50.

78. Quoted in *Inventos.*

79. Asad, *Formations of the Secular,* 27.

80. This quote is from Virginia Woolf, *To the Lighthouse* (New York: Harcourt, Brace, Jovanovich, 1989).

81. Ozomatli, "Cumbia de los Muertos," on *Ozomatli,* Almo Sounds, 1998.

82. T. S. Eliot, "Burnt Norton," in *The Four Quartets* (New York: Mariner Books, 1968).

Index

Abraham, 59, 60, 62, 69

the aesthetic contours of soul: mysticism, music, and festivity, 25–30; African American Christianity, 29; capitalism, 28; the Catholics, 28–29; concept of the soul in the Middle Ages, 26; Descartes, René, 29; great chain of being, 28; Gregory of Nyssa, 26; Hart, David Bentley, 25–26; incorporeal conception of the soul, 29; Latin baroque Christianity, 29–30; liberal arts, 26–27; music as revelatory of the pattern of the universe, 27; Navajo Night Chant, 25; Nicolas of Cusa, 25; Nietzsche, Friedrich, 27; Protestant Christianity, 28; Teresa of Ávila, 27

African American Christianity, 29

Afro-Latin hip-hop in the Americas, 213–15; Castor, Jimmy, 213; forerunners of rap in Latin America, 214; percussion beats, 213, 260n34; Perry, Imani, 214; *sabor Latino*, 215; and traditional Latin music, 215

Afro-Latin religion and hip-hop, 221–27; African gods, 223; ancestral rhythms, 222–23; *cabildos* (Catholic societies and guilds), 221; "Canto a Elewa y Changó" (Orishas), 223–24; *cantos* to the Orishas, 222; Causa, Hermanos de, 227; "Chango 'ta Beni" (Olivencia), 222; cross-cultural encounters, 225;

EPG and ancestral rhythms, 222; Judith (biblical), 226; "Muralla" (Cuarta Imagen), 222–23; Orishas, 222; Santa Barbara and Shango, 224–26; "Tengo" (Causa), 227

Afro-Latin soul, 10–12

Afro-Latin soul and hip-hop, 204–34; African and Spanish fusions, 206; Afro-Latin hip-hop in the Americas, 213–15; Afro-Latin religion and hip-hop, 221–27; Afro-Latin soul in the Americas: the *son*, 209–13; Catholic baroque in the Americas, 206–8; exile and indigenous motifs, 227–234; grammatology as an instrument of empire, 206; *mestizaje* (cultural miscegenation), 205; "third world" context of Afro-Latin hip-hop, 215–221

Afro-Latin soul in the Americas: the *son*, 209–13; Bambaataa, Afrika, 213; *batá* drum, 212; bolero, 211; "Cajón de Muerto"; a *son*, 211–12; Catholicism, 209; dangers of, 211; development of the *son*, 210; early history of *son*, 210–11; Farr, Jory, 210, 212; Feijóo, Samuel, on, 210; Flores, Juan, 213; folkloric sense of the *son*, 210; hip-hop and worship as defiance, 213; migration of African slaves to Cuba, 209; origins of *son*, 211; the Orishas (African ancestors and deities), 209; Ortiz,

265